HELPING FAMILIAR STRANGERS

WORLDS IN CRISIS: REFUGEES, ASYLUM, AND FORCED MIGRATION

Elizabeth Cullen Dunn and Georgina Ramsay, editors

HELPING FAMILIAR STRANGERS

Refugee Diaspora Organizations and Humanitarianism

LOUISE OLLIFF

INDIANA UNIVERSITY PRESS

This book is a publication of

Indiana University Press
Office of Scholarly Publishing
Herman B Wells Library 350
1320 East 10th Street
Bloomington, Indiana 47405 USA

iupress.org

 The paper used in this publication meets the minimum requirements of the American National Standard for Information Sciences—Permanence of Paper for Printed Library Materials, ANSI Z39.48-1992.

Manufactured in the United States of America

First printing 2022

Cataloging information is available from the Library of Congress.

ISBN 978-0-253-06355-7 (hardback)
ISBN 978-0-253-06356-4 (paperback)
ISBN 978-0-253-06357-1 (ebook)

CONTENTS

PREFACE

WHILE MANY OF THE WORDS in the following chapters initially found form in a doctoral thesis, this book is really the culmination of nearly two decades of work. Prior to starting a doctorate at the University of Melbourne in 2014, I had worked for nongovernmental organizations (NGOs) in Australia on refugee policy, research, and advocacy for over ten years; I had been an executive committee member of one refugee diaspora organization (RDO) for five years; and I had long-standing links with many other RDOs through my professional and volunteer networks. On a personal level, my husband arrived in Australia as a refugee in the 1990s, and the years I have spent with him, his family, his friends, and his community have greatly informed my understanding of the everyday experiences of forced displacement. In short, I was already embedded in the field prior to starting a PhD, and my positionality had implications for how I went about the research that underlies this book.

To begin with, my decision to pursue doctoral research was very much informed by a sense of injustice that the RDOs that I was frequently coming across in my work and personal life seemed to be invisible or count for little to the organizations and institutions that claim a mandate to work *for refugees*. The invisibility of RDOs was apparent, for instance, when I traveled to Geneva in 2015 for both my work with the Refugee Council of Australia and for PhD fieldwork. My work role at the time was to support Australian NGO and refugee community advocates participating in a series of formal meetings between NGOs and the United Nations High Commissioner for Refugees (UNHCR). This coordination role gave me access and opportunities to observe discussions involving both senior representatives of humanitarian organizations and refugee diaspora advocates who were among the Australian delegation.

One meeting I participated in involved senior representatives of UNHCR's Africa Bureau and five delegates from Australian NGOs. Among these delegates was a refugee support agency senior manager, Dr. Melika Sheikh-Eldin, who had herself arrived in Australia as a refugee originally from Eritrea. At the meeting, Dr. Sheikh-Eldin asked UNHCR for an update on plans to support young Eritreans accessing education in the notoriously underresourced Shegerab refugee camp in eastern Sudan. She was told that due to issues with external security threats and Sudanese authorities, NGOs were constrained in what they could do at Shegerab at that time. Dr. Sheikh-Eldin responded by remarking that an organization in Melbourne—an RDO—had recently raised funds and built three permanent classrooms at a site designated as a school in Shegerab and that those in the Eritrean diaspora might be willing to help. A UNHCR representative dismissed this claim, saying, "That's not possible; the school must be outside the camp." But I knew, as others did, that it *was* inside the camp. I knew because one of the people who traveled to Shegerab to negotiate and oversee the construction of this school building was an Eritrean Australian man from Melbourne whom I knew very well. I had spoken to him in some detail about this project, both while he was in Sudan and after his return. I had seen videos taken from a car window that showed the boundaries of the camp and the road that led to the dusty school site, with its ugly cinder-block building, newly cemented. I knew it was possible for a humanitarian organization to get things done inside this camp; it might just be a different sort of organization to the ones that this representative of UNHCR had in mind.

The feeling of injustice that led me to embark on doctoral research was fueled by my desire to make visible the breathtaking generosity and acts of kindness that I had seen time and time again in the actions of those involved in RDOs and to counter the jarring narrative of *refugees as burden* or *refugees as threat* that so dominates public discourse in Australia, as it does in many parts of the world. I started out wanting to be a stronger advocate and ally for RDOs and hoping that I could do this by contributing some rigorous research to support their cause. I lay out my position here as an activist with an investment in the field of refugee diaspora humanitarianism because I want to acknowledge the effect that this had on how I undertook this research. But I also want to suggest that my positionality—my embeddedness and investment in RDOs—was fundamental to being able to access this multisited, rapidly changing, and at times elusive field and that I actively strove to be self-reflexive—to understand the light I cast on the field and to dampen my desire to see the world in a particular way (Fine 1993, 286).

For researchers undertaking study of a field in which they are deeply immersed, Pierre Bourdieu reminds us that it is "with difficulty" that "genuinely scientific" research can be undertaken because the beliefs of the field ("what goes without saying") are shared (2010). Yet Bourdieu does not diminish the potential of scholarly endeavor for someone immersed in the field of study, affirming the value of prior knowledge as long as it is subjected to examination and disclosure to self and others. Bourdieu's own research in the field in which he was immersed in *Homo Academicus* (1988), for example, shows how reflexivity and a relentless pursuit of empirical rigor can result in valuable insights into a particular social world. In terms of how one is reflexive in these circumstances, a Bourdieuian approach speaks of a "painful amputation" of the enchanted beliefs one holds (Bourdieu et al. 2010, 6). For me, I may have been (and still am) invested in the idea that refugee diaspora humanitarianism is a good thing, and it was a somewhat painful process to disinvest myself of this belief and to allow myself to be subject to the "gravitational forces that pull you into a social field" (Bourdieu 1993, cited in Hage 2005, 465) and reveal a much messier reality.

Being embedded and invested was significant because it gave me access to a range of people, networks, and situations in which RDOs were working that I may otherwise have struggled to access. Without having spent years developing relationships with people involved in RDOs, I doubt I would have been able to organize the number and variety of interviews with RDOs that I did or to pursue more philosophical and challenging discussions with individuals with whom I had stronger connections. Without my affiliation with the Refugee Council of Australia, my ability to access international discussions on refugee protection—particularly the more intimate ones involving senior representatives of humanitarian organizations and refugee diaspora advocates—would likewise have been much different. Indeed, George Marcus provides an insightful discussion about how access and objectivity for an embedded ethnographer undertaking multisited research can lead to productive and unique insights. He writes, "In certain sites, one seems to be working with, and in others one seems to be working against, changing sets of subjects. This condition of shifting personal positions in relation to one's subjects and other active discourses in a field that overlap with one's own generates a definite sense of doing more than just ethnography, and it is this quality that provides a sense of being an activist for and against positioning in even the most self-perceived apolitical fieldworker" (1995, 113–114).

This description of having to position oneself differently depending on the site rang true in my own experience of undertaking fieldwork. When talking to or observing people involved in RDOs in Australia, humanitarian professionals in Geneva, or people whom RDOs were trying to help in Indonesia and Thailand, I was acutely aware of my own positioning on the question of refugee diaspora humanitarianism. My position shifted as I sought to understand and connect to people in different sites. In Thailand, when I met with refugees who were engaging with RDOs, I was confronted by their views that those in the diaspora were not doing enough. I was forced to reevaluate my own belief in and position as an advocate *for* refugee diaspora humanitarianism and to see my own position as ultimately mutable. This, I hope, led to a richer and deeper exploration of the complexities underlying RDOs' acts of helping, which I hope I do justice to in the pages that follow.

Of course, just as my foray into understanding refugee diaspora humanitarianism did not start when I began my doctoral research, so too has it continued beyond completing my PhD in 2018. Since then, I have remained involved in supporting RDOs in a voluntary capacity and collaborating with refugee diaspora advocates and organizations, whose perspectives and experiences are drawn on in the following chapters.

OVERVIEW

This book is organized into seven chapters that tell the story of refugee resettlement as a structuring experience that leads to diaspora communities in Australia forming voluntary organizations to help "their people" overseas. Chapter 1 begins by setting the scene and the backdrop to understanding refugee diaspora humanitarianism, situating this study at the intersections of refugee studies, humanitarianism studies, and scholarly interest in diaspora networks and transnationalism. Chapter 2 then explores the contours of the concept of humanitarianism and the international refugee regime as the dominant structure governing responses to forced displacement, highlighting the significant challenges and shortcomings of both the international refugee regime and humanitarian system in responding to forced displacement.

Chapter 3 provides the broad brushstrokes of an ecology of refugee diaspora humanitarianism, defining RDOs and what they do. This chapter describes how the structuring experience of third-country resettlement leads to a tendency among diaspora communities to mobilize to help those they leave behind, even while there is considerable variation in the ways, means, and contexts in which refugee diaspora humanitarianism takes place. Chapter 4 then explores the question of *why* people involved in RDOs choose to organize and act in this way, describing the recurring narratives of suffering that refugee diaspora humanitarians evoke, as well as the moral forces, affect, and undercurrents of power that compel action and reflect the distinct histories and positionalities of resettled refugees.

Chapters 4 and 5 both concern the modalities of refugee diaspora humanitarianism. While the RDOs described in this book were involved in a wide range of activities, there are crosscutting themes that speak of the distinct ways refugee diasporas in Australia go about transnational helping. Chapter 4 focuses on questions of governance, accountability, and economies, while chapter 5 looks at the ways diaspora humanitarians move, organize, and act transnationally; how they are seen or not seen, depending on context; what they know and do not know; and how they utilize social networks to get things done. Taken together, these chapters maintain that RDOs have distinct capacities to respond to humanitarian needs in forced displacement contexts.

Chapter 6 explores the role that refugee diaspora humanitarianism does or could play in the international refugee regime. The intersections between humanitarianism and the international refugee regime are revisited in order to imagine how RDOs fit within and challenge understandings and practices of protection and humanitarian intervention. This chapter also highlights the potential for RDOs to challenge the disempowering tropes of refugees as victims or threat and to recognize and enable the unique contributions and possibilities of refugee diaspora networks as solidaristic transnational actors that respond in times of crisis and need.

Finally, chapter 7 reflects on the significance of RDOs within the international refugee regime and how to understand grassroots actors—including those forcibly displaced—organizing and acting to support one another, despite or because of the failings of global governance systems. RDOs and their helping work, this discussion concludes, should be considered as a thread within broader tapestries of care, appreciating that a diversity of care practices is significant in and of itself.

ACKNOWLEDGMENTS

I WOULD LIKE TO ACKNOWLEDGE the village that raised this book. In particular, my thanks to the editorial team at Indiana University Press for their patience and care in ushering this book from proposal through to publication. It was a long journey that was completed in the context of a global pandemic and an author juggling multiple work commitments, none of which involved time to work on a book! A heartfelt thank-you to the reviewers who offered their considerable expertise and time to read, comment, and shape this book. Your thoughtful and considered input has made this work far stronger than it would have otherwise been.

This book would not have been possible if I had not completed my doctoral dissertation first. My thanks again to my PhD supervisors, Bina Fernandez and Andy Dawson, for their welcome and wise guidance, constructive critiques, and consistent support and encouragement, and to the two assessors of my dissertation, Cindy Horst and Susan Banki, whose expertise I respect and value highly and whose assessment on my doctoral thesis also informed revisions to this monograph. Thanks also to the many others on my PhD journey who read and commented on chapter drafts, shared their expertise over coffees or email, or otherwise listened to me work through my ideas and my struggles: Faisal Al-Asaad, Tess Altman, Denise Cauchi, Jeff Crisp, Joe Cropp, Erika Feller, Paul Green, Lenka Hadravova, James Hathaway, Mingo Heiduk, Emma Hoskins, Uma Kothari, Marnie Lloyd, Awoh Emmanuel Lohkoko, Mythily Meher, Effie Mitchell, Melissa Phillips, Mediya Rangi, Marika Sosnowski, Shukufa Tahiri, Leah Tang, Thu-Trang Tran, and Hadi Zaher. I wish to also acknowledge all of my esteemed colleagues at the Refugee Council of Australia, but particularly Paul Power, whose integrity, leadership, and willingness to step back and give the floor to people who speak from lived experience is partly why I embarked on this research in the first place.

I would like to express enormous gratitude to my family for supporting me in so many ways and giving me the time and space that allowed me to see this research and now book through: to Abderahim, thank you for being the quiet and unwavering voice of justice in my head and my heart; to Amina and Sophia, our children, I hope you grow to be as compassionate and caring as the people I have written about; and to my parents and sisters, for the countless times and ways you have helped me get to where I am today. I write in this book about the importance of families in shaping the values of those who help, and I would like to think I am an example of this. Thank you especially to my sister, Linda Muir, who created the visuals for this book.

This book is about people who try to help others and whose actions often go unnoticed. I wish I could name you all, but instead I wish to acknowledge all who freely gave (more of) their time to speak to me about what they do and why. My appreciation for the breathtaking generosity and weighty load carried by refugee diaspora humanitarians has only grown through this process. You are truly remarkable.

INTRODUCTION

THE ACT OF HELPING A stranger in need is a complicated one. It involves a person perceiving another's suffering, feeling compelled to do something about it, and, importantly, acting with the intention of alleviating this suffering. The act of helping strangers in need—humanitarianism—manifests in multifarious ways. While the term *humanitarianism* has become almost synonymous with practices dominated by large Western organizational actors with remarkably similar genealogies, in fact humanitarians and humanitarianisms come in many shapes and sizes. Erica Bornstein writes about this in terms of the "subtle shades of humanitarian efforts—differentiated by varied imperatives, impulses, and systems of obligation and assistance" and with varying visibility (2012, 11). She writes that "alongside the heroic efforts of professional aid workers and the dramatic suffering of disaster victims are those who provide care inaudibly, without recognition and without status" (Bornstein 2012, 11).

This book is about one of these less visible humanitarian actors—refugee diaspora organizations (RDOs)—and the complicated impulses, practices, and relationships between these actors and the "familiar strangers" they try to help.[1] It is about everyday humanitarianism, the complex moralities and motivations that underlie acts of helping, and the social world and practices of organizations that are mostly unseen by more powerful humanitarian actors. This book is also about muddying the lines between those who suffer and those who help and exploring the implications of refugee diaspora humanitarianism as a distinct form of transnational engagement—one that is shaped by the politics, histories, and positionalities of people who have direct personal connection to, or experience of, forced displacement. This is about people who struggle to do good and to fill gaps left by deeply flawed global governance systems.

To give a flavor of what this book is about, I want to begin with a story about a very small group of people who have experienced life as refugees, were resettled, and are remaking their lives in new countries and how they continue to help those who are in the precarious situation they left behind.

In 2014, a small group of Hazara refugees living in Indonesia used a US$200 donation to set up a school, the Cisarua Refugee Learning Centre (CRLC). This school was started in a context in which access by refugees to government or humanitarian assistance is extremely limited. If a person is found to be a refugee in Indonesia, the Indonesian government does not consider local integration an option, and resettlement to a third country can take many years, if not decades. Refugees are denied the right to work in Indonesia, and while a small number are eligible for some support from nongovernment and multilateral organizations, most survive through remittances sent by family and friends overseas and their own savings. While the CRLC began modestly, it quickly grew, and by 2020, it had over twenty volunteer refugee teachers and up to three hundred students. CRLC may have been the first, but it is not the only refugee-led initiative in Indonesia filling gaps in protection and support for those stuck in protracted limbo; there were at least eleven refugee-led schools and an estimated 1,800 refugees accessing education through refugee community initiatives by 2020 (Cisarua Learning, n.d.).

The success story of CRLC has much to do with the global networks of supporters that have been drawn to this school and the refugee community living in Cisarua. CRLC's operating budget of roughly US$50,000 a year in 2020 is funded almost entirely through donations from supporters in countries in the Global North, predominantly Australia.[2] This global support network has been amplified through the resettlement of three of CRLC's founders and early leaders—Muzafar Ali, who was resettled to Australia in 2015; Khadim Dai, who resettled in the United States in 2016; and Tahira Razai, who resettled in Canada in 2017. Shortly after arriving in Australia, for example, Muzafar cofounded Cisarua Learning Inc., an Australia-registered public benevolent institution set up to fundraise and support the CRLC and other refugee-led initiatives in Indonesia and elsewhere. Beyond mobilizing financial support, Muzafar and Tahira both continue to be actively involved in accompanying the CRLC management team as the school adapts to the ever-changing local context and community needs. In many ways, the bridge that was created through resettlement processes continues to be crossed, as information, resources, and support flow between the refugee community in Cisarua, those who have spent time in Cisarua as refugees, and the friends and supporters in resettlement countries like Australia, the United States, and Canada who have been gathered along the way.

This global network of supporters was evident when Cisarua Learning Inc. held a twelve-hour online telethon in November 2019 to raise money for CRLC and three other refugee-led schools in Indonesia. The telethon was broadcast live from CRLC and hosted by leaders from the school. It also involved Muzafar, Khadim, and Tahira videoconferencing in from Adelaide, Los Angeles, and Toronto, at times speaking candidly of their own time at CRLC and its impact on their lives since. Muzafar described his experiences in Cisarua in 2013, with four friends pooling US$7.50 to rent a sound system to gather the community for an Eid celebration at a time when refugees were afraid to come together, before discussing the present, "where we are trying to raise funds for more than 1,000 students" (CRLC 2019). He continued: "I think this is a remarkable feat that refugees have achieved. We started off trying to reach out locally, but now we're reaching out globally." Muzafar also spoke about his plans to return to Indonesia in the future as part of a university student volunteer placement and hoped to spend three months "with my community." He said, "I will keep learning, because you guys have achieved enormously since I left . . . and I will try to support you with whatever energy I have" (CRLC 2019).

The point of this story is not to suggest that Muzafar, Tahira, and Khadim are the only, or even the main, reasons for CRLC's continuing success in providing much-needed educational opportunities to refugees in Indonesia. The point is to highlight how different people are able to use their positionality to act in different ways to mobilize assistance for people living in very difficult situations. Muzafar, Khadim, and Tahira were instrumental in starting CRLC, but their departure from Indonesia is not the end of their connection to this school or the community it serves. Refugee resettlement is often the start of a new chapter in helping, as I hope this book shows. Resettlement has provided Muzafar, Tahira, and Khadim with opportunities to build bridges between the refugee community they once lived their day-to-day lives among and people in Australia, Canada, and the United States they now meet and who may otherwise have little access or insights into the plight of refugees living in Indonesia. These transnational networks of care and support are the primary focus of this book.

A BACKDROP OF GLOBAL DISPLACEMENT

The backdrop to this story is the much bigger narrative of global movements of people and, more specifically, experiences of and responses to forced displacement. At the end of 2021, 89.3 million persons were reported to have been forcibly displaced worldwide as a result of persecution, conflict, generalized violence, and human rights violations (UNHCR 2022). This equates to over 1 percent (one in eighty-eight people) of the world's population. The international refugee regime can be understood as the dominant structure governing global responses to this forced displacement. This structure's "solidity in time and space" (Giddens 1984) comes in the legal form of the United Nations 1951 Convention and 1967 Protocol relating to the Status of Refugees as well as the institutional form of the United Nations High Commissioner for Refugees (UNHCR) and its mandate. Together, this institution and laws articulate three "durable solutions" to forced displacement: the repatriation of refugees to their country of origin at the earliest possible stage when it is safe to do so, local integration in countries of first asylum, and resettlement in a new country (UNHCR 2004). In short, the international refugee regime is about putting people "in place" and, in particular, territorializing people within a state (Malkki 1992).

Yet there is growing recognition that the international refugee regime is failing to provide effective solutions to forced displacement. The option of voluntary and safe repatriation for the vast majority of refugees has become less realizable in the context of the increasingly complex and intractable causes of forced displacement that make return untenable in the short or even longer term. At the same time, the options of local integration into countries of asylum or third-country resettlement have been diminished by the unwillingness or lack of capacity of states. To illustrate this in numbers, of the 89.3 million people recognized as in need of international protection in 2021, only 5.8 million (6.5%) found a durable solution.[3] The lack of effectiveness in realizing the solutions espoused by the international refugee regime has resulted in two notable trends: a steady rise in the number of people living in protracted refugee situations with no durable solution in sight and the increasing irregularity of movement of people seeking protection and failing to find it, resulting in more and more people living precarious lives "in the margins of the world" (Agier 2008).

HUMANITARIANISM, TRANSNATIONALISM, AND REFUGEE DIASPORAS

Research on refugee diaspora humanitarianism sits at the intersection of a number of fields, although not squarely in any. For instance, this scholarship is very much interested in critical perspectives on the practices and ethics of humanitarianism, but, as we will see in the next chapter, only if one accepts a much broader understanding of what constitutes *humanitarianism* or a *humanitarian actor.* As Julia Pacitto and Elena Fiddian-Qasmiyeh suggest, academic work on the history of responses to refugees has extensively "focused on the development and functioning of the institutionalized international regime . . . and has thus, similar to humanitarian studies, sidelined 'other' forms of refugee assistance and protection in the history of humanitarian responses to refugees" (2013, 10). This book, then, represents a contribution to writing *the other* into humanitarian scholarship. In writing about other forms of organized compassion, it is hoped that a deeper and broader understanding of what it means to help a suffering stranger may emerge that sits outside—and at times challenges—dominant humanitarian understandings and practices. As Pacitto and Fiddian-Qasmiyeh rightly argue, "The enduring influence of the Northern-dominated international regime in the humanitarian arena should not be trivialized, nor should the capacity of Southern stakeholders, including refugees and forcibly displaced persons themselves, to exert agency as actors in the humanitarian sphere" (2013, 25).

Second, this book builds on scholarship on diaspora communities and their transnational engagements, placing importance on diaspora transnationalism that takes place in spaces between the binary of *homelands* and *hostlands* and beyond the considerable focus that has been given to the political engagements (both positive and negative) and the economic development potential of diaspora networks. Instead, this research builds on important work that has emerged on transnational care practices within refugee communities at a family or household level (see Al-Sharmani 2010; Horst 2008b; Johnson and Stoll 2008; Monsutti 2004; Soh-Leong 2009), expanding this to the associational or collective engagements of refugee diasporas in acts of caring for *a people*, wherever they are in the world.

Third, this research straddles refugee studies on resettlement and the refugee experience, viewing resettlement as a structuring event and a precursor to new forms of mobility and connection between people and places of displacement. Indeed, I intentionally sought out RDOs that were formed by people who had arrived in Australia as refugees or humanitarian entrants, as I wanted to know how having been a refugee shaped their ideas and practices of helping. Perhaps this will help us go beyond emplaced understandings of resettlement that focus on integration experiences (see Neumann et al. 2014) or how refugees dream of and negotiate resettlement processes (De Montclos 2008; Horst 2006a; Sandvik 2009) and see refugees living in host and resettlement countries as connected and moving between these spaces in different and ongoing ways. This book, then, explores the experience of resettled refugees through a lens of mobility (Hannam et al. 2006) and with a recognition that resettlement "has the capacity to influence far more lives than simply those of the refugees selected for relocation" (Piper et al. 2013, 2–3).

This research shows that being granted the opportunity to live permanently and legally in wealthy countries like Australia, Canada, or the United States is significant; it *means something*, not only to those who are resettled and to those who are left behind but also to the larger system of international refugee protection.

Resettlement is a movement that "marks" people "in a way that the ordinary everyday movement people engage in when they move around does not" (Hage 2005, 469). It creates new configurations of expectations, capacity, belonging, and obligation. As Michael Collyer points out, "Resettlement significantly alters the position refugees occupy in their social networks" (2006, 97). Moreover, and echoing Margaret Piper, Paul Power and Graham Thom, "Resettlement is an issue that deserves to be taken seriously by those charged with shaping its policy and those delivering it on the ground. The better it is understood, the more effectively it can be used" (2013, 1).

Lastly, this research offers a contribution to the anthropology of the good literature. In his seminal article "Beyond the Suffering Subject," Joel Robbins argues, "We have learned so much in the last few decades about how human beings can disregard and do violence to one another. A fully rounded anthropology of the good will have to throw light on other ways of relating" (2013, 458). While Robbins is careful not to suggest that anthropology turns away from questions of suffering, he implores scholars to explore "the promise [that] suffering slot anthropology always at least implicitly makes: that there must be better ways to live than the ones it documents" (2013, 458). Sherry Ortner (2016) takes this further, calling for scholars to integrate the important work undertaken since the 1980s that focuses on power, inequality, and violence ("dark anthropology") and work that is more positive or "hopeful" (Jansen and Lofving 2009) in outlook. In this, Ortner calls for the anthropology of the good to be "the anthropology of critique, resistance and activism" (2016, 60). It is this call to understand better ways to live—in all their messiness and in a world where there is cause to feel dark—that this book seeks to answer. In the context of mass forced movements of people and protracted displacement, there is a need for anthropology to continue to focus on questions of loss, displacement, and suffering. But there is also a need to look beyond the suffering and at the possibilities grounded in "those ways of thinking, feeling, and acting that increase the horizons of hope" (Appadurai 2013, 295).

The anthropology of humanitarianism—of which this book may be counted—offers us examples of what this anthropology of the good could offer. In providing ethnographic accounts of the ways different actors try to help in the name of humanity, anthropologists including Liisa Malkki, Didier Fassin, Miriam Ticktin, Ilana Feldman, Erica Bornstein, Raymond Apthorpe, and Mariella Pandolfi offer us warnings as well as threads of hope. As Ticktin argues, this "new anthropological work has pushed back at diagnoses and condemnations of humanitarianism, as well as at anthropological sympathies with the humanitarian project. Instead, it demonstrates how humanitarianism as a project is morphing, for which we need new analytics. Without knowing what, precisely, humanitarianism is and where its boundaries lie, a different anthropological approach—focusing on ambiguities, limits, and constraints—has taken shape" (2014, 281). It is my hope that this account of refugee diaspora humanitarianism gives life to the idea that there are possibilities to resist, empower, and act for good and that therein lies a multitude of ambiguities, limits, and constraints.

RESEARCHING REFUGEE DIASPORA HUMANITARIANISM

The field of refugee diaspora humanitarianism is one that is transnational, dispersed, mobile, and diverse. It comprises an unknown number of relatively small groups of people who come together to form organizations or initiatives that aim to provide assistance to people in need in other parts of the world. These organizations—RDOs—are formed by people who self-identify in a diasporic way with a people who face persecution and have been forcibly displaced from a homeland. The RDOs in this study did not necessarily claim to represent a community in the way that we often think about diaspora associations or organizations. Most were not seeking to be a representational body for a self-identified community but were, in practice, embedded within diasporic social networks since they draw heavily on the support—both financial contributions and voluntary labor—of people who self-identify in a similar (diasporic) way.

While this research could have been conducted in any number of countries where refugee diaspora communities have formed—Europe, North America, and Oceania—for practicality and access, one primary site was chosen: Australia. But refugee diaspora humanitarianism is in no way unique to Australia-based diasporas, with excellent work being undertaken in other parts of the world indicating similar patterns of diasporic mobilization and action in response to displacement (see DEMAC 2016b for European experience; Sweis 2019 for US context). Furthermore, many of the RDOs in this study were affiliated with sister organizations or mobilized support from members of diaspora communities in other parts of the world. Indeed, the field of refugee diaspora humanitarianism needs to be understood as geographically noncontiguous and mobile. Undertaking research in such a field is no small feat. While I spent most of my time immersed in activities and engaging with individuals involved in RDOs located in Melbourne, the membership and leadership of these organizations are often dispersed in different cities across the (large) Australian continent or overseas, and their work is undertaken in different parts of the world, where they have connections to a displaced population. To varying degrees, those involved in RDOs travel between these different sites—cities and countries where their communities primarily reside—to organize and mobilize support, back and forth to the humanitarian contexts in which their organizations' activities are focused (which are themselves often changing as people move), and to the places where decisions about (dominant) humanitarian responses are made, in Geneva and New York.

To give an illustration of this, one of the RDOs profiled in chapter 2 is the Assyrian Aid Society–Australia (AAS–A). In 2014, just prior to starting my fieldwork, an estimated 32,000 out of the 35,000-strong Iraqi Christian population were forced from their homes in Mosul when armed insurgents occupied the city. The AAS–A committee, which was based mostly in Sydney, immediately mobilized funds from Assyrian Australians living in different parts of the country and worked with the Assyrian Aid Society–Iraq (AAS–I) to fund emergency relief efforts. AAS–I itself was forced to relocate its operations during this time, moving along with those fleeing Mosul and setting up mobile distribution points for material aid in different parts of Northern Iraq. Two of the committee members of AAS–A traveled from Sydney to New York during this period to advocate at a UN meeting on indigenous rights, speaking as representatives of AAS–*Iraq*.

In describing the field of refugee diaspora humanitarianism in this way, my research was unavoidably multisited. Here, I draw on George E. Marcus's description of multisited research "designed around chains, paths, threads, conjunctions, or juxtapositions of locations in which the ethnographer establishes some form of literal, physical presence, with an explicit, posited logic of association or connection among sites that in fact defines the argument of the ethnography" (1995, 105). Since I understand the transnational engagements of RDOs as having implications for refugee communities and the international refugee regime, it was necessary for me to follow these organizations to where their effects were felt—from the spaces where RDOs organize and mobilize support, to the humanitarian contexts in which they work, to the places where international humanitarian responses are governed, and all the travel in between. My research design, then, was to "follow the people" (Marcus 1995)—or, perhaps more accurately, to follow the organizations.

While I considered the main actors in my field to be organizations (RDOs), this is not an organizational ethnography. To start with, twenty-six different RDOs make an appearance in this book, and it was neither my intention nor a possibility to provide a detailed portrait of each of these. Although I originally conceived of this research as focusing on one or two case study RDOs, it became clear as my fieldwork progressed that such a design was not feasible. This was due to the very loose and informal structure of RDOs. It was hard to see how one would productively spend a year or more "deeply hanging out" with a group of people who may meet face-to-face only a few times a year, live in different places spread across considerable distances, and organize sporadically.[4] Instead, I decided to talk to as many people involved in RDOs as I could to see what I could learn about different approaches to helping within refugee diaspora communities and whether there were common threads. In reaching out to representatives of different RDOs early on, I quickly learned that there *are* commonalities in the ways in which these organizations work. It then made sense to design my research around a cross section of RDOs and to be opportunistic in "hanging out" with as many people and RDO-related activities as possible.

After spending time with people involved in a range of RDOs, I soon began to see these types of organizations as shared ideas that have effect, rather than as formal entities that can be discerned through their organizational structure, policies, physicality, culture, and histories. Unlike other ethnographic studies that take an organization as their object of inquiry (cf. Agier 2011; Schwartzman 1992; Wigley 2006), RDOs are much harder to grasp. While many of the RDOs in this study were incorporated associations in Australia, in practice they were loose in structure, small, and informal, and almost all had no physical presence. There was no office to meet in, and there were very few written documents or policies to refer to. It is for this reason that I chose to place equal emphasis on interviews with people involved in RDOs—to privilege the individual actor worldview as much as observing and participating in the activities of, or interactions within, organizations. Moreover, it quickly became apparent that the small number of individuals who are motivated to create or sustain an RDO—who invest so much time, resources, and energy into this pursuit—are fundamentally important to the nature and effect of these organizations. The people I spent time with or interviewed were those who were invested in an RDO in some way, either as an organizer, supporter, or beneficiary. As figure 0.1 illustrates, interviewees represented a significantly diverse group in terms of diasporic affiliation, gender, age, refugee experience, recency of arrival, and profession.

Along with interviews with key informants, the data were gathered through ethnographic fieldwork over an eighteen-month period (2015–2016) and involved participant observation with RDOs and actors they engaged with (representatives of other humanitarian organizations, RDO supporters, and beneficiaries). Fieldwork was conducted in Australia, Switzerland, Thailand, Indonesia, in transit and online (fig. 0.2). It involved participating in or observing the day-to-day operations and activities of different RDOs, including fundraising events, planning meetings, community awareness–raising activities, online discussion forums, social media groups (i.e., Facebook groups), and annual general meetings. When the opportunity arose, my fieldwork extended to traveling with five members of one RDO to Jakarta, Indonesia, to join their efforts over six days in trying to help a group of asylum seekers from their community (Oromo from Ethiopia). In 2016, another opportunity came up to travel to the Thai-Burma border to visit a site where a Karenni RDO had been actively engaged (Ban Noi Soi refugee camp). While I did not travel with members of the RDO on this occasion, the RDO

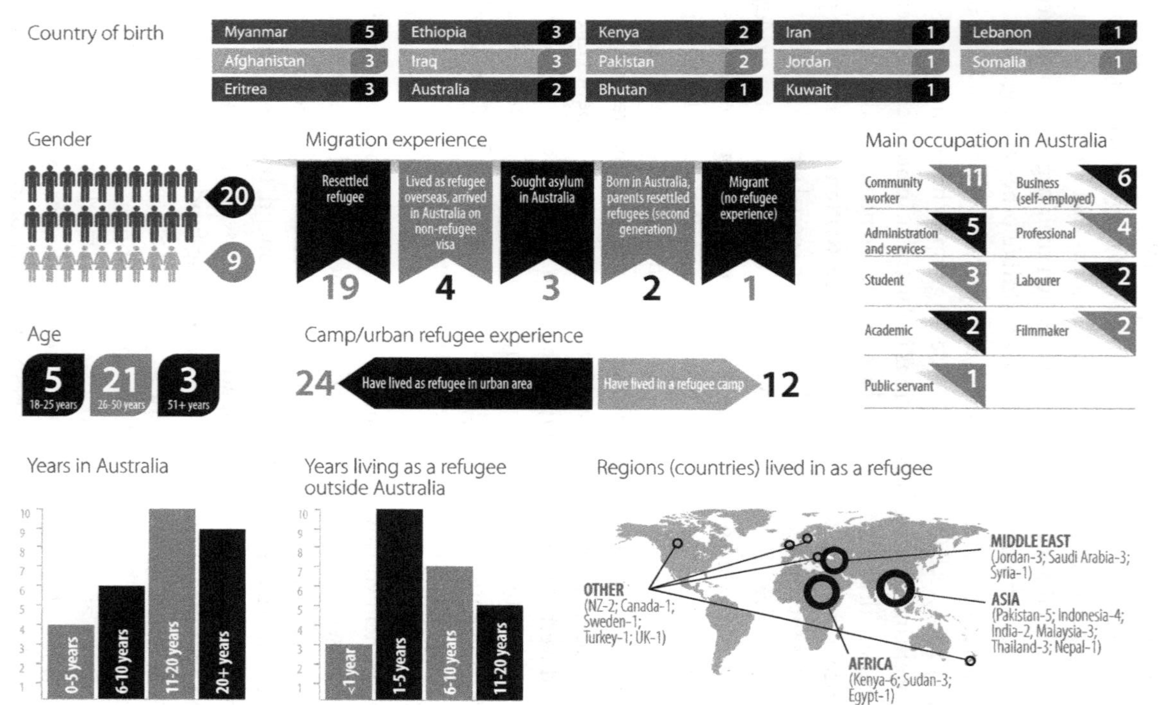

Figure 0.1 Profile of interviewees from RDOs.

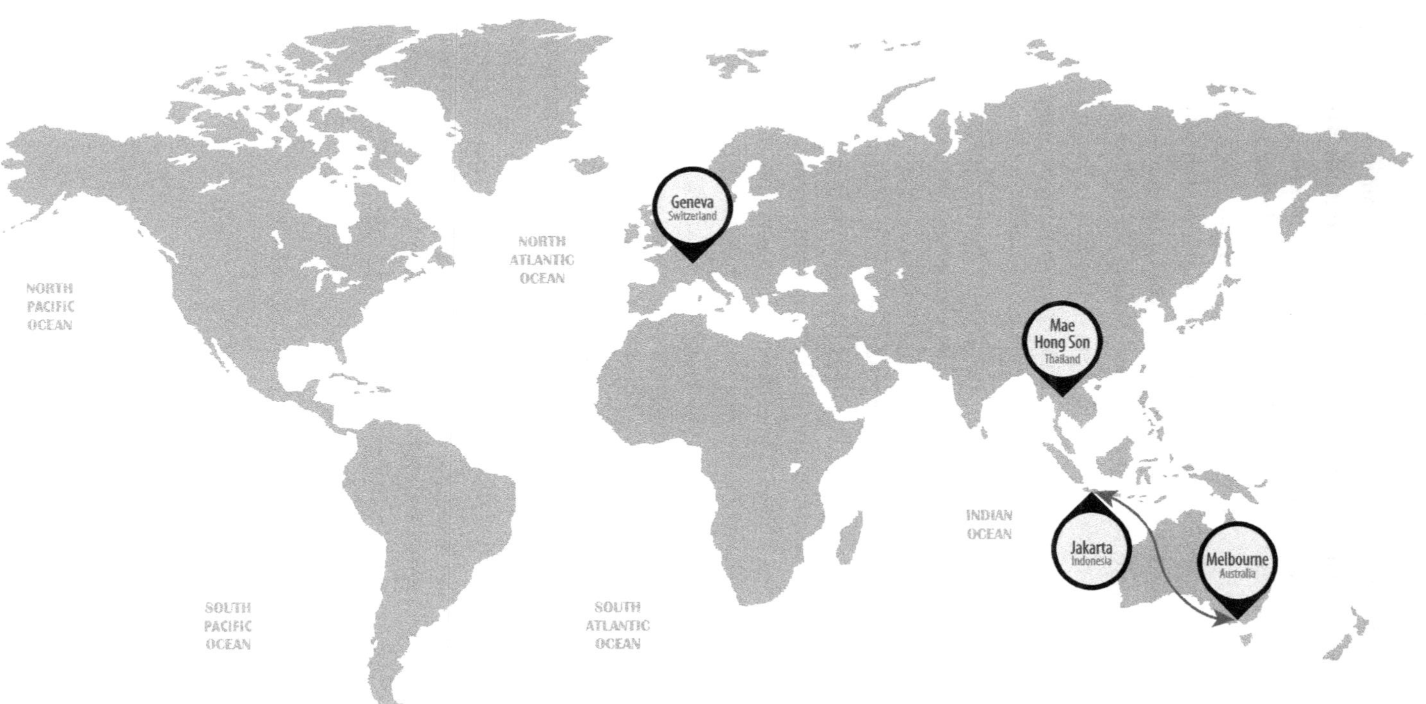

Figure 0.2 Fieldwork sites.

facilitated my visit through its connections with local community-based organizations (CBOs) based in Mae Hong Son, a village just outside Ban Noi Soi camp, and I met with representatives from a number of different CBOs and observed their activities over two days. Finally, fieldwork was undertaken in Geneva at and around the annual UNHCR NGO Consultations in July 2015, where more than five hundred delegates from over two hundred NGOs and ninety-one countries working in international refugee protection were in attendance. This fieldwork was enabled by my role as both a doctoral researcher and an employee of the Refugee Council of Australia. Participation in the Australian NGO delegation to Geneva allowed me to observe the interaction of refugee diaspora advocates (from Assyrian, South Sudanese, Hazara, Eritrean, and Bhutanese communities) with other humanitarian actors and to engage in formal and informal discussions.

Although I have already pointed to the challenges of researching refugee diaspora humanitarianism, I considered it important to try to view the world of RDOs using an anthropological approach—that is, "from the ground level" (Ortner 1984). As Fassin writes of the importance of ethnography in deepening our understanding of humanitarianism: "Ethnography provides insights into the convictions and doubts of the actors, their blind spots and their lucidity, their prejudices and their reflexivity: we owe our informants the respect of restoring these dialectical tensions" (2010b, 13). And, while interviews gave me a window into how the key actors involved in RDOs understood (or wished to represent) their own actions, it was the "friction" (Tsing 2005) that I observed while traveling with RDO members or participating in their activities that added a different dimension to these actors' words. Listening to the way people framed their actions when addressing different audiences and observing body language when different people interacted allowed me to reap much deeper insights into the "always incomplete and sometimes discomforting picture" (Bornstein and Redfield 2010, 253) of refugee diaspora humanitarianism than I could have through interviews alone. As Bornstein and Peter Redfield suggest, "Both devils and angels, as it were, reside in the details" (2010, 253).

ABBREVIATIONS

AAS–A	Assyrian Aid Society–Australia
AAS–I	Assyrian Aid Society–Iraq
ABF	Australian Border Force
AGD	Age, gender, diversity
AOCAV	Australian Oromo Community Association in Victoria
ASPIRE	Australian Society for Palestinian Iraqi Refugees Emergency
CBO	Community-based organization
CBP	Community-based protection
CRLC	Cisarua Refugee Learning Centre
CTD	Convention travel document
CWS	Church World Service
DEMAC	Diaspora Emergency Action and Coordination (ECHO) project
DGR	Deductible gift recipient
DLN	Diaspora Learning Network
EAHA	Eritrean Australian Humanitarian Aid
ECHO	European Union's Humanitarian Aid and Civil Protection department
ECOSOC	United Nations Economic and Social Council
FAO	Food and Agriculture Organization
ICRC	International Committee of the Red Cross
ICT	Information and communication technologies
IDP	Internally displaced person
IFRC	International Federation of Red Cross and Red Crescent Societies
IHL	International Humanitarian Law
INGO	International nongovernmental organization

IOM	International Organization for Migration
JRS	Jesuit Refugee Services
KnFA	Karenni Federation of Australia
KnRC	Karenni Refugee Committee (Thailand)
MSF	Médecins Sans Frontières
NGI	Nongovernmental individual
NGO	Nongovernmental organization
NRV	Network for Refugee Voices
OCHA	Office for the Coordination of Humanitarian Affairs
PRS	Protracted refugee situation
RCOA	Refugee Council of Australia
RDO	Refugee diaspora organization
RHP	Refugee and Humanitarian Program (Australian government)
RSD	Refugee status determination
STARTTS	Service for the Treatment and Rehabilitation of Torture and Trauma Survivors (Australia)
UN	United Nations
UNDP	United Nations Development Programme
UNHCR	United Nations High Commissioner for Refugees
UNICEF	United Nations Children's Fund
UNRWA	United Nations Relief and Works Agency for Palestine Refugees in the Near East
WASH	Water, sanitation, and hygiene
WFP	World Food Program
WHO	World Health Organization

HELPING FAMILIAR STRANGERS

ONE

HUMANITARIANISM AND THE INTERNATIONAL REFUGEE REGIME

A CENTRAL PREMISE OF THIS book is that refugee diaspora organizations (RDOs) helping forcibly displaced people elsewhere in the world are humanitarian actors. For some, this is an uncontroversial statement; for others, questions will be raised as to whether nontraditional actors like RDOs should be placed under the umbrella of humanitarianism and what it means for practices of humanitarian intervention if the concept is stretched to include a more diverse set of actors and actions. This unease could be felt, for example, when a leading humanitarian organization, Médecins Sans Frontières (MSF), pulled out from participating in the World Humanitarian Summit in 2016. One senior MSF executive believed the "liberal application" of the humanitarian label—which saw the inclusion of disaster-affected people, Southern nongovernmental organizations (NGOs), the private sector, and diaspora groups in the summit—was "unhelpful" because it let states off the hook and muddied what were held to be the fundamental principles (and exceptionalism) of humanitarian action: impartiality, independence, and neutrality (Parker 2016). Furthermore, and as Michael Barnett and Thomas G. Weiss usefully point out, what is at stake when the term *humanitarianism* is more expansively applied goes beyond simply establishing who is admitted as a member of the club:

> Humanitarianism concerns saving lives at risk. . . . Aid workers often undergo considerable hardship and run considerable risks to help those in need. Sometimes their only protection in war zones is the respect that they are conferred by combatants because of the presumption that they are only there to keep people alive. The goals, principles, and relationships to politics are not merely rhetorical flourishes to be buried in documents in filing cabinets or to display on brochures and websites. Rather, such expressions of identity govern

> the means and ends of humanitarian action as well as shape the most effective ways to establish lifelines to vulnerable populations. (Barnett and Weiss 2011, 17)

For Barnett and Weiss, there is utility to retaining a narrow definition of humanitarianism: "If humanitarianism means everything, it might very well mean nothing, stretching the concept to the point of uselessness" (2011, 11). In this chapter, the contours of these perspectives are explored.

HUMANITARIANISM OR HUMANITARIANISMS?

Miriam Ticktin suggests that humanitarianism is, among other things, "an ethos, a cluster of sentiments, a set of laws, a moral imperative to intervene, and a form of government" (2014, 274). That this concept has been deployed in such disparate ways means that two people writing about humanitarianism can, in effect, be writing about very different things. One way of clarifying these different ideas is to start with the broadest sense in which the concept has been used—*humanitarianism as an ethos*, or, to use a lay definition, "an active belief in the value of human life" (Wikipedia, n.d.)—and then to focus more narrowly on *humanitarianism as practice*.

HUMANITARIANISM AS ETHOS

In its broadest sense, *humanitarianism* has been taken to mean an ethos or "cluster of sentiments" that places value on human beings and compels action. Scholars who take this wider view of humanitarianism see the centrality of questions of morality in distinguishing humanitarians from other types of actors (Fassin 2010b; Feldman and Ticktin 2010; Pacitto and Fiddian-Qasmiyeh 2013; Ticktin 2014; Wilson and Brown 2009). Moreover, humanitarian morality involves the idea of a "common humanity"—of all humans being fundamentally equal and all lives being valued.[1] Humanitarian morality has been historically linked to the rise of human rights discourse and liberal altruism in Europe and America (see Laqueur 2009) and is said to differentiate humanitarian acts from other acts of caring, such as the actions of states toward citizens or socially and culturally prescribed acts of caring for family or friends. Superficially, humanitarians care for people in need *because they are human* and they recognize their suffering, not because it is their responsibility or duty to care. Although boundaries of responsibility are malleable, humanitarianism has come to mean the crossing of boundaries—of "going beyond the call of duty" (Barnett 2011, 19).

As a hypothetical example, the Japanese government may respond to an earthquake in its territory by funding emergency services, providing temporary food and shelter for earthquake-affected families, and supporting the rehabilitation and recovery of local communities, but its actions would not usually be framed as humanitarian. In the context of Japan as a wealthy welfare state, there is an expectation that the government has the capacity and responsibility to assist its citizens in the case of a natural disaster. However, were the earthquake to have taken place in the Solomon Islands—another sovereign state where the government may have fewer resources to respond to those affected by a disaster—and the Japanese government sent the same emergency responders, provided food and shelter, and offered to assist in the rehabilitation and recovery of local communities, its actions *would* likely be framed as humanitarian. This is because the Japanese government has no clear obligation to help the people of the Solomon Islands but may evoke a *moral* imperative to act. Another example is to consider whether sending money to help a relative or friend who is in need—perhaps they were caught up in the hypothetical earthquake in the Solomon Islands or Japan and lost their home—would be considered a humanitarian act. Again, while there may be a moral imperative to help, it has been argued that obligations to family or friends differ from the moral sentiments that underlie obligations to a "common humanity" (see Bornstein 2012, 8–9), hence the idea of humanitarians transcending boundaries and "saving strangers" (Wheeler 2000).

With this definition in mind—of humanitarianism necessarily involving a moral imperative to come to the aid of a fellow human and the idea of there being a "common humanity"—there are many potential actors, actions, and contexts that could be described as humanitarian. We can see this in the loose way in which the humanitarian label is used to describe a range of actors and situations. For example, a humanitarian act could be one that takes place on a microlevel (an act of compassion by one individual toward a stranger in need) or on a much grander scale (as in the case above of a government responding to a disaster in another country). There are some excellent monographs that illustrate this more expansive definition of humanitarianism. Didier Fassin's *Humanitarian Reason: A Moral History of the Present* (2010b) includes a wide range of humanitarian actors and contexts. The "objects" of humanitarianism Fassin describes are "the victims of poverty, homelessness, unemployment, and exile, as well as of disasters, famines, epidemics and wars—in short, every situation characterized by precariousness" (2010b, x). Ilana Feldman and Miriam Ticktin's *In the Name of Humanity* similarly brings together a wide array of contexts and actors that are linked by their common evocation of "humanity" as a force of "threat and care" (2010).

An important caveat to note here is that to be considered a humanitarian actor, one does not have to be motivated *only* by a moral imperative. We could easily identify other motivations behind why so-called humanitarians respond in the ways that they do (see, for example, De Lauri 2019 on the figure of the "humanitarian soldier" in Afghanistan). What is key is that moral sentiments are centrally espoused and entangled in the actions that follow. This is well articulated by Fassin, who develops the idea of "humanitarian reason" as "a consensual force" that is "morally driven" and "politically ambiguous" (2010b, xii). Fassin writes: "In contemporary societies, where inequalities have reached an unprecedented level, humanitarianism elicits the fantasy of a global moral community that may still be viable and the expectation that solidarity may have redeeming powers. This secular imaginary of communion and redemption implies a sudden awareness of the fundamentally unequal human condition and an ethical necessity to not remain passive about it in the name of solidarity—however ephemeral this awareness is, and whatever limited impact this necessity has" (2010b, xii).

Fassin is particularly interested in the way humanitarian reason "serves both to define and to justify discourses and practices of the government of human beings" (2010b, 2). For Fassin, humanitarianism involves paradoxes of emancipation (alleviating suffering) and domination (control over the people one is "saving"). He provides a collection of ethnographic accounts of how humanitarian reason animates disparate actors and actions that then lead to dominant forms of humanitarian government, which Fassin is ultimately critical of. At the heart of his critique is the idea that humanitarianism does not address the causes of human suffering. He suggests that humanitarianism may be more about those who benefit from global injustices and inequalities feeling better about themselves than redressing these injustices and inequalities. He sees humanitarianism as complicit with the globalizing forces of neoliberal capitalism and the interests of powerful nation-states that benefit unequally from this system and are dominant in their engagement with humanitarianism. Finally, Fassin draws on the work of Giorgio Agamben (2005) to argue that humanitarian reason pays more attention to biological life, or "bare life" (*zoē*), than biographical life (*bios*), "the life through which they could, independently, give a meaning to their own existence" (Fassin 2010b, 254).[2] These ideas will be returned to in the final chapter of this monograph, when we consider what the acts of RDOs tell us about humanitarianism.

HUMANITARIANISM AS PRACTICE

One focus within this area of study is on dominant humanitarian practices, or humanitarian government (see Agier 2010; Barnett 2005; 2011; Barnett and Weiss 2011; Fassin 2010b; Guilhot 2012; Reid-Henry 2014; Salehyan 2005; Sezgin 2015). In this literature, definitions of humanitarianism tend to draw on iterations of what the "high priests of humanitarianism"—the International Committee of the Red Cross (ICRC)—define as humanitarian action: "That involving both assistance and protection in times of man-made and natural disasters and governed by the aspirational four core humanitarian principles developed by the ICRC in

1986 and subsequently adopted by conventional actors: humanity, impartiality, neutrality, and independence" (DEMAC 2016b, 10; GHA 2014).

There is an articulation of context and temporality to this understanding; that humanitarian intervention is what is done to protect people and to reestablish the sovereignty of the nation-state in the aftermath of disasters, until such time as the state becomes the source of protection for people within its territory.[3] Michael Barnett's *Empire of Humanity* (2011) is particularly insightful as a history of the evolution of this dominant form of humanitarian government. Since the First World War, Barnett contends, the organization of humanitarian action has "largely followed the tremendous internationalization, institutionalization, and rationalization of global affairs. Today there exists an international humanitarian order" (Barnett 2011, 21). This humanitarian order has been described as a "globalized apparatus" and a form of "moving sovereignty" (Agier 2010, 32).

The globalized apparatus of the international humanitarian order consists of a surprisingly few, and very large, institutional actors. To know who these are, look to the structures within the Office for the Coordination of Humanitarian Affairs (OCHA), the part of the United Nations (UN) secretariat responsible for "bringing together humanitarian actors to ensure a coherent response to emergencies."[4] While the OCHA mandate is broadly intended to "coordinate effective and principled humanitarian action in partnership with national and international actors"—and therefore works with a range of different actors—there is a group of lead agencies that OCHA works closely with and that are mostly affiliated with the UN system. Nine organizations have been designated as lead agencies in the OCHA emergency cluster response system, with other international nongovernmental organizations (INGOs) and NGOs working in partnership with these lead agencies: Food and Agriculture Organization, International Federation of Red Cross and Red Crescent Societies, International Organization for Migration (IOM), Office of the United Nations High Commissioner for Refugees (UNHCR), Save the Children, United Nations Children's Fund, United Nations Development Programme, World Food Programme, and World Health Organization.[5]

The reference to this system as an international humanitarian *order* implies both a hierarchy and a structure of interrelationships (see also Barnett and Weiss 2011; Redfield and Bornstein 2010, 18–19). Indeed, hierarchy is apparent when looking at trends in global humanitarian funding showing which actors receive the lion's share (fig. 1.1). The Global Humanitarian Assistance Report (2019), for instance, recorded that in 2018, US$28.9 billion was given to humanitarian relief by government and private donors. Of this, 51.4 percent (US$14.7 billion) went to multilateral organizations (i.e., UN agencies), 34.3 percent (US$9.8 billion) went to NGOs, 7.7 percent (US$2.2 billion) went to Red Cross and Red

Crescent Societies, and 4.9 percent (US$1.4 billion) went directly to public sector responses (Development Initiatives 2019, 63). Of the 3.1 percent of humanitarian funding that was granted to local or national actors in 2018, the majority went to national governments (2.6 percent), with a meager 0.3 percent of donor funding going to national NGOs and 0.1 percent to local NGOs (Development Initiatives 2019, 64).

Many of the scholars who have focused on dominant humanitarian practices and the international humanitarian order have done so critically, highlighting many of the tensions therein. There have been critiques that international humanitarianism is a "creature of the world it aspires to civilize," replete with concepts of Western liberalism (Barnett 2011, 9; Reid-Henry 2014); that the espoused universality of humanitarian principles are inconsistently applied in the messy reality of conflicts, disasters, and global inequalities, and that humanitarianism is always implicated in politics (Agier 2011; Barnett 2005; De Lauri 2019; Fassin 2010b; Smillie and Minear 2004; Walters 2010); that humanitarianism is "defined by the paradox of emancipation and domination" inasmuch as it seeks to govern those it seeks to save (Agier 2011; Barnett 2011, 11; Fassin 2010a; Harrell-Bond 2002); that it involves a "hierarchy of humanity" that distances humanitarian actors from the people they serve (Fassin 2010c; Krause 2014); that the practices of dominant humanitarian organizations limit and diminish the ways in which those in the West understand, connect, and act in solidarity with "vulnerable others" (Chouliaraki 2013; Fassin 2010a; Harrell-Bond 2002; Krause 2014; Richey and Ponte 2011); and that it is about meeting the needs of others as well as (increasingly) meeting the needs of humanitarian actors themselves (Fassin 2010a; Krause 2014; Malkki 2015; Redfield 2012).

These critical insights are important and necessary in understanding the actors, actions, contexts, and drivers of this international humanitarian order. Yet if we were to understand humanitarianism *only* in the way that is defined in this literature and by dominant humanitarian practices, then RDOs may well be excluded from discussions. After all, they have limited interaction, impact, or visibility within this international order. There are also questions about how RDOs embody or aspire to embody the aspirational humanitarian principles of humanity, impartiality, neutrality, and independence when they are explicitly connected to *the particular* (a homeland, a people) as opposed to *the universal* (humanity, humanness). RDOs do not seem to fit within this understanding of humanitarian practice or government (see Sweis 2019 and also the discussion on morality and motivations in chap. 3).

Of course, we may choose to call RDOs something else—aid organizations, rather than humanitarian organizations—but then the idea of who is a legitimate humanitarian becomes narrower. This is an idea that Hugo Slim—former head

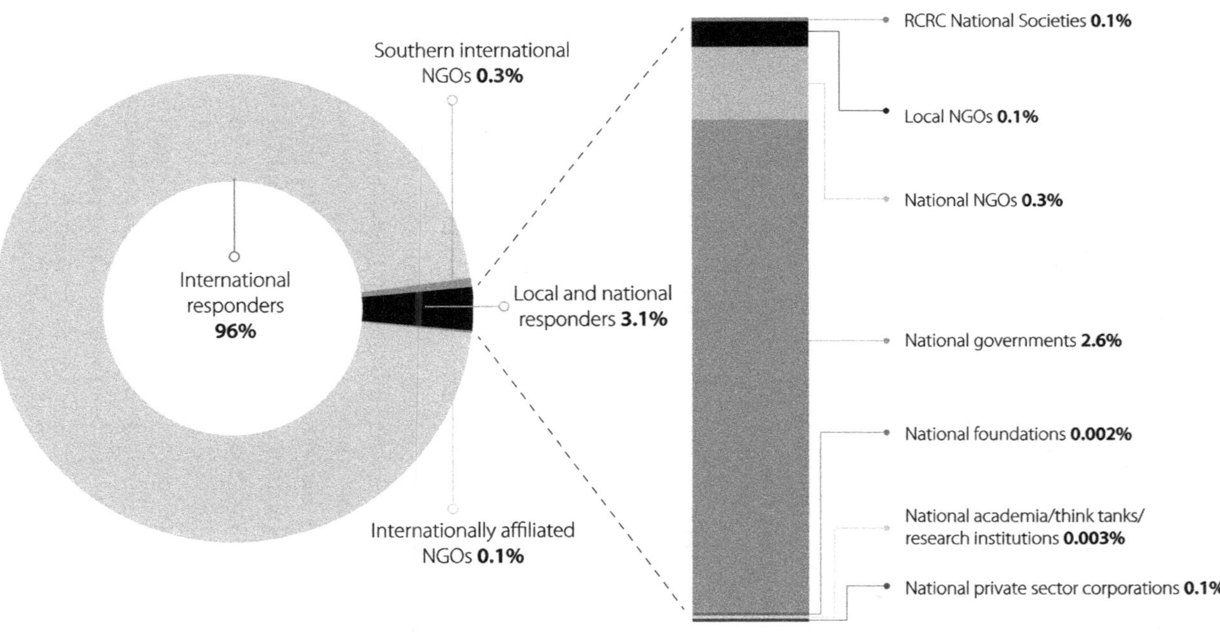

Figure 1.1 Direct humanitarian funding by actor type, 2018.
Source: Development Initiatives 2019, 64.

of policy for ICRC—also takes issue with. Slim writes that the conflict among those who would see humanitarianism as defined by a particular set of professional actors is a case of "professionalism gone mad": "I wonder if there is an analogy between humanitarianism and humour. Laughter is a universal good. What would the world be like if only clowns were allowed to be funny and make people laugh? This would be a terrible world that confined humour to a professional class and restricted a universal human desire and capacity. At times, it can sound as if NGO humanitarians are suggesting something similar about humanitarian action. It is something they want everyone to value and enjoy but which only they are allowed to do" (2003).

It is not hard to see why so much of the humanitarianism literature thus far has focused on the dominant practices, histories, and narratives of the international humanitarian order. However, there is a tendency in this literature to sideline or simply ignore the fact that there are diverse practices of caring for strangers in times of crisis. Barnett himself acknowledges that "we live in a world of humanitarianisms, not humanitarianism" (2011, 10), even while his work is centrally focused on dominant practices.

OTHER HUMANITARIANISMS

The ideas of humanitarianism as an ethos as well as a practice do not necessarily conflict with each other or my own understanding. However, I wish to emphasize two additional points about how the concept of humanitarianism is deployed in this book and applied to the work of RDOs. First, the idea of humanitarianism as an ethos or cluster of sentiments that places value on human beings and compels action in response to human suffering is not the unique domain of Western or European traditions. There are many different and evolving traditions of compassion that evoke the need to care for suffering strangers. Second, recognizing that there are dominant humanitarian practices should not delimit bringing other humanitarian actors into this picture and understanding their own distinct histories, practices, and motivations. Indeed, more care should be taken by scholars to recognize the diversity of humanitarian practices, even when focused on more powerful actors.

The argument for adopting a more diverse understanding of humanitarianism is important because, while much has been written about dominant forms of humanitarianism, very little has been written about other traditions. Scholars such as Fassin have been criticized for their Western bias in understanding humanitarianism as the domain of the powerful and as rooted in European and Christian traditions (see Guilhot 2012; Kloos 2012).[6] Stephan Kloos suggests that by implicitly taking Western notions of the human as universal, Fassin "ends up ignoring cultural and moral diversity where they would appear to be most pertinent, namely in international humanitarian governance" (2012, 339). Julia Pacitto and Elena Fiddian-Qasmiyeh further argue that there is value in "writing the 'other' into humanitarian discourse" (2013, 4) because it may broaden and deepen our understanding of other forms of humanitarianism that can challenge the dominant humanitarian institutions in various ways to think or act differently. Indeed, these authors contend that while "the enduring influence of the Northern-dominated international regime in the humanitarian arena should not be trivialized, nor should the capacity of Southern stakeholders, including refugees and forcibly displaced persons themselves, to exert agency as actors in the humanitarian sphere" (Pacitto and Fiddian-Qasmiyeh 2013, 2). As to what these other humanitarian traditions are, there is surprisingly little written. Some notable exceptions are the emerging literature on Islamic aid (Benthall and Lacey 2014), Eastern traditions of charity as they are applied to humanitarian contexts (O'Hagan and Hirono 2014), and Southern humanitarian actors more generally (Pacitto and Fiddian-Qasmiyeh 2013). Ethnographic studies by Erica Bornstein (2012) on humanitarianism in New Delhi and Rania Kassab Sweis (2019) on Syrian-American doctors responding to the Syrian Civil War are two excellent examples of anthropologists writing *the other* into scholarship on humanitarianism.

As to the importance of bringing diverse humanitarian practices into view in debates about the international humanitarian order, it is worth noting that this order should not be seen as a "seamless, coherent, and all-encompassing conduit for individualizing and depoliticizing neoliberal discourses and biopolitical technologies" (Robins 2009, 639–640). As much of the literature on dominant humanitarian practices shows, there are complex struggles and significant stakes in how actors respond to suffering. Richard Ashby Wilson and Richard D. Brown warn that one should "be careful not to over systematize this loosely bounded ethic of moral and political action" (2009, 4). Barnett also argues that "to the extent that humanitarianism is developing and organizing outside the existing, Western-dominated system . . . then there are good reasons to believe that humanitarianism is entering a new stage. More interactions among different networks might change the very character of humanitarianism, perhaps making it more universal, perhaps less so" (2011, 15–16). As such, Barnett urges scholars to write the history of other humanitarian traditions and to consider the interactions between different actors (see also O'Hagan and Hirono 2014).

In sum, humanitarianism has been used to mean and explore many and varied things. It has been deployed as an ethos, as a set of laws, and as an evolving and dominant practice (humanitarian government). I do not wish to challenge these ideas but to suggest that making distinctions between different forms of humanitarianism is both useful and necessary (hence *refugee diaspora* humanitarianism). Recognizing the distinct and situated moralities and practices of different humanitarian actors should not preclude them from being under the same umbrella. As Bornstein usefully points out, "Most scholars of . . . humanitarianism would agree that sponsoring the education of an orphan or giving to beggars on an urban street is not usually considered to be in the same category as the institutional complex of international humanitarian aid. Yet the two forms are linked through the gift—connecting those who are excluded from resources with those who are willing and able to actively engage" (2012, 12). Humanitarianism, then, is about the connections made between different people—those in need and those who act in response—and these connections are likely to vary significantly depending on who the person, organization, or institution is that is doing the helping and how they understand or relate to the person or people in need. As such, there is not one humanitarian reason; there are potentially very many.

FORCED DISPLACEMENT AND THE INTERNATIONAL REFUGEE REGIME

Humanitarianism can be seen in many contexts and can involve different actors and actions. This book is interested in humanitarianism that specifically focuses on one group of strangers-in-need—persons of concern to the international refugee regime: refugees, internally displaced persons (IDPs), and asylum seekers. These strangers-in-need exist within the field of refugee protection—a field that has effect on all that come within its boundaries (forcibly displaced people, humanitarian actors, states, and international laws).[7] I first introduce the concept of forced displacement and refugees before discussing the field of refugee protection.

WHAT IS A REFUGEE?

Refugees exist within much broader and overlapping experiences of forced displacement. Forcibly displaced populations who do not fall under the mandate of the international refugee regime but who share many similarities include those who have been displaced by environmental disasters, state fragility, livelihood failure, or development projects (Türk 2011). While recognizing that there would be overlaps in the engagement of diasporas in helping other forcibly displaced populations, this book is centrally concerned with the refugee label—what it signifies and the implications of this system of classification (Uehling 1998)—and I have purposefully narrowed my focus to this particular experience of forced displacement.

The term *refugee* has a very specific legal meaning set out in the 1951 Convention Relating to the Status of Refugees (UN Refugee Convention) and its 1967 Protocol as "any person who owing to a well-founded fear of being persecuted for reasons of race, religion, nationality, membership of a particular social group or political opinion, is outside the country of his/her nationality and is unable, or owing to such fear, is unwilling to avail himself/herself of the protection of that country" (Article 1A, Refugee Convention, 189 UNTS 137).

According to this legal definition, refugees lack the protection of their own governments and benefit from an internationally endorsed protection framework, supplemented by constitutional, legislative, and "soft law" guidelines (Feller 2006). While the UNHCR mandate has been significantly stretched over recent years to include support for other forcibly displaced populations, refugees are still the prime *raison d'être* of UNHCR, which was specifically created in 1950 to ensure their protection and assistance (Loescheret al. 2008).[8] Other groups who also fall under the mandate of UNHCR are people seeking international protection who have not yet gone through a refugee status determination process (asylum seekers) and people who have not crossed an international border but otherwise meet the refugee definition (IDPs).

What, then, does it mean to be a *person of concern* to the international refugee regime? Being labeled a refugee or seeking to be recognized as a refugee requires entering the field of refugee protection. Refugee protection can be conceptualized as a field because a person who crosses an international border and claims, seeks to claim, or is conferred the legal status of *refugee* has no intrinsic properties that mark them as a refugee. They could be classified in many alternate ways—as an undocumented migrant, temporary visitor, tourist, businessperson, and so on. However, once a person claims protection by applying for refugee status determination or being recognized as a *prima facie* refugee, they enter a social world with very real effects and defined by multiple actors with varying positions, power, and stakes.[9] These effects are both real and symbolic.

THE INTERNATIONAL REFUGEE REGIME

Entering the field of refugee protection involves direct engagement with the international refugee regime. This regime can be understood as a dominant structure governing global responses to particular situations of forced displacement. Anthony Giddens describes the most important aspects of structure as the "rules and resources recursively involved in institutions" (1984, 24) that allow "the 'binding' of time-space in social systems" (1984, 17). Drawing on this idea, the international refugee regime's solidity in time and space comes in the (legal) form of the 1951 Refugee Convention and 1967 Protocol as well as the (institutional) form of the UNHCR and its 1950 mandate. Together, the institution and laws articulate three preferred solutions to forced displacement—the repatriation of refugees to their country at the earliest possible stage, local integration in countries of first asylum, and resettlement in a new country—otherwise referred to as the Durable Solutions Framework (UNHCR 2004). At the time of writing, over eighty-nine million people were displaced from their homes by conflict and persecution and included under the UNHCR mandate (UNHCR 2022). That is, around 1 percent of the world's population could be considered within the field of refugee protection.

The solutions to displacement articulated by the international refugee regime are about putting people "in place" and, in particular, territorializing people within a state (Malkki 1992). The purpose of the refugee regime is to ensure that substitute protection is provided by "the international community" for people who flee their homes because their own state is unwilling or unable to ensure access to their most fundamental rights and until a time in which their original or a new state can provide effective ongoing protection (Betts 2010, 361). This regime is currently dominated by an emphasis on repatriation as the preferred solution, even while this has become less realizable (Bessa 2009). At the same time, local integration and third-country resettlement are solutions for only a small fraction of refugees. To put this in numbers, out of the 79.5 million persons of concern to UNHCR in 2019 (pre-pandemic), only 107,800 were resettled to a third country, 5.6 million returned home, and 55,000 were recorded as locally integrated in that year (UNHCR 2020a).[10] This represents the realization of a durable solution for a meager 7.3 percent of the population of concern to UNHCR.[11] The limited solutions for those within the refugee regime have resulted in a growing number of people living in protracted refugee situations and relying on the international community for protection and support, as well as an increasing irregularity of movement of people seeking protection further afield and failing to find it.

The effects of the field of refugee protection on those who are its central objects (refugees, asylum seekers, IDPs) are multifold and can be understood from many perspectives. I focus here on legal protection, institutional support, and symbolic effects.

Legal Protection

The effects of being labeled a refugee are usually discussed in terms of legal protection, the most widely understood and held being the principle of *non-refoulement*. Non-refoulement in international law forbids "the rendering of a true victim of persecution to his or her persecutor" (UNHCR 2014b)—in other words, sending a person back to a place where their life will be in danger. Other than the principle of non-refoulement, there is very little clarity about what *refugee protection* means in practice, as it relates to both international and domestic laws that vary considerably and are inconsistently applied in different countries and contexts. James Hathaway suggests that protection is hard to define because "there is no universally accepted standard of quality of life, nor of the role that government should play in meeting the hopes and needs of its citizenry. This plurality of experience and outlook restricts any attempt to define in absolute terms the nature of the duty of protection which a state owes to its people" (2005, 105–106). Dallal Stevens argues that the lack of clarity about what is meant by refugee protection and the variations and proliferation of protection concepts have diluted the meaning such that protection can be associated with fewer rights obligations by states toward refugees within their territory (2013, 234). While it is impossible to make a definitive statement about what being labeled a refugee will mean in terms of legal protection, some of the rights that it may afford include the right to remain (not be detained or deported); the right to government services (e.g., education, health, social, and income support); the right to work, own property, enter into legal contracts, and attain identity documents; the right to a pathway to citizenship (full political rights); and the right to apply for and attain resettlement in a third country.

Institutional Responses

Being designated a refugee has the potential to entitle a person to institutional support, particularly from those organizations mandated to work with refugees. In many contexts where states have limited capacity, this support is provided by UNHCR, implementing partners (often NGOs), and other humanitarian organizations representing the international community. As with legal protection, what this means in practice varies considerably depending on context. For example, if a person seeks asylum in Australia, UNHCR offers no practical support, as the Australian government has domestic laws and policies that afford those seeking protection some rights as well as institutional support.[12] However, in situations of mass displacement following conflict or in protracted refugee situations, UNHCR and other humanitarian organizations may play a more central role in assisting those under their mandate. These institutional supports range from the provision of assistance to meet basic needs (e.g., emergency housing, food, water, sanitation, hygiene, primary health, and security) to more sustained supports (e.g., for livelihoods, education, training, and community development). Depending on the constraints on institutional resources and the legal environment for refugees, entitlement to access these supports can be restricted or limited, making the institutional effects of being classified as *a refugee* contingent on access.

Symbolic Effects

Finally, entering the field of refugee protection has symbolic effect. As Liisa Malkki (1996) suggests, becoming a refugee entails having an identity that is conferred. This identity is often bound to concepts of vulnerability, pathologization, suffering, and loss. A refugee's personal history—whether they were a doctor, a businesswoman, or a former member of parliament—is erased within the field of refugee protection. Drawing on the work of Michel Foucault, Malkki argues that the term *refugees* denotes "an objectified, undifferentiated mass that is meaningful primarily as an aberration of categories and an object of 'therapeutic interventions'" (1992, 33). Refugees become suffering subjects or objects of vulnerability to be helped: "The homogenizing, humanitarian images of refugees work to obscure their actual sociopolitical circumstances—erasing the specific, historical, local politics of particular refugees, and retreating instead to the depoliticizing, dehistoricizing register of a more abstract and universal suffering" (Malkki 1995, 13).

The effect of this symbolic conferral of the refugee label can be illustrated in the way that refugees who help are treated as an anomaly and considered newsworthy.[13] Take, for example, the following headlines from a simple Google search of "refugees help out":

- "Syrian Refugee Saves the Day after Ontario Bride Has Dress Mishap"[14]
- "Refugees Volunteer as Firefighters in Australia"[15]
- "Meet the Syrian Refugee Leading the Help for Flood Victims in England"[16]
- "Refugee Who Came to Lancaster County Helps Louisiana Flood Victims as Red Cross Volunteer"[17]
- "Former African Refugee Now Helping North Queensland Seniors Regain Strength and Stay Fit"[18]

What presumably makes these stories newsworthy is that the refugees are acting as helpers. Replacing the word *refugee* with an alternative designation in the above further illustrates the symbolic effect of the refugee label.[19] In all these cases, the refugee could have been labeled in alternate ways as a person who is helping in their local community, but instead they are valorized or seen as exceptions for helping others.

Take, for example, the first story of the Syrian refugee who "saves the day" in Canada. This story was first posted on Facebook by a wedding photographer and was subsequently reported in the Huffington Post after the story went viral on social media. The story is about a man, Halil Dudu, who fixed a broken zipper on a bride's dress on her wedding day. Dudu, who is a master tailor by profession, was staying in the house next door to the bride and came to the rescue after a member of the wedding party knocked on his door to ask for some pliers. Dudu offered to fix the zipper, and did so. The situation is described in the article as "incredible," leading one to question *In what way?* It was certainly incredibly lucky that the person who had exactly the skills needed to fix a problem was coincidentally found next door. But if Dudu had been a Canadian-born master tailor who happened to be having lunch with friends when a frantic request came to help with a bride's broken zipper, would this story have made international news? I would guess *no*. What is incredible in this story and in the response to the story is that Dudu was also a refugee from Syria. The subtext is that refugees are to be helped, not do the helping. Perhaps more telling is the tendency within this and other articles to refer to these actions as refugees *paying back* their local communities, subtly diminishing their actions and their power by suggesting their contributions are transactional—a clearing of debt for having been helped rather than an act of compassion or goodwill that is usually attributed to people who help. Dudu is reported in the article as saying, "I was so excited and so happy [to] help Canadian people like other people helped [me]." The idea of repaying *the gift* of resettlement is further explored in chapter 3.

HUMANITARIAN BORDERS AND THE EVERYDAY LIVES OF REFUGEES

Having briefly laid out what refugee protection means for those who are central to this field, I turn now to how this field intersects with humanitarianism. If helping people in need is at the core of humanitarianism, then humanitarian action targeting refugees must be calibrated to their needs. In this, refugees and humanitarianism can be said to be intertwined in a number of ways: first, by conceptualizing the international refugee regime as a form of humanitarian government and its failings as a source of suffering in and of itself; second, through understanding how humanitarianism is implicated in the control of borders and mobility (humanitarian borders); and last, through the multitude of humanitarian actors who feel compelled in different ways to ease the suffering of refugees and who refugees turn to for help.

In terms of this first and primary intersection, it is beyond the scope of this book to offer an in-depth analysis of the international refugee regime as a system of humanitarian government. This has been ably done by others (see, for example, Agier 2008; Betts 2010; Loescher et al. 2008).[20] The second intersection relating to humanitarian borders will also receive only rudimentary acknowledgment here, for there is growing and important work that explores the complex and troubling relationship between Northern borders, constraints on mobility, and the provision of humanitarian assistance. It has been argued for some time that the proliferation of humanitarian action in borderlands—including the externalization of territorial borders—needs to be understood as part of the exercise of power and control masked as compassion (see Walters 2010; Williams 2015). There is, for example, ample evidence that the flow of aid from the Global North and forced migrants from the South move in opposite directions, illustrated by the seismic increase in aid flows to the EU borderlands of Turkey, Lebanon, and Greece from 2015 as a measure to stem the flow of refugees trying to enter Europe (Tsourapas 2019). These are troubling because the idea of *humanitarianism* becomes further tainted in these very obvious juxtapositions of control and compassion. This is perhaps even more starkly illustrated in the case of Australia, whereby the reimposition of a violent offshore immigration detention complex on remote Pacific Islands in 2013 (see Tofighian 2020) was and still is articulated in compassionate or humanitarian terms as "saving refugees from drowning at sea" (Little and Vaughan-Williams 2017). I do not wish to weigh in on these important debates, because in many ways, they are more interested in questions of power exercised by dominant actors—states and Northern actors—and in which refugee diaspora humanitarianism can be understood as partly a consequence of the exercise of control described by the humanitarian borders idea and the resulting failures of the international community to protect those who are displaced. Instead, I am interested in the third intersection—everyday humanitarianism and the multitude of actors who step in to help refugees in the spaces created by border regimes and the international refugee regime, with all its possibilities and failings. One may think of this in relation to James Ferguson and Akhil Gupta's concept of "transnational governmentality"—nonstate actors (NGOs, activists, international organizations) who govern in zones the state has ceded or abandoned (see also Agier 2008; Fassin 2010a). Ferguson and Gupta argue that "the outsourcing of the functions of the state to NGOs and other ostensibly non-state agencies . . . is a key feature, not only of the operation of national states, but of an emerging system of transnational governmentality" (2002, 990).

Indeed, there are many ways in which we can see refugees looking to nonstate actors to meet their basic needs, particularly as most live in host countries that have very little capacity to provide for refugees within their borders, even if there is a willingness to do so. In 2018, for example, a third of the global refugee population (6.7 million people) was living in the Least Developed Countries (UNHCR 2019). At the same time, and as Wilson and Brown point out, "there is no obvious legally-constituted international setting for those in dire need of humanitarian assistance to pursue their claims against a potential state provider, even if such a claim could be acknowledged as a right. Consequently, potential recipients are more reliant upon the moral impulses of those who provide assistance or aid" (2009, 8). This reliance on humanitarian assistance is troubling when one considers how sporadic or deficient institutional humanitarian responses can be and how much depends on the context in which refugees find themselves.

HUMANITARIAN CONTEXTS

The following is an attempt to loosely sketch the contexts in which humanitarian actors are focused on persons of concern to the international refugee regime. These can be broken down in terms of *spaces* (i.e., refugees in camps, refugees outside camps, internally displaced, and asylum seekers) or *temporality* (i.e., from emergencies to protracted refugee situations).[21] A humanitarian context could thus be described using dimensions of both space and time (see fig. 1.2). Furthermore, there are conventional ways that dominant humanitarian actors coordinate their response in the aftermath of a displacement crisis, as large numbers of people are fleeing immediate violence and key agencies set up temporary camps to respond and administer to urgent needs within a fluid environment. This is one refugee camp context. But a refugee camp that has existed with a relatively stable population for forty years could still be considered a humanitarian context if those administering to the needs of encamped refugees are primarily humanitarian actors. As we will see in chapter 2, the RDOs that participated in this study were acting in all these contexts.

Spaces

Refugees in Camps

Much has been written about the suffering of refugees in camps (see Agier 2010; 2011; De Montclos and Kagwanja 2000; Horst 2008a; Lischer 2005; Turner 2016). The causes of suffering in refugee camps are frequently attributed to camps as a system of humanitarian government. Discussion about *refugee warehousing* in camps has highlighted, for example, the lack of basic rights and freedoms and the violence of confining people to a limited space and administering to their needs (see US Committee for Refugees and Immigrants 2004). While setting up refugee camps has not been a preferred policy of UNHCR for some years, in practice, 28.6 percent of refugees were living in planned/managed camps at the end of 2016 (UNHCR 2017, 55). But beyond the broader critique of camps as a (violent) system of humanitarian government, there are also critiques of how humanitarian actors address the needs of encamped refugees. Some have argued that the *actions* of humanitarian organizations in camps can be disempowering and dehumanizing (Harrell-Bond 2002) and others that it is the *inaction* of humanitarian actors that causes suffering (Agier 2010). For example, in Thailand—where I conducted fieldwork and where the Thai government does not allow the free

TIME				
	Emergencies/crisis situations		Protracted situations	
Spaces	Needs	Response	Needs	Response
Refugee camps	Safety from violence and persecution in home country. Basic needs e.g. shelter, WASH, food, medical.	Coordination, setting up and management of camps. Aid provision (focus on more urgent needs). Refugee status determination (RSD), identity documents	Basic, social and community needs (including livelihoods, education). Safety from violence and exploitation in country of origin and asylum. Rights, freedom.	Aid provision (basic needs, social and community services). Camp management and policing. Advocacy and support for durable solutions, rights etc.
Refugees outside camps	Safety from violence and persecution in home country. Basic needs.	Aid provision (focus on more urgent needs). Advocacy and support to access housing, services. Status recognition.	Safety from violence and exploitation in country of asylum and origin. Basic, social and community needs. Rights (e.g. to work, education, access justice).	Advocacy and support for durable solutions, rights etc. Aid provision (basic needs, social and community services).
Internally displaced	Safety from violence and persecution. Basic needs.	Coordination, setting up and management of IDP camps OR creating safe spaces in non-camp settings (e.g. military, policing, peacekeepers). Aid provision (focus on more urgent needs).	Integration into local communities. Access to social and community services. Access to justice (e.g. compensation for property taken or destroyed).	Multi-level advocacy. Aid provision (basic needs, social and community services). Camp management and policing.
Asylum seekers	Safety from violence and persecution in home country. Access to legal process (RSD) and status. Basic needs.	RSD processing and legal support. Aid provision (focus on more urgent needs).	Safety from violence and exploitation in country of asylum (e.g. trafficking, smugglers). Basic, social and community needs. Legal rights and freedoms (e.g. legal status, not subject to arbitrary detention, access to justice system).	Multi-level advocacy. Aid provision (basic needs, social and community services). Legal services (including support for RSD).

Figure 1.2 Humanitarian spaces, needs, and responses over time.

movement of refugees from Myanmar outside of nine long-established border camps—informants spoke of the shifting of resources by aid agencies away from camps toward activities preparing for or supporting repatriation to Myanmar. For those in Thai refugee camps, then, the experience of humanitarianism was initially one of (forced) reliance and is now shifting to concerns about the *lack of* humanitarian or other kinds of support that would allow those who do not feel safe to return to Myanmar to live in safety and dignity.[22]

Refugees outside Camps

At the end of 2016, 63 percent of refugees lived outside camps in private accommodation in urban and rural areas (UNHCR 2017, 55). The needs of refugees living outside camps clearly vary depending on local context but are often associated with lack of legal protection and insecurity; lack of access to work, an income, an education, and health, legal, and other services; and vulnerability to exploitation and abuse without the effective protection of the state or recourse to justice. In these contexts, refugees interact with humanitarian actors who either advocate on their behalf or provide the services and support that may otherwise be available to (nonrefugee) resident populations. Again, to use one of my fieldwork sites as an example, Indonesia is not a signatory to the Refugee Convention. Refugees registered with UNHCR in Indonesia either live in the community with limited protections and rights or are detained in immigration detention centers. Those living in the community are unable to legally work, and their uncertain legal status makes them susceptible to exploitation, discrimination, and abuse. Refugees in these contexts without their own safety net (e.g., family networks, savings) may be reliant on humanitarian actors for basic income, housing, education, and health and legal services, surviving or thriving depending on the capacity of humanitarian actors to meet their needs.

Internally Displaced

There is growing recognition that IDPs whose experiences of persecution, insecurity, violence, and flight are comparable to those of refugees face similar challenges to those who cross an international border: they struggle to meet their basic needs and to access services and longer-term security.[23] For example, IDPs in Iraq were targets of a number of RDO activities in this study because neither the Iraqi government nor many humanitarian actors could easily provide emergency relief due to the volatile and insecure areas in which they sought refuge. IDPs' needs are often unmet because of the failings of the international refugee regime to articulate any longer-term or durable solutions for people who have not crossed an international border. Addressing the needs of IDPs is also potentially more difficult for humanitarian actors because of their more limited capacity to mobilize funding and support for interventions targeting citizens within a sovereign state.

Asylum Seekers

There is a significant and growing body of literature on the needs of people who are seeking international protection and have not (yet) had their status determined (see Agier 2008; Essed and Wesenbeek 2004; Gleeson 2016; Higgins 2017; JSS 2015; McAdam and Chong 2014; Missbach 2015). People seeking asylum often experience violence and insecurity, dangerous journeys, exploitation and abuse, detention and the denial of liberties and rights, and a lack of access to basic services. The spaces of those seeking asylum can be thought of less as physical places and more as territories (legal, geographical) that they move through. Humanitarians respond to the needs of asylum seekers as advocates and as providers of basic services. The Australian government, for example, is legally responsible for ensuring the basic needs and rights of asylum seekers. In reality, however, government policy has led to state-sanctioned violence and deprivation of those seeking asylum. As with refugees in other urban settings, asylum seekers in Australia may be residing in an affluent, stable society but are not afforded the protections of living safely and in dignity in this context. Tess Altman describes this as a "neoliberally induced humanitarian crisis," whereby denying asylum seekers the right to work and/or providing a living allowance well below the poverty line results in a forced reliance on humanitarian actors to survive (2015; see also JSS 2015).

Temporality

With all the spaces sketched above, situations and needs change over time and present different possibilities for humanitarian action. While humanitarianism in its dominant form is closely associated with responses to immediate and unfolding crises—to what Barnett calls "emergency humanitarianism" (2011)—the contemporary picture is that few conflict situations resolve quickly and large numbers of the world's displaced people live as refugees for many years, if not decades. The continuum between emergency and protracted refugee situations and who and what the responses should be along this continuum are a central challenge for the international humanitarian order. The need to reconsider the temporariness of humanitarian interventions has been highlighted by scholars and practitioners alike, who acknowledge that humanitarian actors need to consider and plan for how, for example, temporary shelters may realistically become homes for people for much longer periods of time (Brun and Fábos 2015; Frerks 2004). A key and unresolved concern is how to bridge the gap between providing relief in emergency situations and ensuring appropriate responses to protracted refugee situations that somehow fall "between relief and development" (Frerks

2004). This is particularly challenging when considering that it is much easier to mobilize resources—both public and private—in the immediate aftermath or spectacle of a disaster than it is to sustain or impel action as disaster turns into a slow and unremarkable "condition of life" (Feldman 2012, 155; Malkki 1996).

LIVING WITH AND WITHIN FLAWED GOVERNANCE SYSTEMS

Having sketched out the ways in which humanitarian actors are involved in the lives of refugees, it is worth noting that most literature that has focused on this intersection has explored dominant humanitarian actors and responses—those best described as being at the more powerful end of the international humanitarian order. While these actors and dominant forms of humanitarian practice are undeniably important, they also face significant and well-documented shortcomings. Refugees, asylum seekers, and IDPs continue to suffer despite, or sometimes even because of, the existence of (dominant) humanitarian actors. I refer here to the practices of refugee camps described earlier (Agier 2010) and of critiques that have been leveled at humanitarian actors, including UN agencies, for their complicity in acts of violence (see Crisp 2018; Forsythe 2009). This is where a deeper understanding of how other humanitarians are engaged in helping refugees is important. It is not to say that other ways of helping will be or are any less flawed, but that we need to go beyond critique of dominant forms of humanitarian government and look at possibilities for how things could be done differently.

The significance of dominant humanitarian actors in the everyday lives of refugees must also be questioned. This is not a new argument. Several scholars have questioned the bias in refugee studies on visible humanitarian actors and the role they play in the everyday lives of refugees. Oliver Bakewell warns that access to and the experiences of refugees are often filtered through the eyes of policy makers and practitioners and that this can skew their resulting importance in the picture (2008; see also Harrell-Bond and Voutira 2007). This idea was reflected in my own fieldwork experiences, with a number of exchanges being memorable in this regard. In Indonesia, I spent two days visiting community-based organizations (CBOs) set up by refugees and asylum seekers. I visited these CBOs with members of a local Indonesian-Oromo association. The Indonesian-based Oromo asylum seekers were struggling to meet their basic needs and were keen to find out from other refugees how they had managed to survive in Indonesia. One of the people the Indonesia-based Oromo asylum seekers met was an Iranian man who had been living in Jakarta for some years and had been involved in setting up an effective support network. As he was explaining what his group was doing, he leaned toward members of the Indonesian-Oromo association and said, "Listen, no one will help you. IOM, UNHCR, JRS, CWS . . . don't bother. You have to help yourselves."[24] The next day, when we visited a different CBO outside Jakarta, the cofounder used almost exactly the same words: "No one else is going to help you. You are on your own."

The advice that was passed from one refugee to another—that they were *on their own*—was not because formal humanitarian organizations in Indonesia were doing nothing. Rather, they were communicating the very limited capacity of these institutional actors and their importance in their everyday lives. This sentiment best describes the contexts in which refugee diaspora humanitarianism takes place. It takes place, in part, *because* of the failings of the international refugee regime to realize durable solutions for people "out of place" and *because* of the limitations of dominant humanitarian actors and systems to effectively respond to the diverse temporal and spatial contexts that people central to the international refugee regime inhabit.

TWO

THE ECOLOGY OF REFUGEE DIASPORA HUMANITARIANISM

THIS CHAPTER LAYS THE FOUNDATION for exploring questions of *why, how,* and *to what effect* refugee diaspora communities are engaged in helping "familiar strangers." Before addressing these more substantive questions, I first discuss what is meant by the term *refugee diasporas,* particularly in the Australian context. I then describe what refugee diaspora organizations (RDOs) do in the simplest of terms; this description is not intended to provide commentary or analysis of what these actions mean, but rather to give the reader a sense of who is involved in RDOs, where they are working, and what they are doing. I present this through a snapshot of the characteristics of twenty-six RDOs that participated in this study, as well as a descriptive illustration of five RDOs, selected to highlight the diversity of people, contexts, and practices. This chapter lays out the broad brushstrokes of an ecology of refugee diaspora humanitarianism.

REFUGEE DIASPORAS

This study is focused on *refugee diasporas*—on helpers who have personal experience of the international refugee regime and who identify in a diasporic way. When using the term *diaspora,* I draw on Khachig Tölölyan's work in conceptualizing four main, overlapping dimensions to the diaspora concept: (1) diasporas are "born of catastrophe" and are shaped by the centrality of "memory, commemoration and mourning"; (2) diasporas are a subset of ethnic minorities distinguished by culture/collective identity that preserves homeland language or religious, social, and cultural practice but that allows for degrees of "biculturalism"; (3) diaspora is a "process of collective identification and form of identity," not a fixed concept and social formation; and (4) diaspora is part of an "uncertain, indeterminate process of diasporization" (2007). In further clarifying what I mean by diasporas in this book, I make two key points: there is value in seeing *refugee* diasporas as a subset and diasporic self-identification has effect; it *does* things.

Refugee Diaspora as a Subset

While a much broader group of diasporas in Australia could have been included in this research, I purposefully focused on refugees as a subset of diasporas because of their (past) relationship with the international refugee regime. As this study is interested in humanitarian responses to refugees, it seems that those who identify in a diasporic way and who have spent time as refugees and as objects of humanitarian responses will have distinct knowledge, experiences, and networks that inform their own acts of helping.[1]

A question that arises from this is whether there is utility in including diasporas from vastly different backgrounds under the one umbrella. For argument's sake, what are the commonalities between a Bhutanese RDO and one established by Eritrean Australians? In response, I suggest that there is utility in linking refugee diasporas together because of the commonalities they share as having experienced life as refugees. Although it is important to keep sight of the "specific histories of displacement and dwelling" and the "ambivalent politics of diaspora in view" (Clifford 1994, 313), it is also possible to see common threads in the experiences of those who have engaged with the international refugee regime and then resettled in a third country.[2] As was argued in the previous chapter, coming within the field of refugee protection is a structuring experience with multiple effects. Other scholars have likewise suggested that there is utility in applying diaspora as a conceptual tool for understanding the particular experiences, beliefs, and practices of refugees as a subset of diasporas (see Butler 2001; Malkki 1995; Van Hear 2006, 2009; Wahlbeck 2002). Kim Butler, for example, argues that the reasons for dispersal—categorized by "degrees of volition"—will result in different types of relationships between diasporas, their homelands, and their host societies (Butler 2001; see also Wahlbeck 2002).

What Refugee Diaspora Communities Do

In developing the concept of refugee diasporas, Nicholas Van Hear suggests that "if displacement persists and people consolidate themselves in their territories of refuge, complex relations will develop among these different domains of what we may call the 'refugee diaspora': that is, among those at home, those in neighbouring territories, and those spread further afield" (2006, 9). In this, Van Hear focuses on refugee diasporas' *transnational* engagements—the interrelationships between groups of people who are dispersed—rather than on the effects of diasporic identification on local lives and communities. What Van Hear (1998, 2006, 2009) suggests is that interrelationships between different groups of refugee diasporas have effect—they *do* things. He conceptualizes key differentials in the interrelationships of refugee diasporas spatially, with the "near diaspora" being those in neighboring territories and the "wider diaspora" being those further from the homeland, mostly in countries he describes as affluent (e.g., the United States, parts of Europe, and Australia). Van Hear suggests that at least three sets of relations emerge from this understanding of refugee diaspora: between the homeland or territory of origin and the neighboring country of first asylum, between the neighboring country of first asylum and the wider diaspora, and between the homeland and the wider diaspora (2006, 11).

As to what exactly refugee diasporas do, there has been a tendency in research to focus on the political and economic dimensions of refugee diasporas' transnational engagements and on the relationships between diasporas and homelands (see Brinkerhoff 2012; Collier 2000; Fullilove 2008; Nyberg-Sørensen 2007; Sharma et al. 2011; Williams 2012; Zinterer 2005). Paul Collier, for example, focuses on the role of diasporas in financing and exacerbating conflict, emphasizing the "romanticized attachments to their group of origin" and their propensity to "nurse grievances as a form of asserting continued belonging" (2000, 14). However, more recent studies of diaspora transnationalism provide a more discriminating view, suggesting that "the influence of diasporas is rarely consistent across whole groups and often shifts over time" (Van Hear and Cohen 2017, 172). Van Hear and Robin Cohen develop a useful schema for understanding these varying and shifting transnational engagements, arguing that there is value in distinguishing three spheres of diaspora engagement: "The largely private and personal sphere of the household and the extended family; the more public sphere of the 'known community,' by which is meant collectivities of people who know one another or know of one another; and the largely public sphere of the 'imagined community,' which includes the transnational political field, among other arenas" (2017, 172–173).

The transnational engagements of the RDOs in this study fit best within this second sphere, engagement with the "known community" (see fig. 2.1). Indeed, Van Hear and Cohen list the activities of diaspora-based welfare organizations to provide relief for the victims of conflict among those taking place within this sphere.

Distinguishing different spheres and sites of diaspora engagement is useful because it allows us to see the plurality of diasporas' overlapping transnational engagements—and of collective acts of helping (humanitarianism) as only one

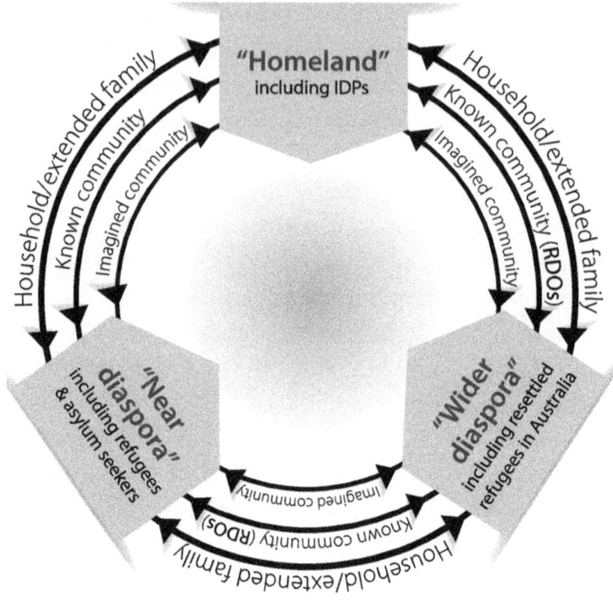

Figure 2.1 Spheres and sites of refugee diasporas' transnational engagements.

small piece in this. As Van Hear and Cohen suggest—and as was made apparent in this research—those in the diaspora are often pulled in multiple directions by "a portfolio of obligations" across these different spheres (2017).

Understanding the plurality of spheres and sites of transnational engagements also helps to avoid generalizing statements about the effects of refugee diasporas, particularly to conflict-affected societies. For example, the effects of remittance-sending practices between households and extended families have received considerable attention (see Hansen 2004; Horst 2008b; Lum et al. 2013; Monsutti 2004; Poole 2013; Shandy 2006), as has the political activism within "imagined communities" (Betts and Jones 2016; Danforth 1995; Koinova 2011; Missbach 2013; Mojab and Gorman 2007), with varying conclusions drawn. For those interested in imagined communities and long-distance politics, diasporas have been cast as either the makers or breakers of peace. For those interested in household survival, diasporas are vital lifelines for conflict-affected communities. Yet these engagements happen simultaneously. Those in the diaspora can be sending money to families caught up in a conflict while also lobbying or otherwise supporting parties to a conflict.

In this study, then, it should be clear that humanitarianism is but one aspect of refugee diasporas' transnational engagements and may take place at the same time as other engagements and with mixed effects. While it was not within the scope of this research to explore these simultaneous engagements, I do not want to dismiss their existence nor suggest that the acts of helping described in this study are necessarily of primary importance in the "portfolio of obligations" of those involved in RDOs. Yet it remains important to understand acts of collective helping within "known communities," just as it remains important to understand other spheres of diaspora engagement. As Van Hear and Cohen suggest, activities in the "known community" may have a slightly different value and effect in helping to "repair the social fabric shredded by years of conflict, not least by helping to re-establish social linkages ruptured during war, and re-building trust and confidence" (2017, 173), an idea that will be returned to in chapter 7.

In sum, the diaspora concept is useful because it allows us to see how people identify collectively and in dynamic ways as a consequence of migration. It helps us understand relationships between groups of people across space and time and their effect. Placing the people and organizations in this study within this context also allows us to see refugee diaspora humanitarianism as part of a complex web of transnational practices.

REFUGEE DIASPORAS IN AUSTRALIA

Figure 2.2 provides a visual representation of refugee diasporas in the context of Australia. The larger group of "ethnic minorities" could be considered anyone who migrated to Australia or is the descendent of a migrant. In Australia, this would mean almost the entire population, although if we focus on more recent migrant experience, this equates to roughly half the population.[3] The circle of "refugee and humanitarian entrants" is anyone who arrived in Australia under the Refugee and Humanitarian Program (RHP). This is a discrete and identifiable group defined by visa category (discussed below). The shape depicting *diasporas* would more accurately be drawn and redrawn as constantly moving, acknowledging that diasporas are fluid, as people identify collectively in different ways and at different points in time.

I begin with the more straightforward and discrete group of refugee and humanitarian entrants before addressing the amorphous question of diasporic identification and association in the Australian context.

Refugee and Humanitarian Entrants

Australia has a long history of accepting refugees, displaced persons, and others fleeing persecution for permanent settlement. Refugee historians have pointed to arrivals of groups fleeing persecution as early as the 1830s, with Germans fleeing religious persecution in Russia settling in South Australia (Price 1990). However,

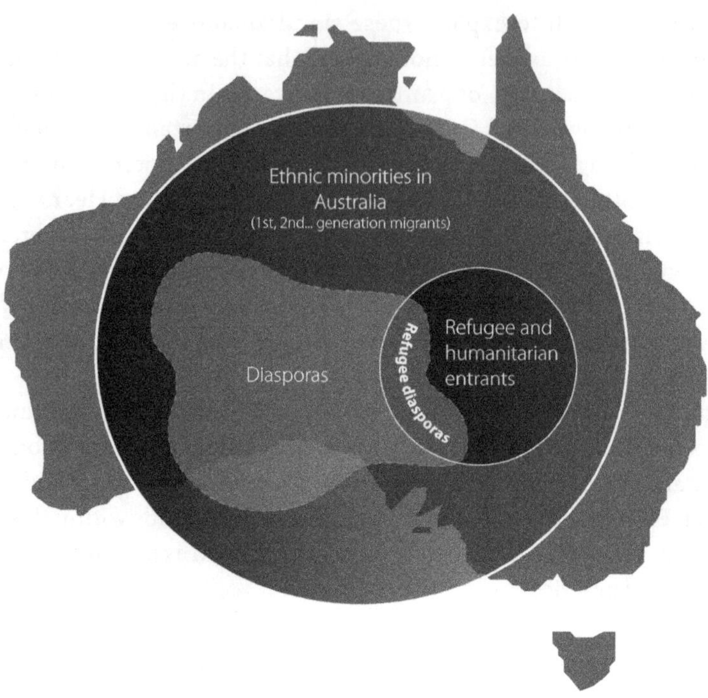

Figure 2.2 Refugee diasporas in Australia.

Charles Price and others (Hugo et al., 2011) point to 1938 as the year in which Australia began to play a major role globally in refugee resettlement by accepting large groups of Jews fleeing Nazi Germany. Even then, it was not until the latter years of World War II that involvement in refugee issues became a major element in Australian government policy, and it was not until 1978 that refugee-humanitarian migration became a subprogram within Australia's larger immigration program (Hugo et al. 2011, 4–5). It has been estimated that, since Federation, over 800,000 refugee and humanitarian entrants have settled in Australia (Refugee Council of Australia, n.d.).

Since its inception, Australia's RHP has provided permanent settlement to a relatively stable number of people each year, with an average of 13,880 refugee and humanitarian visas granted per annum between 1985 and 2020 (see fig. 2.3). The size of the RHP has hovered between 11,000 and 20,000 annually and sits within a much larger and tightly controlled migration program (ibid.). In terms of composition, table 2.1 shows the top countries of birth of refugee and humanitarian arrivals since 1991. Many countries on the list still have ongoing conflict or sizable populations that have been displaced elsewhere in the world. Since the

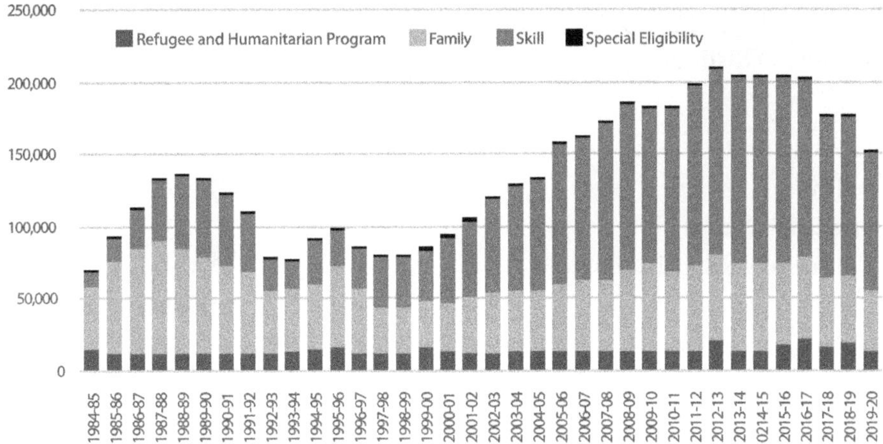

Figure 2.3 Permanent migrants to Australia: Visa grants by migration stream, 1984–1985 to 2019–2020. Source: Data up to 2012–2013 taken from Phillips and Simon-Davies (2014, 3). Data from 2012–2013 to 2019–2020 taken from the Australian Government Department of Home Affairs website, accessed February 22, 2021, https://www.homeaffairs.gov.au/research-and-statistics/statistics/visa-statistics/live/migration-program.

1970s, Australia has progressively narrowed its focus to resettling refugees from three main geographical regions: Asia Pacific, the Middle East, and Africa.

Australia has historically provided permanent visas to those who have been recognized as refugees in other countries and are then resettled to Australia as a third country (*resettled* refugees; see fig. 2.4). The proportion of the RHP made of people who have been found to be refugees in Australia (onshore protection visas) has historically been low, mainly due to the geographical distance between Australia and countries where most of the world's refugees have originated, as well as to Australia's highly controlled borders heavily restricting legal admission pathways to anyone who is considered likely to seek asylum upon entry (McAdam and Chong 2014).

Diaspora Associations

It is important to note that not all refugee and humanitarian entrants are going to identify or relate to each other in diasporic ways. The people about which this study is focused—resettled refugees who form organizations that help displaced people overseas—do, however, seem to fit this diaspora concept. While I do not want to spend time elaborating on the processes of diasporization, it is important to acknowledge that diaspora associational forms have a long history in Australia

Table 2.1 Top 30 Countries of Birth of Refugee and Humanitarian Entrants, 1991–2020

Country of Birth	No. Visas Granted
Iraq	81,906
Afghanistan	39,877
Sudan**	27,572
Myanmar (Burma)	27,239
China, Peoples Republic of	22,429
Former Yugoslavia	21,642
Syria	20,949
Iran	20,059
Bosnia-Herzegovina	15,100
Vietnam	10,784
Democratic Republic of Congo	9,566
Ethiopia	9,269
Sri Lanka	8,692
Croatia	7,802
Somalia	6,803
Pakistan	5,855
Bhutan	5,266
Eritrea	5,131
Thailand	4,973
Australia*	4,474
Egypt, Arab Republic of*	4,229
Sierra Leone	3,525
Liberia	3,318
El Salvador	3,008
Former U.S.S.R.	2,998
Kenya*	2,997
Indonesia*	2,787
Nepal*	2,318
Lebanon	2,245
Cambodia	2,219

* Most likely includes children born to refugees from other countries: Kenya (e.g., children of refugees from Ethiopia, Sudan, South Sudan, Somalia); Nepal (Bhutan, as well as Nepalese); Turkey (Iraq, Syria, Kurdish); Tanzania (Congolese, Burundi, Rwanda); Thailand (Burma); India (Burma, Somalia, Iran, and others); Malaysia (Burma and others); Egypt (Horn of

tied to the country's settler-colonial history; Australia's population has significantly transformed over two centuries through mass migration, the violent displacement and domination of indigenous peoples, and its evolution as a pluralist multicultural society within the modern system of nation-states.[4]

Multiculturalism has been an official government policy in Australia since the 1970s and the end of the White Australia policy. What this multiculturalism means, of course, is highly debatable (see Hage 2012). However, at a legal and policy level, there is an articulation of "the rights of all to celebrate, practice and maintain their cultural traditions within the law and free from discrimination" (Commonwealth of Australia 2011). Different tiers of government support multiculturalism through initiatives such as the establishment of multicultural advisory councils, antiracism strategies and legislation, policies and programs to increase access to and equity in government services, and provide funding for multicultural arts, festivals, and sports. Multicultural policies have enabled the expression of language, culture, and associational forms of people who have settled in Australia. There are, for example, "ethnic communities' councils" across all states and territories in Australia whose members are ethnic associations.

Australian multiculturalism is significant for understanding why resettled refugees form organizations and why they do so as clearly identifiable ethnic associations. Not only is there official endorsement of people celebrating, practicing and maintaining cultural traditions, there are also laws that govern and support the establishment of community-based organizations (incorporated associations) and allow groups to apply for funding. Indeed, there is a long history in Australia of ethno-specific or migrant-support organizations being established by different waves of settlers and playing a pivotal role in people's lives by providing support, advice, advocacy, and a sense of belonging (Jakubowicz 2002). However, this is not to say that RDOs only form because of government policy. As one interviewee who works with refugee communities in Sydney contends: "People need to associate. They need to belong and the first place you belong are [with]

Africa); Uganda, Zimbabwe (other African); Indonesia (Afghanistan, Iran, East Timor, West Papuan)

** Includes people born in what is now South Sudan.

Source: Data from 1991 to 2015 taken from Australian Government Settlement Reporting database, accessed April 1, 2016. Data from 2015 to 2020 has been taken from the Australian Government annual report on the humanitarian programme for 2019–2020 and only includes top ten countries of birth.

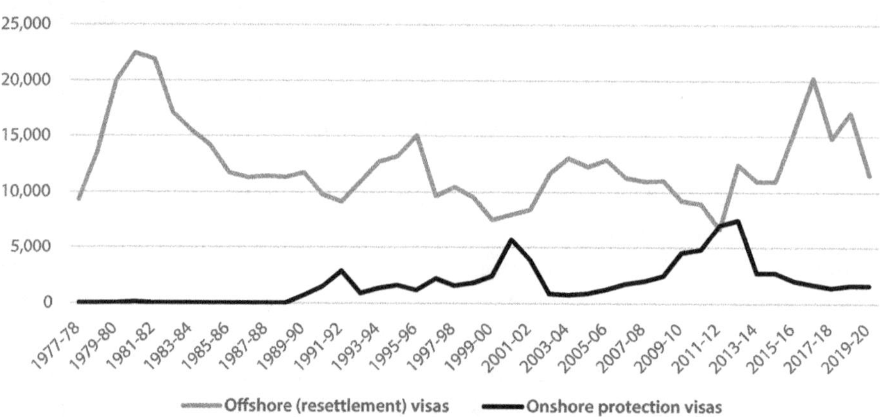

Figure 2.4 Refugee and humanitarian visas by offshore and onshore streams, 1977–2020. Source: 1977-2012 data is Australian Government data cited on Refugee Council of Australia website, accessed October 3, 2017, https://www.refugeecouncil.org.au/getfacts/statistics/aust/australias-refugee-humanitarian-program-visa-grants-stream-1977-78-2011-12/; 2012–2016 data from Department of Immigration and Border Protection annual reports, accessed October 3, 2017, https:/www.border.gov.au/about/reports-publications/reports/annual; 2016–2020 data from Department of Home Affairs annual reports, accessed February 22, 2021, https://www.homeaffairs.gov.au/research-and-stats/files/australia-offshore-humanitarian-program-2019-20.pdf.

people who speak the same language as you; who understand what you've been through. And this whole networks-for-mutual-support, I think it's something that people develop. It's a survival strategy. . . in situations of war and violence, when you don't have government to provide you protection, or a government does the opposite of providing protection, so you need to find a way of getting together and supporting each other. . . . So, people form organizations fairly quickly."[5]

Indeed, in mapping out potential RDOs to recruit for this study, I quickly identified over a hundred organizations. While not all were involved in acts of helping people overseas, all involved people who had arrived in Australia predominantly as refugees and who wished to associate as a self-identified collective (diaspora).

REFUGEE DIASPORA ORGANIZATIONS

The following section outlines some of the characteristics of the twenty-six RDOs that participated in this research. This is intended only to provide the reader with a feel for the diversity and particularities of these organizations. The categories and labels used could, of course, be problematized. For example, how meaningful is *country of origin* as a signifier for diasporas that do not self-identify with a nation-state? While many of the labels I have used have been chosen by the participants themselves, others should be taken as a rough marker for what is likely a much more complex reality.

The twenty-six "organizations or groups" (RDOs) that participated in this research were selected because they satisfied two main criteria: (1) they were formed and led by people who identify as being from the same community as the population targeted by their actions, and (2) they were involved in helping in a refugee situation outside Australia.[6] In working out which diaspora communities to recruit for this study, I decided to focus on the top countries of origin for refugee and humanitarian arrivals and excluded communities where there were no significant displaced populations overseas.[7] Diaspora communities from the top fifteen countries of origin at the time that met the criteria were from *Iraq, Afghanistan, Sudan/South Sudan, Iran, Burma (Myanmar)*, Sri Lanka, *Ethiopia*, Sierra Leone, Democratic Republic of Congo, *Bhutan*, Liberia, Somalia, *Syria, Eritrea*, and Burundi. RDOs from nine of these countries of origin participated in this research (italicized).

Characteristics

Table 2.2 provides a summary of the demographics of the diaspora communities in Australia associated with the participating RDOs (how they self-identified), who their interventions were targeting, and where they were working (humanitarian context).

Demographics

The majority (81%) of the RDOs in this study were working with target communities that they self-identified with (i.e., they were helping familiar strangers). Of the RDOs that were working with a broader target group, all also incorporated people that they self-identified with. However, there were interesting ways that groups self-identified. For example, the RDO that identified as South Sudanese purposefully included members of different ethnic backgrounds (e.g., Dinka, Nuer) within the RDO's governance structure and in its fundraising activities in Australia. The target beneficiaries were those internally displaced in South Sudan due to a conflict that has exacerbated ethnic divisions. Careful decisions were made by the RDO's organizing committee to ensure that beneficiaries were not selected based on ethnic affiliation.

Humanitarian Contexts

RDOs were working across different humanitarian *spaces*, with ten working with internally displaced, twelve working in refugee camp settings, and fifteen working

Table 2.2 Overview of Demographics of RDOs, Target Beneficiaries, and Characteristics of Humanitarian Contexts in Which RDOs Are Working

RDO	Country of Origin	Community	Country where RDO Is Working	Characteristics of Humanitarian Context						Target Beneficiaries
				IDPs	Refugee - camp	Refugee - urban	Protracted refugee situation	Complex emergency	Other*	
1	Afghanistan	Hazara	Afghanistan	•					•	Afghan (including Hazara)
2	Afghanistan	Hazara	Indonesia			•			•	Any (majority Hazara)
3	Afghanistan	Hazara	Pakistan			•	•			Hazara
4	Afghanistan	Hazara	Pakistan			•	•			Hazara
5	Afghanistan	Hazara women	Pakistan/Iran			•	•			Hazara women
6	Bhutan	Lhotsampa	Nepal		•		•		•	Lhotsampa/Nepalese
7	Burma	Karen	Thailand		•		•			Karen
8	Burma	Karen	Thailand/Burma	•	•		•		•	Karen
9	Burma	Karenni	Thailand/Burma	•	•		•		•	Karenni
10	Burma	Rohingya	Global		•	•	•		•	Rohingya
11	Burma	Zo	Malaysia			•	•			Zo
12	Ethiopia	Ogaden	Kenya		•		•			Ogaden
13	Ethiopia	Oromo	Indonesia			•			•	Oromo
14	Ethiopia	Oromo	Global		•	•	•		•	Oromo

RDO	Country of Origin	Community	Country where RDO Is Working	Characteristics of Humanitarian Context						Target Beneficiaries
				IDPs	Refugee - camp	Refugee - urban	Protracted refugee situation	Complex emergency	Other*	
15	Ethiopia	Oromo	Yemen/Horn of Africa		•	•	•	•		Oromo
16	Eritrea	Eritrean	Sudan		•	•	•			Eritrean
17	Eritrea	Eritrean	Sudan		•	•	•			Eritrean
18	Eritrea	Eritrean	Yemen/Egypt/Horn of Africa		•	•	•			Eritrean
19	Iran	Baha'i	Iran						•	Iranian (majority Baha'i) women
20	Iraq	Chaldean	Iraq	•				•		Iraqi Christians
21	Iraq	Iraqi	Iraq	•				•		Iraqi (any)
22	Iraq	Mandaean	Iraq/Syria/Jordan	•		•		•		Mandaean
23	Iraq/Syria	Assyrian	Iraq	•				•		Assyrian
24	Iraq/Syria/ Lebanon	Eastern Orthodox	Syria/Lebanon	•		•		•		Iraqi/Syrian Christians
25	Palestine	Palestinian	Lebanon/Iraq		•	•		•		Palestinian
26	South Sudan	South Sudanese	South Sudan	•				•		South Sudanese
				10	12	15	15	8	9	

* *Other* includes helping people who are currently and directly experiencing persecution but have not left their country of origin (addressing root causes of displacement), helping returnees to reestablish themselves, helping local populations in humanitarian emergencies (natural disasters) in countries that host refugees, and helping refugees or asylum seekers in transit countries.

with refugees living outside camps. The limitations and possibilities for RDOs working in these different spaces varied. For example, working with internally displaced persons (IDPs) within countries where RDO members may have an ambivalent relationship to the state (e.g., they have fled due to state-sanctioned persecution) may constrain the scope and type of help that they can offer. Providing aid to people in refugee camps also involves different possibilities and constraints for RDOs. Where access to a camp population is restricted by formal humanitarian governance structures, RDOs must either fly under the radar or partner with organizations with access to these camps. While moving in and out of urban environments may be easier for members of RDOs with Australian passports or travel documents, establishing relationships with local host communities and coordinating with other humanitarian actors can be harder in these contexts, particularly where a host government questions the right for refugees to live within their borders or wishes assistance to be directed to local citizen populations who may have similar needs.

Regarding *temporal* dimensions, fifteen RDOs were working in protracted refugee situations and eight were involved in responses to "complex crises" (IASC 1994). However, nine of the participating RDOs were working with neither long-term displaced nor those in complex emergencies. These I have categorized as *other* and include a wide array of humanitarian contexts: helping people who are currently and directly experiencing persecution but have not left their country of origin (addressing root causes of displacement), helping returnees to reestablish themselves in their country of origin, helping local populations in humanitarian emergencies (natural disasters) in countries that host refugees, and helping refugees or asylum seekers in transit countries where they have limited protection.

Activities

It is hard to characterize the activities that RDOs were involved in. As Diaspora Emergency Action and Coordination (DEMAC) well describes, "Diaspora organizations can be considered as multimandate organizations that couple relief and recovery with political, economic and social reform, linking relief, rehabilitation and development and thereby challenging the typical notions associated with humanitarian aid" (2016b, 6). That is, RDOs may be involved in activities that do not fit easily into dominant humanitarian practice frameworks. Table 2.3 illustrates the broad types of activities that representatives from participating RDOs described. These categories are not mutually exclusive. For example, some groups were providing material aid as emergency relief (i.e., collecting and sending clothes or medical supplies from Australia), and others were simply funding emergency relief (i.e., sending money to local organizations undertaking relief activities). Some RDOs were involved in a wide range of activities simultaneously

Table 2.3 Types of Humanitarian Interventions Described by Participating RDOs

RDO	Diaspora	Location	Type of Intervention								
			Advocacy	Education	Material aid	Emergency relief	Migration	Health	Infrastructure	Livelihoods	Women's empowerment
1	Assyrian	Iraq	•	•		•			•		
2	Baha'i	Iran	•							•	•
3	Iraqi Muslim	Iraq	•		•	•	•				
4	Chaldean	Iraq			•	•					
5	Eastern Orthodox	Syria/Lebanon	•		•		•	•			
6	Eritrean	Sudan		•				•	•		
7	Eritrean	Sudan			•	•					
8	Eritrean	Yemen/Egypt/ Horn of Africa		•							
9	Hazara	Indonesia		•							
10	Hazara	Pakistan		•							
11	Hazara	Pakistan	•	•	•						
12	Hazara	Pakistan/Iran						•		•	•
13	Hazara	Afghanistan			•				•		•
14	Karen	Thailand	•	•		•	•				
15	Karen	Thailand/Burma		•	•			•	•		
16	Karenni	Thailand/Burma		•		•				•	
17	Lhotsampa	Nepal				•		•			
18	Mandaean	Iraq/Syria/Jordan	•			•	•				
19	Ogaden	Kenya	•	•	•		•		•		
20	Oromo	Indonesia	•			•	•				
21	Oromo	Global									
22	Oromo	Yemen/Horn of Africa		•	•	•		•			
23	Palestinian	Lebanon/Iraq	•				•				
24	Rohingya	Global	•	•			•				
25	South Sudanese	South Sudan			•					•	
26	Zo	Malaysia	•				•				
Total			13	12	10	10	9	6	5	4	3

or as opportunities arose. This table shows that the type of activities RDOs were most commonly involved with were advocacy (n=13), education projects (n=12), material aid (n=10), emergency relief (n=10), and migration support (n=9).[8] This is only a rough indication of the types of activities that these RDO were involved in, as the data was gathered from interviews that were semistructured, and interviewees were asked to self-report on what their organization was doing to help. This meant that preidentified categories were not used to capture the nature of interventions in a systematic way. Some of the participating RDOs may therefore have been involved in other activities that were not mentioned in interviews.

It should also be noted that capturing RDO activities in this way tends to privilege certain understandings of what constitutes helping: those that can be easily named and measured. For example, when I asked, "What does your organization do to help?" the interviewees tended to draw on dominant humanitarian discourses when describing activities. Yet it was apparent through my fieldwork that there are many less measurable things that RDOs do to help, which speaks of what Michael Barnett writes when he laments the professionalization and bureaucratization of international humanitarian practice: "The desire to measure places a premium on numbers—for instance, lives lost and saved, people fed, children inoculated—to the neglect of non-quantifiable goals such as witnessing, being present, conferring dignity, and demonstrating solidarity. Is it possible to quantify, for instance, the reuniting of families, the providing of burial shrouds, or the reducing of fear and anxiety in individuals who are in desperate situations?" (2011, 216). As I explore later, the RDOs in this study were involved in helping in ways that were harder to quantify and that seemed more about witnessing, comforting, and demonstrating solidarity than about simply saving lives.

CASE STUDIES

The following case studies represent a cross section of the demographics, humanitarian contexts, and types of activities characterized above and are included here to give the reader a feel for what these characteristics mean.

Oromo Diaspora Humanitarianism in Indonesia

People from the Oromia region of Ethiopia (see map 2.1) have been displaced for many decades due to what has been described as a long pattern of often preemptive and brutal suppression by the Ethiopian state of even suggestions of dissent (Amnesty International 2014). Oromo people—with an estimated global population of twenty-five million—have been dispersed and formed diaspora communities in many parts of the world, with the largest in the United States, Canada, Australia, Kenya, Sudan, Egypt, Yemen, Saudi Arabia, and Djibouti.

Oromo in Australia predominantly arrived as refugee and humanitarian entrants and as family migrants in waves, starting from the mid-1980s.[9] While the Oromo community in Australia is well established and now includes many young adults who were born and have grown up in Australia, the political struggle for Oromo self-determination and rights within Ethiopia that began in the 1980s remains pertinent, and, at the time of this fieldwork, those identifying as Oromo were still being granted refugee status in Australia and being resettled from elsewhere.

The Australian Oromo Community Association in Victoria (AOCAV) is a not-for-profit, volunteer-run incorporated association that was established in 1984. AOCAV is one of numerous Oromo diaspora organizations in Australia that have been formed with various political, cultural, and social purposes. The main work of AOCAV is centered on the cultural and community development of the Oromo community in the state of Victoria, where AOCAV estimates approximately five thousand community members reside.[10] The activities of AOCAV include the provision of information and support programs, cultural events and festivals, sports and recreation programs, advocacy services, and settlement support. While AOCAV does not include international aid and advocacy among its stated aims, the association's website profiles activities that have focused on helping Oromo people in other countries. AOCAV is governed by a volunteer committee made up of people who identify as Oromo. The organization has a small office and one part-time paid staff member, who is funded by the Victorian (subnational) government to work on a community education program relating to family violence. All other activities are self-funded and run by volunteers.

In 2015, AOCAV became involved in supporting a group of Oromo asylum seekers living in Indonesia. As Indonesia is not a signatory to the Refugee Convention, the protection gaps there are significant. Asylum seekers and refugees face arbitrary arrest, indefinite harsh detention, and substantial discrimination in terms of housing, are not permitted to work, and have extremely limited access to health services or education. Access to humanitarian assistance in Indonesia is scarce, and refugee status determination processes, which are conducted by the United Nations High Commissioner for Refugees (UNHCR), can take years. The Indonesian government does not consider local integration a possibility for refugees, and resettlement to a third country can take many years.[11] While a small number of refugees and asylum seekers in Indonesia are eligible for some support from nongovernmental organizations (NGOs) (housing, income, education), most survive through their own means, and, at the time of fieldwork, some were giving themselves up to be detained in immigration detention centers so they could access desperately needed food and shelter (Missbach 2015).

In 2014, a member of AOCAV traveled to Indonesia for business and by chance met a group of Oromo asylum seekers standing outside the UNHCR office in

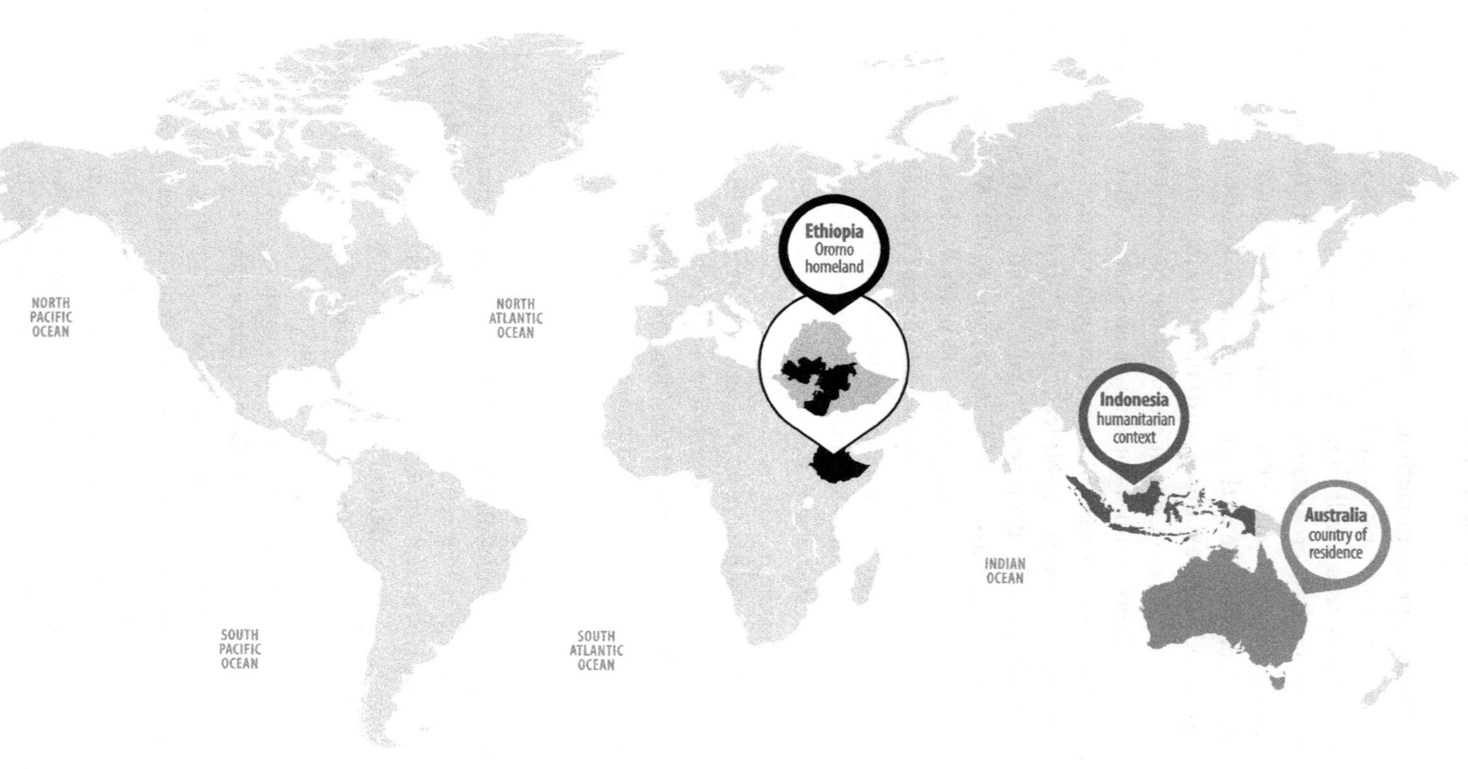
NORTH PACIFIC OCEAN
NORTH ATLANTIC OCEAN
Ethiopia
Oromo homeland
Indonesia
humanitarian context
Australia
country of residence
INDIAN OCEAN
SOUTH PACIFIC OCEAN
SOUTH ATLANTIC OCEAN

Map 2.1

Jakarta. Upon hearing about the difficult situation the people were facing, the AOCAV member returned to Australia and spread the word. What followed was a mobilization of interest and resources that eventuated in a delegation of five Oromo-Australians traveling (self-funded) to Indonesia in 2015 to try to help the two hundred or so Oromo who had sought asylum there.[12] Over a week, AOCAV held a series of meetings to bring together Oromo asylum seekers, hear their concerns, support the development of a newly formed Oromo community association in Indonesia, and identify different ways that the Oromo diaspora community in Australia and other parts of the world could help. AOCAV also set up a series of meetings between Indonesia-based humanitarian organizations, UNHCR, and members of the Indonesia-based Oromo community to discuss their concerns, including about interpreter use by UNHCR. A small amount of financial support was provided by AOCAV members to those identified as particularly vulnerable (mostly female-headed households with small children), and a commitment was made by AOCAV to support the local Indonesia-based Oromo association as it developed and to try to assist with migration pathways (i.e., visa sponsorship) for those found to be refugees in the future.

Eritrean Diaspora Humanitarianism in Sudan

At the time of Eritrea's independence in 1993, roughly one million Eritreans had fled the armed conflict with Ethiopia and settled in neighboring Sudan, in various Middle Eastern countries, and in Europe, North America, and Australia (see map 2.2). As Nicole Hirt writes, in spite of an initial "liberation euphoria" (2015), only a small number of Eritreans returned from exile and stayed, while the vast majority chose to remain in their respective host countries. Eritreans arrived in Australia as refugee and humanitarian entrants and as family migrants in waves, with the greatest numbers arriving in the 1990s. Like the Oromo, the Eritrean diaspora in Australia is made up of these earlier resettled refugees who are now well-established, second-generation Eritrean Australians who were born or have grown up in Australia, as well as Eritreans who have more recently arrived through refugee resettlement, family sponsorship (mostly marriage), or other visa categories, including some who have sought protection after arrival. The 2016 census recorded 4,301 Eritrea-born residents in Australia, an increase of 51 percent from the 2011 census. In addition, 7,557 persons indicated their mother was born in Eritrea and 7,973 that their father was Eritrea-born. However, members of the Eritrean diaspora estimate their community as much larger, taking into account the second generation.

Eritrean Australian Humanitarian Aid (EAHA) is an Eritrean RDO established for the sole purpose of helping Eritrean refugees overseas. EAHA was formed in 2009 "to provide humanitarian assistance to improve the living

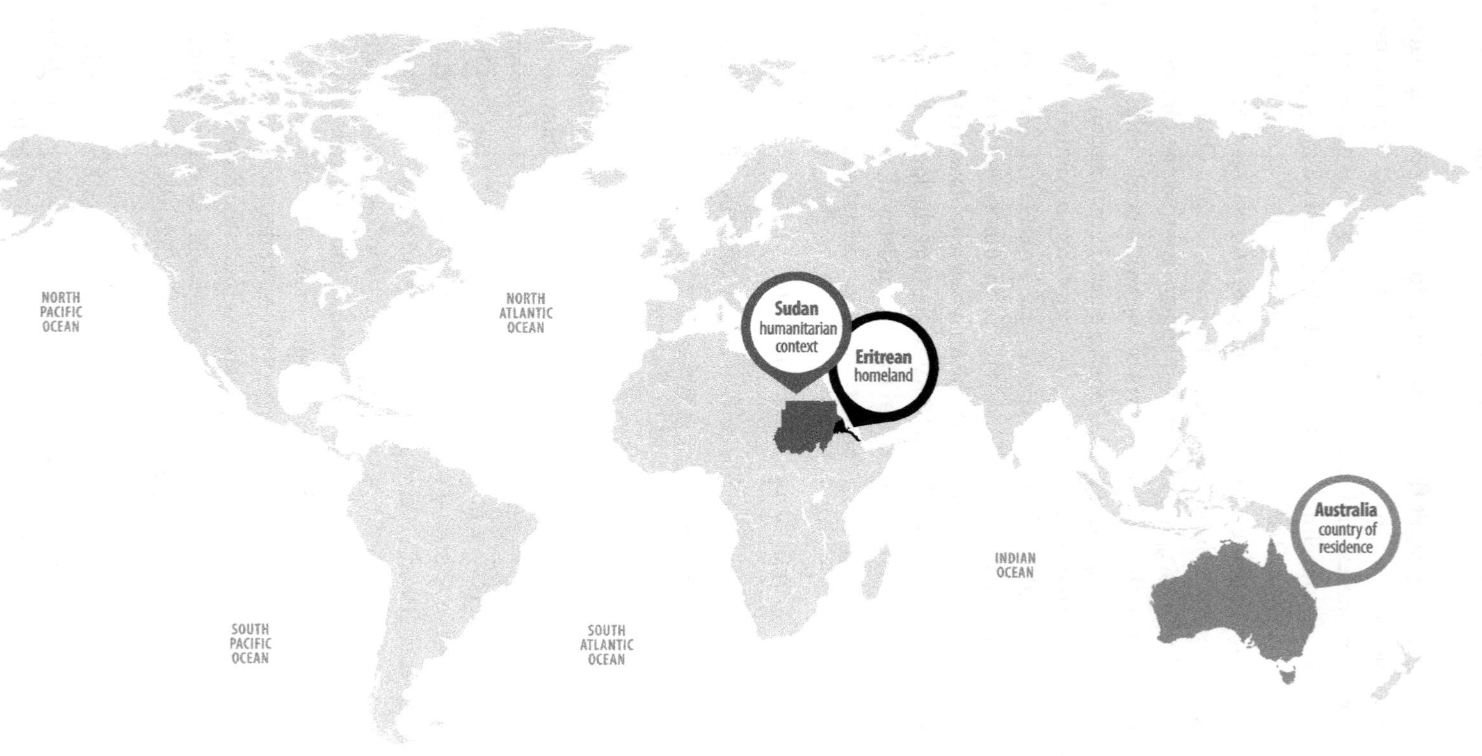
NORTH PACIFIC OCEAN
NORTH ATLANTIC OCEAN
Sudan
humanitarian context
Eritrean
homeland
Australia
country of residence
INDIAN OCEAN
SOUTH PACIFIC OCEAN
SOUTH ATLANTIC OCEAN

Map 2.2

conditions, educational and health needs of Eritrean refugees living in camps" (EAHA, n.d.). EAHA is an incorporated association that was registered as a charity organization with the Australian Charities and Not-for-profits Commission in 2015. The organization is run by a small volunteer committee of management mostly involving people who identify as Eritrean. EAHA raises funds for its humanitarian work by holding community fundraising dinners and barbecues at public events, the latter with the support of a local rotary club.

EAHA's humanitarian work has been focused on one of Africa's most protracted refugee situations: Eritreans in Eastern Sudan. In refugee camps and towns in Sudan, Eritreans who have been living as refugees for four decades reside alongside more recent arrivals who continue crossing the border (UNHCR 2014a). As a report by the UN Human Rights Council Special Rapporteur on human rights in Eritrea describes, young Eritreans are mostly fleeing an intensified recruitment drive by the Eritrean state into mandatory and open-ended national service (OHCHR 2015). UNHCR describes Sudan as being at the crossroads of the Horn of Africa's large, complex and constantly evolving migration routes and both a temporary and long-term host to an extensive population of refugees, asylum seekers, and other persons of concern, numbering some 990,000 in 2020 (121,000 of these being Eritrean) (UNHCR 2020b, 1). Eritrean refugees live in a particularly complex situation in Sudan due to political tensions and a lack of security, and an overall shortfall of funding for humanitarian assistance has meant there are considerable unmet needs, such as local infrastructure with the capacity to absorb increasing numbers of refugees.[13]

In terms of its activities, EAHA has mobilized resources largely from within the Eritrean diaspora community in Melbourne to undertake small projects that can best be described as material aid with an education focus. This has included funding and overseeing the construction and maintenance of school buildings in both urban and refugee camp settings, purchasing and distributing school stationery and supplies, collecting and sending a shipping container of school supplies and computers, and supplementing teachers' salaries in community-run schools. EAHA has also undertaken maintenance work in a medical clinic and has been involved in a fundraising and community education project involving refugee schoolchildren in Sudan collaborating with schoolchildren in Melbourne to produce a book, *Words and Pictures*, in 2015. EAHA has identified needs and implemented projects through members traveling to and from Sudan.

Karenni Diaspora Humanitarianism in Thailand

The Karenni diaspora originates from Karenni State in eastern Burma (Myanmar) (see map 2.3). The Karenni have been described as a diverse population whose "experiences at the hands of the Burmese army or others inside Karenni

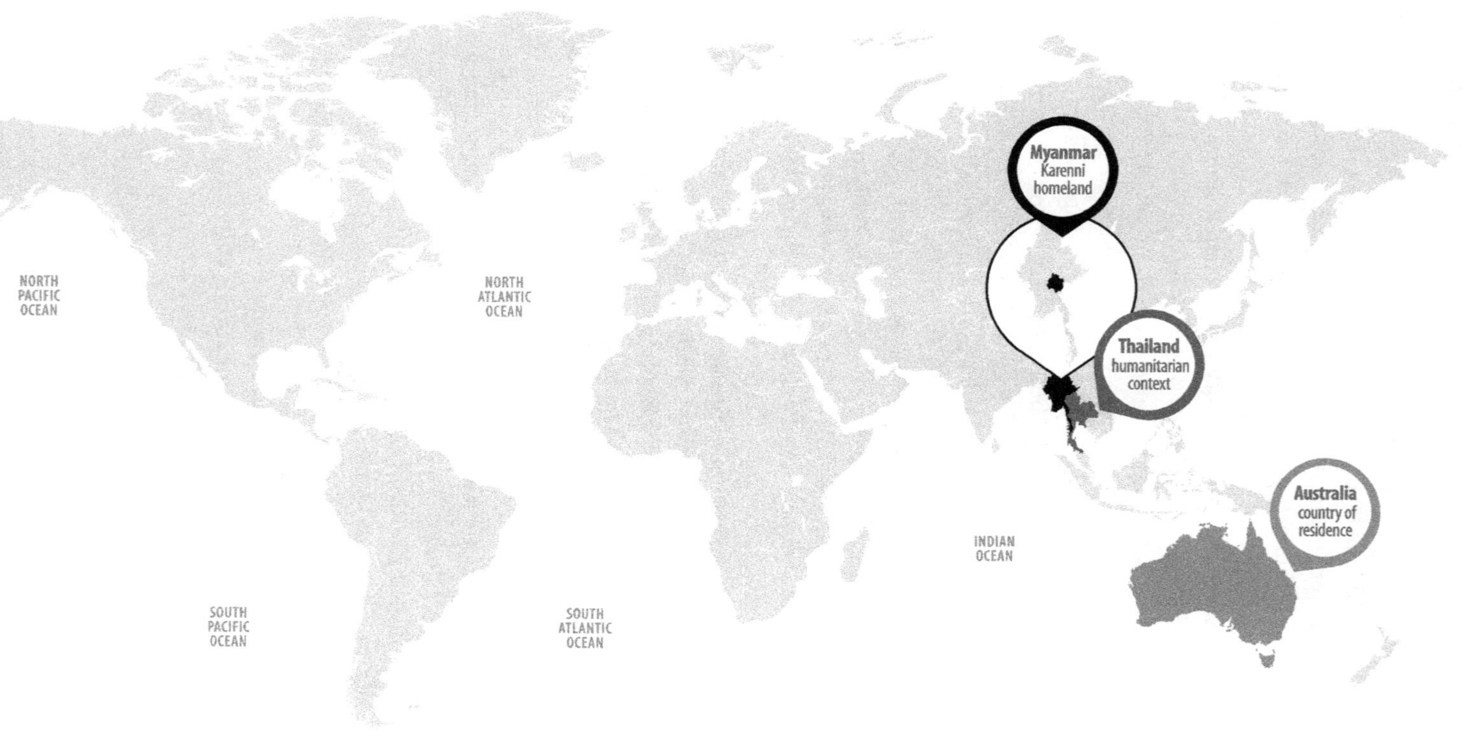
NORTH PACIFIC OCEAN
NORTH ATLANTIC OCEAN
Myanmar
Karenni homeland
Thailand
humanitarian context
Australia
country of residence
INDIAN OCEAN
SOUTH PACIFIC OCEAN
SOUTH ATLANTIC OCEAN

Map 2.3

State and subsequent displacement have brought together people who are in many ways disparate" (Dudley 2006, 2). As Sandra Dudley argues, "diversity is a characteristic of the population inside Karenni State and has been concentrated still further by the distillation process of displacement and subsequent coming together in the relatively confined spaces of the refugee camps" (2006, 2). The Karenni diaspora predominantly resides in Thailand—with an estimated population of 22,000 living in refugee camps—with smaller populations in the United States, Canada, Australia, New Zealand, and the Nordic states. The 2016 census recorded 32,656 Myanmar-born people in Australia, but this is not broken down by ethnic groups. Community informants estimated the Karenni community in Australia to number around two thousand people in 2017. Almost all have been resettled through the RHP, with the majority arriving in the decade from 2005.

The Karenni Federation of Australia (KnFA) was registered as an incorporated association in 2010 and is a not-for-profit organization run by a volunteer committee of management. At the time of writing, the president of KnFA was in Victoria, but membership and activities are carried out by subcommittees or affiliated local Karenni organizations in different cities throughout Australia. KnFA is focused predominantly on advocating for and supporting the integration of new arrivals and the cultural and social development of the Karenni community in Australia.

In 2016, 22,000 people from Karenni State were estimated to reside predominantly in two refugee camps along the Thai-Burma border. They are among 120,000 refugees, mostly ethnic minorities from Burma, in nine Thai border camps that have existed in various forms since the 1980s. While there were increasing talks of repatriation of refugees from these camps during the period of my fieldwork, there was also widespread fears among refugee communities in Thailand about the prospect of safe and dignified return.[14] The Thai government has long restricted movement in and out of border camps, and refugees are unable to legally work, making these populations highly reliant on aid, remittances, and informal activities. At the same time, humanitarian assistance to camps on the Thai-Burma border had been progressively withdrawn, as aid agencies began shifting their focus to areas in Myanmar where refugees were expected to return. As such, survival in camps in Thailand has become more precarious, and fewer external actors are channeling resources to help these populations.

On March 22, 2013, and then again on April 7, 2015, fires broke out in camps on the Thai-Burma border where refugees from Karenni State reside, destroying hundreds of homes, killing thirty-six people, and resulting in thousands becoming homeless (Radio Free Asia 2015). After both fires, KnFA mobilized funding from within the Karenni community in Australia and sent this to the Karenni Refugee Committee (KnRC) in Thailand. The funds were then distributed as cash by KnRC to all affected families in the camp, with those whose homes had been destroyed receiving a greater share. In 2013, the amount raised was AU$67,000 (US$51,000), with AU$9,000 (US$7,000) sent in response to the 2015 fire. A representative of KnFA explained that, while other humanitarian organizations—including UNHCR, Jesuit Refugee Services, the International Rescue Committee, and IOM—responded to these fires and helped to rebuild homes, the cash amount distributed to families by KnFA was intended to allow people to replace other household goods and livestock of their own choosing.

Palestinian Diaspora Humanitarianism on the Iraq-Syria Border

It is difficult to accurately estimate the size of the Palestinian diaspora in Australia, since most entered holding different passports, arrived in relatively small numbers and over decades, and are invisible or inconsistently identified in available population data. The 2016 census included "Gaza and the West Bank" as a category under "country of birth," with 2,939 persons listed. However, since Palestinians have been living across the Middle East since the 1950s, it is likely that many are counted in populations born in Syria, Jordan, Iraq, Lebanon, and Kuwait. In the 2016 census, 10,119 persons indicated they were Palestinian by ancestry. Palestinians have settled permanently in Australia through both the humanitarian and the general migration program.

As with other diaspora communities, there are several Palestinian organizations in Australia with a range of social, cultural, and political objectives. The Australian Society for Palestinian Iraqi Refugees Emergency (ASPIRE) was set up in 2008 with a very specific humanitarian purpose. ASPIRE was registered as an incorporated association in Victoria and operated for approximately six years, ceasing to renew its registration in 2014. While operational, ASPIRE was run by a small volunteer committee of management made up of both Palestinians and non-Palestinians. ASPIRE's founder estimated fifteen people were actively involved in ASPIRE at the peak of its activity, although the organization drew on a much larger network of supporters.

ASPIRE's focus was advocacy and support for a small group of Palestinian refugees stuck on the Iraq-Syria border at Al Hol refugee camp (see map 2.4). Those in Al Hol were Palestinians who had been living as refugees in Iraq for decades—some since the partition in 1947 and others because of the subsequent and ongoing Israel-Palestine conflict. In 2006, many Palestinian refugees fled their homes due to the increasingly brutal armed conflict and the inability of the Iraqi state to effectively protect civilian populations. A few thousand Palestinian-Iraqis reached the Iraq-Syria border, but many were prevented from crossing into Syria due to their lack of documentation.[15] Makeshift camps were set up in no-man's-land in the border region: Al Hol and Al Tanf on the Syrian side of the border and Al Waleed on the Iraq side. Humanitarian agencies—including UNHCR, the

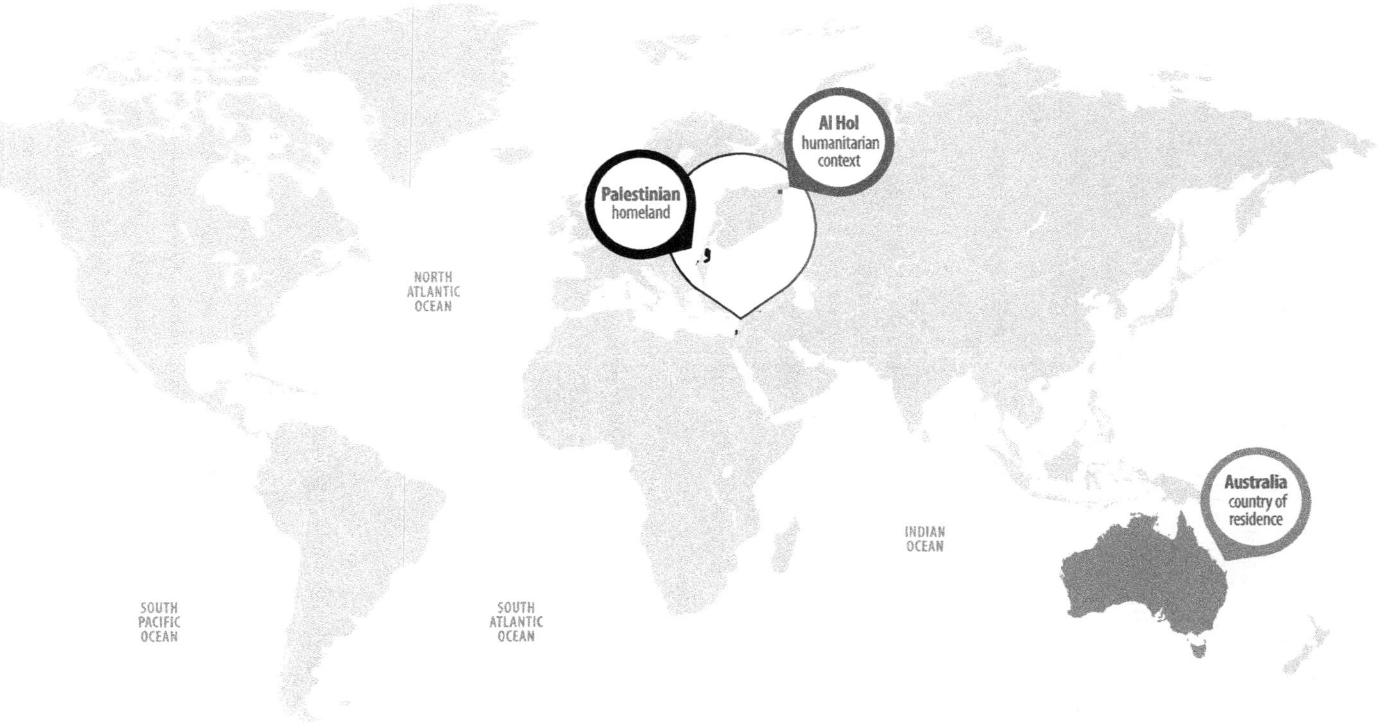
Palestinian
homeland
Al Hol
humanitarian
context
Australia
country of
residence
NORTH
PACIFIC
OCEAN
NORTH
ATLANTIC
OCEAN
SOUTH
PACIFIC
OCEAN
SOUTH
ATLANTIC
OCEAN
INDIAN
OCEAN

Map 2.4

UN Relief and Works Agency for Palestine Refugees in the Near East (UNRWA), UNICEF, the World Food Programme, the Palestinian Red Crescent, and the Syrian Arab Red Crescent—provided basic assistance to refugees in these camps, which are located in incredibly harsh desert areas. Al Tanf camp was eventually closed in 2010, after residents were either resettled to third countries or were relocated to Al Hol.[16] In 2010, the small group of refugees in Al Hol (less than two thousand people) remained living in extremely difficult and unsustainable conditions, unable to move either forward into Syria or back into Iraq.

In its activities, ASPIRE successfully advocated alongside organizations such as Amnesty International for Australia to offer resettlement places to refugees living in Al Hol and was involved in efforts to raise the public's awareness through media campaigns and lobbying. ASPIRE also provided significant practical support to fill in and translate visa application documents to facilitate the resettlement of refugees from Al Hol. This was done in two rounds, one in 2009 and the other in 2010 to 2011, with applications filed for 117 families and representing hundreds of hours of work.[17] To do this, ASPIRE drew together a committed group of professionals with key skills—lawyers, migration agents, advocates, filmmakers, academics, and Arabic translators. ASPIRE's founder traveled to Al Hol in 2010 to identify and work with local camp leaders who could assist in facilitating the visa application process. The outcome of ASPIRE's activities was that fifty-one families were accepted for resettlement and arrived in Australia between 2009 and 2012. Members of ASPIRE also provided settlement support after these families arrived, including on-arrival accommodation.[18]

Assyrian Diaspora Humanitarianism in Iraq

According to the 2016 population census, 23,915 persons in Australia identified their religion as either Assyrian Apostolic or Chaldean Catholic.[19] Assyrians arrived in Australia in several waves from Iraq, Iran, Syria, and Turkey—the countries in which the Assyrian homeland roughly corresponds (see map 2.5).[20] Many were resettled through Australia's humanitarian program following the Iraq-Iran war in the 1980s and 1990s and the Iraq war in 2003, and again from 2009 to the time of publication due to the breakdown in security in Iraq and Syria. Assyrians have also settled in Australia through family reunion within the general migration program. Between 2014 and 2017, the Australian government resettled an additional twelve thousand refugees from Iraq and Syria on top of its regular RHP quota, a large proportion being Christian minorities. Assyrian Australian communities have predominantly settled in the Fairfield and Liverpool areas of Sydney and in the northern suburbs of Melbourne, where there are established Assyrian and Chaldean churches and local community associations.

The Assyrian Aid Society–Australia (AAS–A) was established and became an incorporated association in Australia in 2000 following an outbreak of fighting

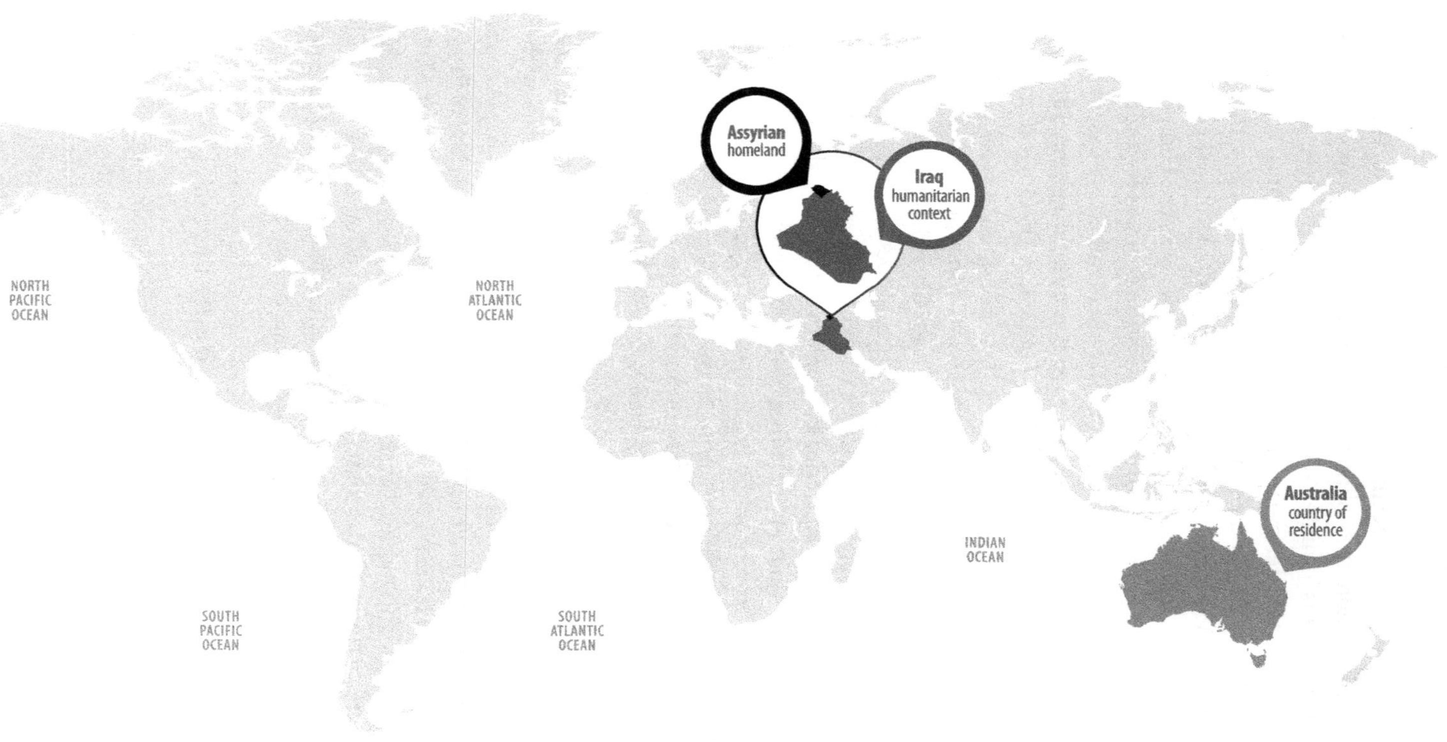
NORTH PACIFIC OCEAN
NORTH ATLANTIC OCEAN
Assyrian homeland
Iraq humanitarian context
SOUTH PACIFIC OCEAN
SOUTH ATLANTIC OCEAN
INDIAN OCEAN
Australia country of residence

Map 2.5

in Iraq and the mass displacement of Assyrians at that time. While AAS–A is a national organization, the voluntary committee of management mostly resides in Sydney. AAS–A is affiliated with the Assyrian Aid Society, a global diaspora movement that has sister organizations in the United States, United Kingdom, Sweden, and New Zealand and whose head office is in Iraq. The Assyrian Aid Society–Iraq (AAS–I) was the first to be established following the Gulf War in 1991 and was granted Special Consultative Status with the United Nations Economic and Social Council in 2011, an application that was facilitated by AAS–A. AAS–A is funded through fees collected from a membership base that comprises almost entirely Assyrian Australians, as well as by holding community fundraising events. AAS–A is not aligned to any political or theological organization.[21]

While AAS–A has been supporting the development work of AAS–I since 2000, the organization became directly involved in relief work in 2014, when an estimated 32,000 out of the 35,000-strong Iraqi Christian population were forced from their homes in Mosul when armed insurgents occupied the city (Otten 2014). At this time, many Assyrians fled to the cities of Erbil and Dohuk in the Nineveh Plains area in northern Iraq, under the control of the Kurdish Regional Government. Access to IDPs in Iraq (including Assyrians) by international humanitarian organizations has been sporadic because of the ongoing instability and violent struggle for control by different armed groups, as well as the lack of humanitarian funding attributed to donor fatigue and the diversion of international aid to meet the acute needs of displaced Syrian and Yemeni populations in the region.[22]

Prior to 2014, AAS–A-funded projects were mostly focused on education and the preservation of the Assyrian language and culture within Iraq. Since the renewed displacement crisis began in 2014, AAS–I activities—with funding support from affiliated diaspora organizations including AAS–A—shifted to include humanitarian relief work. Following the capture of Mosul in June 2014, AAS–A mobilized the Assyrian diaspora in Australia to raise over AU$264,000 (US$208,000).[23] This money was sent directly to AAS–I, which was coordinating relief efforts on the ground. Funding went to a pooled emergency relief fund that was used to purchase and distribute food, clothes, bedding, and hygiene kits and meet other locally identified needs for displaced Assyrians.

DIVERSE WAYS OF HELPING

Entering and then exiting the field of refugee protection—experiencing life as a refugee and then resettling permanently in a third country—is a structuring experience with multiple effects and is likely to lead to situated knowledge, experiences, and networks that inform acts of helping. This chapter shows how refugee diaspora communities in Australia engage in collective acts of helping, with significant variation in the context and scope of their activities. At the same time, refugee diaspora humanitarianism needs to be understood as part of a portfolio of overlapping obligations and engagements. Collective acts of helping to alleviate the suffering of familiar strangers can happen simultaneously alongside other transnational engagements, such as remittance-sending practices and interpersonal networks of support at a family/household level, but also with more political agitation and mobilization to address grievances and transform the landscape of a homeland. While the remainder of this book focuses on the collective helping aspect of refugee diaspora transnationalism, this broader context should not be forgotten. It is the focus of the next four chapters to expand on the *why, how,* and *to what effect* of refugee diaspora humanitarianism and to suggest that there are commonalities in the helping practices of refugee diaspora communities as much as there are variations in form.

THREE

FORCES THAT COMPEL

THE PREVIOUS TWO CHAPTERS PROVIDED a backdrop for understanding what refugee diaspora organizations (RDOs) do within the broader global context of forced displacement and humanitarian responses to people considered out of place. Before moving into a more detailed analysis of the distinct ways in which the RDOs in this study went about helping, I first want to explore the question of *why* these people choose to organize and act in this way. Drawing from the work of Didier Fassin, I want to explore the moral heart of humanitarian action from the (emic) perspectives of diaspora humanitarians themselves, "taking seriously what actors in the humanitarian world do and say, what leads them to debate and act" (2010a, 270). This ensures attention is paid to the complex undercurrents that animate acts of helping familiar strangers. For, as will become apparent in subsequent chapters, the work of RDOs involves considerable investments of time, energy, and resources. To create, implement, and sustain the kinds of activities that RDOs undertake requires significant animating forces. It is the central concern of this chapter to ask *What are the forces that compel refugee diaspora humanitarians?*

HUMANITARIAN MORALITY AND MOTIVATIONS

There is a growing body of literature exploring "forces of compassion" (Bornstein and Redfield 2010) and questions of morality, values, emotions, and motivations underlying humanitarian acts (see Bornstein 2012; Fassin 2010a, 2010b; Fassin and Pandolfi 2010; Feldman and Ticktin 2010; Laqueur 2009; Malkki 2015; Wilson and Brown 2009). This anthropology of humanitarianism has focused on the lifeworld of different actors who claim to act in the name of humanity. While there are some exceptions (see Bornstein 2012; Ghorashi and Boersma

2009; O'Hagan and Hirono 2014; Sweis 2019), most of these studies have taken dominant (Western) humanitarian actors as their focus, tracing the genealogy of reasons and emotions that animate this work. This literature offers insights into humanitarian moralities and motivations that are relevant to this study and have been summarized under three themes: (1) how humanitarianism creates momentum and action (forces of compassion); (2) the complex motivations underlying humanitarian acts; and (3) how humanitarian moralities and motivations are historically, socially, and culturally situated. A reference to these debates is included here because of their relevance to understanding the forces that compel refugee diaspora humanitarians.

Forces of Compassion

Humanitarianism involves a moral economy inasmuch as those who call themselves or their actions *humanitarian* use moral arguments to distinguish their acts from those of others and as a basis for judgment and a justification for actions (Fassin 2010a, 275). Whether we agree or not that there is a single shared value that underlies all self-proclaimed humanitarian acts, it is possible to see how different expressions of moral sentiments create momentum for people to act. When writing of moral sentiments, Fassin refers to the duality of *reason* and *emotions*: "On the one hand, we have what we might call 'humanitarian reason': the principle according to which humans share a condition that inspires solidarity with one another. On the other, we have what we will name 'the humanitarian emotion': the affect by virtue of which human beings feel personally concerned by the situation of others. Even though the morality of political action is generally claimed to be built on reason, behind the humanitarian gesture, there is always an emotion toward the suffering of others, without which this gesture would not come into being" (2010a, 269).

Fassin argues that humanitarianism is built on two figures—suffering victims and the benefactors who assist, protect, and struggle to defend them—who are linked by moral sentiments, affects, and their underlying values. Referencing philosopher Adam Smith, Fassin suggests that affect—particularly sympathy—is what underlies humanitarianism's moral sense, as it is "inscribed in the actors' virtues, judgements, or the actions they take" (2010d, 37). What is meant here is that emotions (pity, compassion, sympathy, empathy) and values (beliefs about what is right or wrong) are central for propelling certain types of actions under the banner of humanitarianism.

Indeed, it is not hard to find examples whereby moral sentiments have given force and legitimacy to acts claimed as humanitarian. Liisa Malkki (2015) illustrates these forces in her detailed account of how the figure of the child is deployed by aid agencies in humanitarian logics and practice to create certain understandings and responses to violent conflict (see also Suski 2009). The articulation of reason and emotion in the attitude held toward *the other* as a "vulnerable human being," Fassin argues, "opens up the possibility for all actors, including victims, to claim the authority of law or to excite sympathy and to play on this tension in order to promote interests and defend causes and even to instrumentalize humanitarian action" (2010a, 272).

What Fassin and others (see Barnett 2011; Bornstein and Redfield 2010; Feldman and Ticktin 2010; Forsythe 2009; Laqueur 2009; Wilson and Brown 2009, 9–10) describe when they write about humanitarian morality, however, leans toward a genealogy of moral sentiments espoused by more powerful humanitarian actors—Western states, supranational bodies, and international aid agencies. They suggest that these actors' moral sentiments draw from understandings of a common humanity, the sanctity of life, and humaneness that are rooted in European or Western philosophy (the Enlightenment period), politics (pre- and post-revolutionary France and the US Declaration of Independence), and Christianity. Fassin writes that "the concept of humanitarian work is still strongly marked by the history of Western thinking on charity" (2010d, 38). The fact that the organizations that have been the primary focus of these analyses—the International Committee of the Red Cross, Médecins Sans Frontières, and the United Nations, for example—originated in one part of Western Europe within a relatively short period of time makes this genealogy of moral sentiments highly relevant.[1] As David P. Forsythe bluntly suggests: "Because the West pays for this [humanitarian] system and mostly leads it, Western attitudes are crucial" (2009, 60). However, questions remain about how universal these moral sentiments are for actors who do not necessarily share these historical roots but also call themselves or their acts *humanitarian*.

Complex Motivations

A second theme to emerge in the anthropology of humanitarianism literature relates to the complex array of motivations underlying humanitarian acts that may be masked or unspoken because of the consensual (moral) force of "humanitarian reason" (Fassin 2010b). The idea that something as complex and diverse as humanitarianism is underwritten by a variety of motivations should be self-evident. As Jacinta O'Hagan and Miwa Hirono (2014) rightly point out, the motives behind humanitarian assistance in all societies are always complex. While an articulation of morality may be core to humanitarianism, this does not preclude there being other motivations. Indeed, a number of scholars have argued that we should look beyond the articulation of moral sentiments if we are to understand the complex dynamics—geopolitics, identity, economic expansionism, or other expressions of power—that animate the world of humanitarianism (see Feldman and Ticktin 2010; Gökalp 2020 for an excellent discussion of the animating forces behind the UAE's "humanitarian diplomacy"). Notable in this literature is Malkki's 2015 ethnography, *The Need to Help*, which takes Finnish Red Cross workers and volunteers as its population of interest. Malkki describes the neediness of these humanitarian actors, whose helping is as much about their own lifeworlds (loneliness, guilt, professional identity) as it is about their capacity to alleviate the suffering of people living far away from contemporary Finnish society. Malkki digs beneath the veneer of humanitarian workers and volunteers as "moral heroes" (Fassin 2010d) to describe a much messier and complex set of animating dynamics.

As to what other motivations or interests are implicated in humanitarian acts, there have been several suggestions. Most notable is a recognition of the dimensions of power and politics in humanitarian endeavor. Miriam Ticktin argues that while some humanitarians claim to be apolitical, humanitarianism is a form of politics that "engages and reproduces a set of power relations," and certain acts of caring that are complicit with unequal power relations may even be considered a form of "antipolitics" (2011, 19). She notes that there is danger in humanitarian actors pretending to be apolitical, since "power is wielded without acknowledging it and therefore without accountability" (Ticktin 2011, 19–20). This sentiment has been echoed by others, particularly when it comes to the role of humanitarian actors within the international refugee regime. Michel Agier, for example, suggests that humanitarian interventions in refugee situations are closely tied to the interests of powerful states and their "war on migrants," with a converse relationship between the flow of humanitarian funding and the mobility of migrant populations (2010; see also Little and Vaughan-Williams 2017; Walters 2010).

Fassin (2010a) and Michael Barnett (2011) have both illustrated the entanglements of humanitarianism with the economic or geostrategic interests of powerful states, using examples such as the deployment of humanitarian sentiments in the 1999 military intervention in Kosovo and the 2003 invasion of Iraq.[2] Closer to the research field, it is not hard to see how humanitarian reason is deployed for political expedience in the Australian government's policies toward people seeking asylum by boat. The Australian government has repeatedly framed asylum deterrence policies as *humanitarian*, even where strong evidence shows these policies cause significant harm to the same people they are meant to be saving (see Gleeson 2016). More importantly, harsh border policies have been shown to be effective in garnering voter support for political parties, suggesting that humanitarian reasons can be deployed for political gain (Higgins 2017; Maley 2016).

The coopting of humanitarian sentiments for reasons of state is perhaps an obvious critique, but also highlighted in this literature is a more sensitive critique of how the humanitarian aid industry itself may have self-serving interests. Large international nongovernmental organizations (INGOs), for example, must vie for a share of a growing, increasingly competitive, and professionalized market (Barnett 2005). Dorothea Hilhorst and Bram Jansen describe this as the "humanitarian arena," whereby agencies use a language of ethical and humane interaction to gain legitimacy (2010). They suggest that INGOs "use the image of the humanitarian space to conceal their own interest in humanitarian action and their intended or unintended political roles" (Hilhorst and Jansen 2010, 119). Defending the humanitarian identity of an organization, then, can also be understood in terms of *field* and *market*. This may be an uncomfortable dynamic to discuss because of the untouchability of those who act in the name of humanity (Fassin 2010d), but it is a necessary piece to understanding how and why actors choose to call themselves *humanitarian*.

Although it is not my intention to provide a full analysis of the complex moralities and motivations of different humanitarian actors, what is highlighted here is the need to question *whose* needs, interests, and power are furthered by deploying humanitarian sentiments, be they advertent or inadvertent. These questions are pertinent for humanitarian actors who wield significant power, but they are also relevant for smaller actors—including RDOs—who also wield power, albeit in smaller, more localized ways.

Diverse Moralities and Motivations

A third theme in the anthropology of humanitarianism literature that is relevant to this study is by far the least developed, and that is the recognition that there are other humanitarian moralities situated in different histories, cultures, and politics that potentially lead to different ways of helping. Erica Bornstein's work (2012) is a significant contribution in this regard, as it explores the performance of "moral good" among wealthy Indians in New Delhi. Bornstein describes a kinship-based model of action that differs from liberal altruism as a driver of humanitarianism—a morality politics she calls "relational empathy" (Bornstein 2012). There is other emerging work on Islamic (Benthall and Lacey 2014) and Eastern (O'Hagan and Hirono 2014) traditions of charity, non-Western "humanitarian diplomacy" (Gökalp 2020), and Southern humanitarian actors more generally (Pacitto and Fiddian-Qasmiyeh 2013), even though this work is still mostly focused on more powerful actors (i.e., states and INGOs). However, even the compelling portraits of the social, cultural, political worlds, and histories of dominant humanitarian actors that are the focus of ethnographers such as Ticktin (2011), Malkki (2015), and Fassin (2010b) suggest the possibility of diverse and situated moralities and motivations; how humanitarian actors perceive a "morally legitimate" sufferer or victim and feel compelled to act is, in fact, "deeply contextual" (Ticktin 2011, 4).

If we accept that moralities and motivations that compel humanitarian actors to help are highly contextual, then diverse moralities and motivations must be discernible if we look at actors situated in different historical, social, cultural, and political contexts. It is to the morality and motivations of refugee diaspora humanitarians that I now turn as I detail how participants in this study talked about *who* they were trying to help, *why* they suffered, and *what compelled them* to do something about it.

NARRATIVES OF SUFFERING

Thomas W. Lacquer suggests that "the extension of compassion to others requires both 'habits of feeling' and 'theories of causation' and it is these two foundational ideas that form the basis of humanitarian narratives" (Laqueur [1989, 204], cited in Suski 2009, 210). In interviews, participants were asked *who* their organizations were trying to help. In the responses elicited—as well as in subsequent discussions about what motivated interviewees on a personal level—several themes emerged. The narratives of interviewees revealed much about how these actors understood suffering and how they perceived injustices and violence, perpetrators and victims. In the following, I discuss both reoccurring *figures of suffering* and the theories of causation that were described by participants in this study.

I begin this section with two caveats. First, I want to acknowledge the danger in oversimplifying the complex inner worlds of people's moralities and motivations. I did not intend this research to focus on understanding why people helped. It was only as my research progressed that I came to see this *why* question as fundamentally important for understanding what is distinct about refugee diaspora humanitarianism. As such, I include my findings here but suggest that these be taken only as a scratching of the surface; it was not within my scope to delve into the complex personal and collective histories that underlie the formation and workings of each RDO. Second, by deconstructing the figures and sources of suffering described by refugee diaspora humanitarians, I do not wish to suggest that there are not real people who experience real violence and injustices. What I mean to show is that figures of suffering are constructed in ways that lead people to understand both problems and solutions in certain ways and to act on this understanding.

"My People"

Many of those I interviewed invoked the phrase *my people* when describing who they were trying to help. They used the collective *we* or *our* when speaking about suffering, drawing themselves into the circle of sufferers, and *a people* as a collective figure of suffering. This may come as no great surprise, considering organizations were selected that self-identified in a diasporic way, with a homeland and people. Take, for example, the following excerpts:

> [We are seeking] human rights for the suffering [of] the Karen [that is] going on. It's advocating to the outside world to know about the Karen sufferings, and then to get support from the international community. . . . We are here because of our Karen struggle, and we believe that our struggle is just. (James)[3]
>
> I think in terms of helping Oromos, not a lot of people know about Oromos, so for us to sit back and say "OK, someone else can help them," we wouldn't be able to do that. . . . I didn't personally come from a refugee background. I was born in Australia, so I didn't see a struggle growing up. But knowing the struggle the Oromos go through, the cause, everything, that's why we went and helped. (Adem)[4]

This figure of *a people* struggling against powerful forces was evoked again and again. The figure was not an individual or a demographic subset but a whole population, undifferentiated by class, gender, or age. The people *all* suffered because they belonged to a group that was persecuted, under threat, or ignored. Even when the subjection of individuals to violence or injustices was talked about, this was often in relation to the impact on the collective, as the following illustrates: "We are a small community. We're not much. We are about, maybe not even eighty thousand . . . so whoever [comes] here [cannot] feel safe. . . . I have to worry about [everyone] else. . . . Like when we heard about three young men that [had] been killed, kidnapped, in Iraq . . . it is affecting the entire land. There is a funeral being done for each one of them everywhere in the world where there are Mandaeans. . . . We're not a big people, so when we lose three, it's huge" (Sarah).[5]

The sense of urgency in protecting, speaking for, or helping *a people* seemed to resonate with interviewees from many different backgrounds—Karen, Oromo, Ogaden, Mandaean, Palestinian, Assyrian, Hazara, Rohingya—and reflected a people bound not by nation-states but by a shared identity. Importantly, this was an identity—a people—under threat. More than one interviewee claimed their people to be "the most persecuted in the world." So, while the perpetrators, violence, and injustices that were perceived varied depending on the different contexts, a common thread was that it was the collective figure of *a people* that suffered.

A common element in this construction of a suffering people was that of voicelessness—of a people whom the world did not see, hear, or care about. Many spoke about their people being unable to get their voices heard, presumably by those who could stop the violence or suffering that they endured. A number described the voices of the people as *inside* trying to reach *outside* or said there were discussions that their people were excluded from. For example: "What we're doing is trying to be the voice for those inside and put their concerns out there"

(Ladan, Ogaden RDO); "Sometimes when you [are] in the deeper jungle area, you cry for help. You pray or you cry out. For some reason, you need help. No one can hear you" (Jordan, Karen RDO); and "For years, we were missing from the discussions. . . . It's only now that this awful, horrible tragedy [has happened]. I mean, why did it have to reach this stage for them to notice us?" (Carmen, Assyrian RDO).[6]

The notion of *a people* was also evident when discussions turned to children. Many of the RDOs in this study were involved in education projects, and interviewees explained this in terms of a familiar children-as-the-future narrative (as per Malkki 2015; Suski 2009). Yet the future envisioned was of *a people,* educated, free, and with a voice that could be heard. The denial of education to children was, therefore, the denial of the future prosperity and hope of a people. One interviewee spoke about the need to invest in schools for refugees because "at least maybe one of these kids is going to be the president of Eritrea tomorrow. So [we] need to have a relaxed man, a happy man; educated. And he [will] say: 'Look, I grew up in a refugee camp. I have been helped by [this organization] when I was going to school.' And for sure, he's going to be a good person" (Berhan).[7]

In sum, the evocation of *a suffering people* who are persecuted and voiceless was a common construct among refugee diaspora humanitarians. Many interviewees identified themselves as part of this body of suffering, even though they were residing in the seeming comfort and safety of Australia, because violence or injustice experienced by one was seen as violence or injustice perpetrated on the collective body of a people. Moreover, the need to help was about protecting or ensuring the future integrity of this collective body.

Social Ruptures

Scholars have often referred to the predominance of the physical body or biopolitics in humanitarian narratives of suffering, which reflect the idea that the suffering that makes us human and shapes (dominant) humanitarian responses is contained within the physical body (Fassin 2010b; Ticktin 2011). In contrast, very few diaspora humanitarians talked specifically about suffering bodies; they more often framed suffering around social ruptures. The more visceral responses to evoke suffering included descriptions of families torn apart, of people suffering because of their inability to fulfill their caring roles, or of people unsupported or alone. Even when suffering bodies were talked about, the discussion was often about those who cared for them. For example, one woman, Sarah, spoke about a boy from Iraq who needed an urgent medical operation. The telling was framed in terms of the father's suffering, not the boy's. The urgent operation "had to be done" because the father had already lost one of his sons, and "he was in shock, and he didn't want to lose the other boy."[8]

The suffering caused by the inability of someone to fulfill an expected caring role was spoken about by many different interviewees. The figure of suffering was not necessarily the person who was being cared for (i.e., a sick person, a child, or the elderly) but the people who were unable or struggled to provide care. In this way, the suffering of a parent not able to care for their child drew a visceral response. Rosanna, for example, spoke about children who were being looked after by their grandmother because their parents were imprisoned. The suffering was of *the parents* who could not look after their children and who had burdened the ailing grandmother with this responsibility. Rosanna explained how her organization helped women prisoners generate an income, including the woman whose children were being cared for by their grandmother, because "when they are [in prison], they depend on their family and they feel very sad."[9]

Within these descriptions of social ruptures and reconfigured caring roles, the most commonly deployed figure of suffering was that of a mother. Mothers' vulnerability was described in terms of them being alone and unsupported: "Young people, they can do some things—laboring or whatever—to survive. I know it's not easy, but they can do [it]. What we need to focus on is women who are alone and women with children" (Hassan).[10] Another interviewee noted, "There was this mother by herself who had seven kids. She's sick. She has no support" (Youssef).[11]

Providing support to ensure mothers could care for their children was a central theme for many. Various anecdotes were shared about how mothers were struggling and RDOs were supporting them. Again, the suffering was framed around the mother in her caring role, not the child or her own suffering as a human being. Take, for example, the following response to why an RDO was focused on supporting a refugee school: "I saw a lady coming, begging the principal, saying, 'I can't pay for my three kids, and I can't let my three kids out of the school, but I'll do my best to get the fees for two kids. So please, let my kids [be] part of this school and I'll pay for the two.' That's on my eye, [and] it gave me a picture of the whole school.... They are suffering from a different kind of poverty, and no one helps them" (Anwar).[12]

In sum, one of the recurring figures of suffering evoked by refugee diaspora humanitarians was that of persons struggling to fulfill their expected—and clearly gendered—caring roles. The cause of suffering was the rupture in social support networks and, most centrally, in the caring roles of families. Those without support, families burdened and torn apart, and those who stepped in to fill caring roles were all spoken of in terms of their needs. It was not the human body that was broken, but social networks of care.

Forgotten Refugees

Before starting fieldwork, I anticipated that those involved in RDOs would talk about refugees as figures of suffering, as I had purposefully recruited organizations helping in refugee situations. Interestingly, very few of my informants spoke with conviction about refugees in this way. My informants more frequently spoke in the terms described above or in more generic ways of *people in need* or *needy people*. As Alaa plainly said when pressed about why he chose to help a group of Palestinian refugees on the Iraq-Syria border: "I just looked at them as people in need."[13] It was only when my informants started to talk about *why* these people were in need that being a refugee factored into narratives of suffering. When diaspora humanitarians spoke about causes of suffering, *being a refugee* meant suffering the injustices of poverty and disempowerment, of being unhelped and forgotten.

Many of my interviewees included themselves in the suffering of refugees, and the more animated responses to my question about who RDOs were helping involved a description of how the interviewees themselves had suffered in the past from being a refugee. One man, Hadi, was talking about "big organizations" that help refugees when he said, "The people who go there [to help refugees from Iraq], they have no idea how we suffer. Whatever they have—even if it's sympathy—it's not the same."[14] Hadi's use of the collective *we* to describe the suffering of Iraqi refugees suggested he understood their suffering from the perspective of one who experienced this suffering, despite having lived in Australia for many years and acquired Australian citizenship.

Another animated response came from John, a man who had more recently resettled in Australia from Malaysia: "One thing that I really, really want [the office of the United Nations High Commissioner for Refugees (UNHCR)] to know is, as a human being, they have to put that human being value, instead of that refugee value.... [Being labeled a refugee is] very influential to our mentality, and it affects [us]. You know, like children. If you [keep saying] 'you cannot do, you cannot do,' it happens. They lose their ability and their self-esteem. Refugees are the same. We've been suffering back there for years with such unkind treatment, so it's not easy to recover [from] our trauma."[15] The trauma, then, comes from being treated not like a human being, but like a refugee—a person who is not valued. The suffering is because of a loss of ability and self-esteem, of being told, like a child, that "you cannot do, you cannot do."

But the suffering of refugees was also spoken about more plainly in terms of the violence of poverty and the inability of people to find enough food to eat or access to health care or education. Sarah said that her organization received emails or phone calls from families in Syria "who are saying they have not eaten anything, just bread."[16] Another man, Anwar, described an encounter when he visited an Eritrean refugee camp in Ethiopia:

> I remember a lady... she explained a lot of things to us. She said: "We get one soap the whole month." And even you can't wash your clothes, you can't wash yourself... and fifteen kilos of grain. And... they give it to the miller so they can

> mill for them, and [the miller] takes half of that, which is 7.5 kilos for a month for a person. And a [cup of] salt, and one cup of lentil, and a cup of oil and nothing else. No sugar, nothing, nothing, nothing. So, for them it was very hard.[17]

Another reoccurring dimension in the narrative of refugee suffering was the perception that refugees are not being helped. One woman, Carmen, put it very plainly: "Our people don't have help. No one helps us . . . except ourselves, and the motto for [our organization] is 'Help us to help them,' because no one does."[18] Others framed the suffering of being a refugee more in terms of the process of having to ask for, or being denied, help. Adem stated, "They thought they were alone with nobody to talk to; nowhere to go. They felt like [they made] no ripple, because they [went] to the UN and [were told], 'No, go back,' and they get no help."[19] Leyla, another interviewee, asked, "Do you know how humiliating it is, just to have to ask for bread? People don't like to be pitied."[20]

As Leyla's words suggest, the suffering of refugees evoked by diaspora humanitarians was often associated with the act of seeking help or to the inadequacy of help available. For some, there was a recognition of the lack of capacity of humanitarian organizations to provide what was needed. For example, one man, Raj, spoke about the lack of health care provided to people with chronic illnesses in refugee camps in Nepal: "I think what [NGOs] look at is how the money will be spent on the greater good rather than spending that money on an individual."[21] But there were others who spoke with vehemence about the dehumanizing process of seeking help and with suspicion about the inadequacy of humanitarian agencies' responses to requests for help. There were some informants who suggested refugees suffered *because of* corruption and disregard by humanitarian agencies that were meant to help them; members of these agencies were depicted as driving around in large white cars and sticking logos everywhere but not providing real help. For example: "When we went to Shegarab [refugee camp] we asked them—because we saw a lot of logos there, you know, UNHCR, Human Appeal, this and that—and we said, 'Look, [you've] got hundreds of organizations here!' They said to us, 'Yes, we see the names, but we didn't see even a glass of water from these people.'"[22]

This narrative of not being helped was closely related to another theme that echoed through many interviews, and that was of refugees as forgotten. My informants described the suffering of refugees not just in terms of poverty or the inadequacy of available assistance, but also in terms of a more existential suffering, as the following excerpts illustrate:

> They see us as their hope. And it makes them really happy to know that there is the Ogaden-Australian community, or the American or the European (community), that actually is thinking about them. You know, not forgetting. . . . So a lot of

> people from the camp who give feedback—either through Facebook or through email or through someone who visits—they send recordings [and] they always say, "Thanks for not giving up on us [or] forgetting that we exist." (Ladan)[23]

> One of the families where our group went [and visited], the last thing they said to them was, "Don't forget." . . . They appreciate [when] you come and support. . . . There [is] no requirement for money or other things. All they need is support and [that you] remember them. (Jordan)[24]

> I think the highlight for me was actually bringing those people together [in Jakarta] . . . it was like "Wow!" They knew the people were here [and] bringing them together and sharing their problems. . . . That they can feel like they're not alone in this world is one of the biggest things for me. (Hassan)[25]

The ways in which diaspora humanitarians describe refugees as people in need clearly link their suffering to the violence of poverty and disablement, of being told they cannot do things for themselves, and of having to ask for help. This idea very directly relates to the failings of the international refugee regime and (dominant) humanitarian responses to forced displacement and has been described in other writings about refugees (see Agier 2008; Harrell-Bond 2002). But these narratives also speak of an existential suffering, of refugees being forgotten. This, perhaps, is an important construct for motivating the types of activities that RDOs undertake. For, if someone suffers because they are forgotten, then an understandable response to alleviate this suffering is to make them feel remembered, which speaks to that which is nonquantifiable in refugee diaspora humanitarianism.

FORCES THAT COMPEL REFUGEE DIASPORA HUMANITARIANS

Having described how refugee diaspora humanitarians conveyed a sense of *who* they are helping—their people, people whose social networks are ruptured, and forgotten refugees—I turn now to *why* individuals felt compelled to do something to address this suffering. The following describes how interviewees explained why they were personally involved in RDOs. These individuals were, for the most part, the leaders or founders of their organizations. They were those whose convictions, values, and interests led them to contribute significant amounts of energy, time, and resources to a voluntary endeavor. Trying to understand what animates these people is important because, in doing so, we may better appreciate the strength of their convictions and potential blind spots, and grasp the direction and shape of the actions that follow. So, it is to the question of *what forces compel diaspora humanitarians* that I address the remainder of this chapter. I have broken these into forces of morality, affect, and power, although there are many overlaps.

Morality

Morality in the descriptive sense refers to "certain codes of conduct put forward by a society or a group (such as a religion), or accepted by an individual for her own behavior" (Gert 2016). Interviewees expressed a variety of beliefs about what they were doing in terms of moral obligations, their sense of personal responsibility, and it being "the right thing to do." Although individual expressions of morality varied—and it is not possible to explore in any detail the various (normative) codes of conduct that were referenced—there were reoccurring themes that were echoed by participants from quite different backgrounds. These have been grouped in terms of selective obligations, faith, family values, and the need to repay the gift.

Selective Obligations

A number of people spoke about their need to act in response to suffering in ways that resonate with how Fassin describes "humanitarian reason"—of acting "in the name of humanity" in a secularized liberal sense (2010b). These people were quick to clarify that they would help anyone in need. They spoke in abstract terms of human rights, human nature, and humanity. Take, for example, Hadi, who spoke about why he was involved in several RDOs:

> It's human nature. Like yesterday I saw on Facebook, it's a little kid, he is singing, "Why [are] we not living together?" It was touching. Because the world is not as we want it. . . . It's human nature to live in peace and live a normal life; no difference between different race or different background. [But] we are not in an ideal world. . . . Because of politics, religion, whatever reasons, we are different now. So, people who do this help are trying to bring it [back] to nature. We don't have the power—we are not politicians, we are not religious figures—but as individuals, we do it on our level.[26]

While those who spoke in these terms may have ascribed to the aspirational humanitarian principles of independence, neutrality, and impartiality, many also expressed the impossibility of serving "all of humanity" (see also DEMAC 2016b, 36). One interaction was illustrative of this perspective for me. In a conversation with Abdul, I mentioned that I had talked to humanitarian professionals who had expressed concern about the capacity of RDOs to adhere to humanitarian principles. Abdul scoffed at this, saying that these humanitarian principles were "the domain of the privileged"—those who had money and power to act at an arm's length from those who suffered. The vehemence in Abdul's response spoke of the deeply personal connections of refugee diaspora humanitarians and the sense that they *could not* distance themselves from the people they are helping. Peter

Redfield discusses this dynamic in his analysis of the tensions and differences between expatriate volunteers and national staff of Médecins Sans Frontières. He describes national staff as "weighed down" by their local connections and unable to demonstrate the (supposed) "passion, devotion, selflessness, rebellious spirit," and "concern for others, not self-interest" of expatriate volunteers who are able to move lightly in and out of humanitarian contexts by virtue of their privilege, highlighting the power asymmetries within dominant humanitarian practice (Redfield 2012; see also Fassin 2010c).

Some people I spoke to also recognized their own limited capacity to serve humanity but saw that they could be effective in trying to alleviate the (very real) suffering of people they shared some affinity with. As Mae Sie says: "Of course I want to help everyone in the world, but it's not possible. So, I do what I can."[27] These people were acting in the name of humanity, but their actions were directed at a group of people they also felt connected to or who they felt they could be more effective in helping. Take, for example, the following explanation given by Ladan: "I am involved because my ancestors are basically from the Ogaden. Not only that, looking at it as a human—reading, watching documentaries about the injustice that is happening in the Ogaden—it's unbearable. . . . So I get myself involved, not even having seen the Ogaden, but I have that connection through my ancestors, and I have that connection as a human being."[28]

The moral imperative to help a person in need is, perhaps, unavoidably selective. Selectivity about *who* we feel obligated to or responsible for is a common human experience. Barnett argues that we all reside in multiple communities and "concentric circles of community produce concentric circles of obligation; as our sense of community thins, so too does our sense of responsibility" (2011, 228). In this vein, obligations to kin may mean a person is willing to make extraordinary sacrifices for a family member in need, while the need to help may be less constant or intense the further removed a sufferer is from a person's own sense of self, belonging, and community. Thomas W. Laqueur is more direct in his critique of the possibility of a liberal morality that would allow us to care for all humans equally: "Humanity in the first instance begins at home, in our own community. Only a very devoted Kantian or hard core utilitarian would believe that anything else is actually possible, and few today would think it desirable. Ethics is about making human communities not about abstract claims, and of course the suffering of those near us means more than the suffering of strangers" (2009, 46).

It was clear that many of those involved in RDOs felt obligated to help *their people* and to the idea of serving their own community, whether that was defined by state, region, ethnicity, religion, or a combination of these. Take, for example, Carmen's response to why she remained involved in an RDO after she had explained some of the significant challenges she had faced: "It's overrated, sleep! . . . As much as we would all like to have more time for ourselves, I don't think I'd really enjoy it now because I'd know what I should be doing. This is like my obligation. But obligation might be a bad word. It's like a voluntary obligation . . . to my people."[29]

Indeed, many other interviewees spoke of *serving* as a kind of moral duty that was part of being a member of a community (see also O'Hagan and Hirono 2014). This sentiment could be heard when I asked Youssef why he and others from his organization traveled to Indonesia to help a group of strangers. He replied simply: "We went for community."[30] His colleague went on to say:

> I think to me it's because I'm Oromo I feel obliged to help every single Oromo in the world who is in trouble. . . . If I come out of a wealthy family, I can afford to [get] a good education, I can afford to get good health [care], I can afford to get the job and the business I want. But by the same token, if somebody came out of a not-so-well-off family, they can't get that education, they can't get that health care. It's wrong that those who are so privileged . . . continue to enjoy it despite the pain of other people. So, I think we've got an obligation to raise [the] concerns of our people who are in trouble. . . . It's [my] responsibility as an Oromo and as an individual. (Hassan)[31]

The idea that it is a personal responsibility to give so that all members of a community are cared for was a sentiment that many shared. As Berhan said of people from his community helping their extended families in times of need: "It's a given thing. . . . Ninety percent of the community has this responsibility on its shoulders."[32] This sense of personal responsibility for the collective has been described elsewhere to explain widespread remittance-sending practices (see Al-Sharmani 2010; Monsutti 2004), but it was also used by interviewees to explain how RDO volunteers are recruited: "I guess [being part of the RDO] is more you just serving your community. Everyone is serving their own community, whether they are here or back home. So, 'can you bring something to serve?'" (Marama).[33]

It was clear that some individuals' self-identification with *a people*—particularly a people under threat—was central to their understanding of their moral obligations. Indeed, the relationships between those involved in RDOs in Australia and the people they were helping was often spoken of in familial terms. They were helping their "brothers and sisters," as Elizabeth says: "Before that, they just saw us as South Sudanese Australians . . . but now that we are letting them know that we haven't forgotten about them and that we do want to help, they're quite proud to be like, 'You guys are our brothers and sisters, and you guys do want to help us out.'"[34] In these instances, describing the relationship between those in the wider diaspora and those they were helping in familial terms has significance. Our responsibilities and obligations to kin carry powerful moral force. This correlates with Bornstein's description of a kinship-based model of action that challenges the idea that humanitarianism is only driven by liberal altruism and the concept of "abstract others" in need, suggesting that practitioners of "relational empathy" turn "strangers into kin" (2012).

Narratives of moral obligation to the collective were not only spoken about in familial terms but also in terms of community solidarity. A video shared by one informant is illustrative of this idea.[35] The video shows a well-known Hazara musician, Zia Sahill, traveling from Australia to Indonesia to visit and perform for a group of Hazara refugees. Sahill arrives in Indonesia and is greeted at the airport by a line of men, attends a feast, and receives a formal welcome. The meal takes place in a large room with about twenty Indonesia-based Hazara men along with the three Hazara Australian musicians. Everyone shakes hands. They eat rice with meat and soft drinks. The soundtrack to the short video is an atmospheric and moody refrain. Halfway through the video clip, one of the Indonesia-based men says in Hazaraghi, "Just like they say, music is food for the spirit. We need it, especially when it is live." Sahill replies, "We too are the messengers of love and friendship. Of the feelings and thoughts of those living in Australia. We have come here with the purpose of bringing their love to you all so that we can be together and at least make you all feel that you are not forgotten." This performance of community solidarity—of remembering—was echoed in interviews when individuals spoke of the need to demonstrate solidarity with *their people*. As Alaa noted, he had a "moral commitment to help Palestinians in need. . . . When we lost Palestine, the only thing we have is solidarity—community solidarity."[36]

Finally, selective obligations were not always spoken about in terms of national, ethnic, or religious communities. Gender also figured prominently for some of my participants, particularly women, who felt compelled to help other women. Indeed, some of the RDOs in this study were formed to alleviate the suffering of refugee women. They sought to address gender inequities within their own ethnic or religious communities. While interviewees may have spoken in broad terms of *my people*, there was a recognition of diversity and intersectional marginalization within communities—of people who suffered more or in specific ways—perhaps reflecting the experiences of those involved in RDOs who relate to refugee women's suffering from their own lived experiences.

Faith

Faith was a strong force guiding many of my participants' involvement in RDOs. Religious beliefs unsurprisingly came to the fore for those involved in RDOs who foregrounded their religion over their national or ethnic identities. Yet even those involved in secular organizations spoke of their personal faith guiding their need to help. Interviewees came from a wide range of faith traditions (Baha'i,

Mandaean, Hindu, and various Muslim and Christian denominations), highlighting that different religious doctrines—as moral codes of conduct—refer to ways followers should act toward those in need. Take the following excerpts:

> There is no exclusion in our policies. I put that down to not only [the RDO], but just the nature of Assyrians being not just hospitable, but very good Christians. (Christian)[37]

> [I do this] for the sake of God first of all. So that I can say, "I believe in God, in the day of doomsday and before him that I did something good for humanity." (Muslim)[38]

> [I do this] because of the principles [of my faith]. We have to help each other, not criticize each other, to love people for who they are. Also, we think education is very important, we believe in equality for men and woman, we don't judge other people, we cannot be involved with politics [and so forth]. I think it helps us to learn how to work with each other. (Baha'i)[39]

> The thing about the Mandaeans, we believe in peace. We do not believe in conflict or killing or things.... If you hit [us, we] don't hit back.... We are all brothers and sisters, and we have to live in harmony, loving each other. (Mandaean)[40]

In some accounts, religious teachings provided very specific guidance as to who and how to help people in need. This was particularly the case for one man, who spoke about the Islamic tradition of *zakat*, which translates as *giving*, and who went into considerable detail about how much one was obliged to give during the holy month of Ramadan (see also O'Hagan and Hirono 2014, 418–419). Some of the RDOs in this study were closely aligned with different Christian denominations (Baptist, Anglican, Eastern Orthodox, and Roman Catholic) and likewise described how the church as an institution played a role in shaping how they chose *who* and *how* to help. Thus, the link that has been made by a number of scholars regarding the centrality of faith to humanitarianism (see Barnett 2011; Benthall and Lacey 2014; Fassin 2010a; Laqueur 2009) was reflected in the ways in which many of my participants spoke about why they volunteered to help others.

Family Values

Another recurring theme that came up in interviews spoke of a different moral force, involving family values. These values were not necessarily framed in terms of faith or cultural beliefs—even if we may be able to clearly see their roots here—but conveyed how people learned what the right thing to do was through the actions and words of family members. Mothers and fathers were a powerful moral force that seemed to shape many of my interviewees' understandings of how to act in response to another's suffering. One of the more poignant explanations for *why help* was told by Joseph and involved a recollection of the actions of his father:

> I enjoy making sure that other people's lives are made simpler. Is it faith? I'd say definitely faith plays a key role, but, at the end of the day, I think it's what my parents would have taught me. I've seen my parents doing things. . . . During the [Israel-Palestine] War in '82, I was twelve at the time. . . . To cut a long story short, this Palestinian man, a stranger, he comes over. [He] knocks on my parents' door . . . and he [asks] for bread. He [said] to my dad [that they were] surrounded; they have no food. He needs food to feed his family. Being in war, people are very cautious. You know, you need to look after your family and at the same time you've got somebody out there knocking on the door; a stranger asking for food. [My father] didn't turn him away. He actually told Mum to make him bread; gave him enough bread and food and things to take to his family. That stayed in my mind.[41]

Anecdotes such as these about lessons learned from parents were numerous. One woman told a story about how her mother took her outside, showed her a trail of ants, and explained how she should not kill even one ant if she can help it. Another informant's mother demonstrated her values by bringing gold to a community event—a "meeting of a hundred women"—and publicly giving it to her daughter in support of the RDO she had established, saying, "Look, I have this much gold which I accumulated for my daughter's marriage. . . . I don't want it. Keep it, sell it, and I want you to start working on a project."[42] One man spoke of his father acting as a traditional mediator in Afghanistan and how, as a child, he had observed his father acting with integrity in support of abused women, even though this challenged powerful patriarchal norms. Two other women—one originally from Iran and the other from Pakistan—spoke at length and with comparable sentiments about their fathers serving as role models who encouraged them to fight for justice and what was right, particularly when it came to gender roles in conservative patriarchal communities. The fathers of both women were credited with shaping their personal convictions. One said, "When I was young, I always asked my father why my eyes are so little. . . . I can see girls with bigger eyes are beautiful. . . . My father would say that your eyes [don't] matter. Your inner eyes matter. People are beautiful from inside, not from outside. . . . I would always think about that. How can someone's inner eyes [be] beautiful? [Today], I can say that, yes, all those people are beautiful whose eyes are beautiful inside."[43]

Distinguishing here between family values and moral codes inscribed in religious or sociocultural traditions is necessary, because these individuals told how their family members challenged what was expected (i.e., social norms). These were people who had been encouraged from childhood to actively challenge injustices and to help people who were in need, even if it meant going against what was expected of them by others in their community.

Repaying the Gift

Finally, there were some people who described why they were helping in terms of a moral obligation to give back. This was touched on in chapter 1, when discussing the symbolic effects of being labeled a refugee and the tendency in resettlement countries for refugees who help to be framed as *repaying* the country that had given them *the gift* of a new start. This sense of moral obligation was echoed by some of my informants, who saw their involvement with an RDO partly as a way of returning the gift of assistance that they had received. They framed their motivation by speaking first about periods in their lives when they had experienced hardship and had been helped, either by a humanitarian organization or by being resettled in Australia. Take, for example, the following two descriptions:

> [We are] raising funds for Caritas Nepal and sending that through to them to do education support there. So, I think, because you already know people and you have been the beneficiary of that program . . . because you have benefited from what they have done, you just want to reciprocate that in some way. (Raj)[44]

> To be honest, I would say I'm in a better position. I'm in a safe, clean environment where I have my next meal. And thinking of those people, who almost have nothing . . . they don't know what their next meal is or even if they have a place to stay. You appreciate a lot what you have, and in your little way, you try to give back. (Mohammed)[45]

In this first quote, the sense of obligation and reciprocity is direct. Raj felt obliged to support an organization he had once benefited from. The second is perhaps a more generalized statement about reciprocity, but one that resonated with many others' descriptions of giving back. In this case, the relationship of reciprocity is not a direct one. The gift that Mohammed was given was a chance to live in a better position. He understood that this was something that others did not enjoy and that those who had not received this gift continued to suffer. It was the situation of imbalance that made Mohammed feel indebted, as there was no just reason for his privilege. This sense of (indirectly) giving back came heavily imbued with feelings of guilt, a point I will return to shortly.

The idea that gifts involve moral obligations and create bonds between people has a long history in anthropology. The important work that was begun by Marcel Mauss and has been built on by many others describes how the giving of a gift is embedded with ideas of reciprocity. Receiving a gift involves norms of obligation to reciprocate in ways that are culturally and socially contextual and create or bind social ties. For some of my participants, however, the context in which they received the gift (of opportunity through resettlement) did not provide a straightforward way of reciprocating. This is highlighted by Fassin, who argues that the humanitarian gift of assistance is founded on the (unrevealed) fact that the gift is unequal: "Recipients of humanitarian assistance cannot offer anything in return, except in the highly asymmetric form of gratitude or in narratives of their distress" (2010d, 45). As a challenge to this assertion, the experiences of this small group of gift recipients seem to suggest an additional means of return. Their involvement in an RDO in Australia could perhaps be understood as an effort to return the gift of assistance that they once received—an attempt to "pay back."

Affect

Affective forces are those that relate to emotions and how we feel about something—to visceral, rather than rationalized, responses. Fassin argues that "behind the humanitarian gesture, there is always an emotion toward the suffering of others" (2010a, 269) and that even though morality and reason are necessary for people to comprehend and respond to the suffering of others, the compulsion to act is more powerful when reason and emotion are combined. Scholars who have addressed questions of humanitarian morality and motivations have described empathy—being able to imagine or "feel oneself" in another's suffering—as integral to humanitarian acts (see Laqueur 2009; Malkki 2015). While empathy was clearly a force that compelled refugee diaspora humanitarians, other emotions could also be discerned, including feelings of guilt, trauma, and pleasure.

Empathy

Empathy requires a person to not only comprehend that another person suffers, but to *feel* their suffering in some way. Richard Ashby Wilson and Richard D. Brown note that empathy inhabits a site further along the emotional register than sympathy: "Whereas a state of sympathy for one says 'I recognize your pain,' in empathy, one says 'I feel your pain'" (2009, 2). Empathy ignites the senses. Moving from being sympathetic to another's plight to feeling empathetic leads to a greater investment in their situation and to the likelihood that action will follow (see also Bornstein 2012, 148–149; Laqueur 2009). For most participants in my study who had once lived as a refugee, their own personal experiences of displacement provided fertile ground for an empathetic response. Interviewees spoke of having *been there* themselves or in ways that suggested they could imagine themselves in this situation. Those who had *been there* imagined others' suffering by drawing on their own experiences—the sights, smells, sounds, feelings, and sensations they could recall or revisit. See, for example, Mohammed's explanation of his motivation for volunteering with an RDO:

> I can say ninety-nine percent of those people [in Sudan] left their country because there is no stability. Whatever they [had] back home meant a lot to them. Maybe these people were not the richest people . . . maybe they were living in a small hut, but it was warm and they had a sense of family and all that—a country, a place. Leaving that and now being in a place where completely, there's nothing, it's just . . . you feel it. In the same way, I felt it as well in my journey. . . . I was in India and Syria and I've seen it, when you know deep inside that you have no place [to] call home, it's just uncertainty. . . . When I think of that, it just gives me that motivation to continue to do what we do.[46]

Another conversation with a man who had been involved for many years helping refugees was particularly pertinent in highlighting the visceral experiences that diaspora humanitarians tap into and how deeply emotional these can be. Hadi and I were speaking about his long-standing volunteerism. He leaned forward at the table as he recalled when he first started helping, his voice catching toward the end:

> I tell you, the first time I did this I think was in 1991 during the Iraqi uprising against Saddam Hussein. . . . I was one of the people who fled the country to Saudi Arabia on the desert border. On our way, it's really . . . it's like a movie . . . because we've been hungry, thirsty, threatened, and all our families are separated . . . and in the desert we walk, and we don't know what's going on or where we're going. . . . How do we live? Because the American army and the French army were on our way, and when they eat they throw away some leftovers . . . so, their leftovers helped us to survive until we got to the border. And when we got there, the Saudis were treating us very bad. [They] let us stay in the desert and they surrounded us with a fence. But before, when we first arrived, people kept coming. [They] were thirsty. . . . I used to fill a bottle of water and walk the opposite way just to see who is the most needy, to give them a bottle of water. . . . And it was really something that, I dunno, now I have tears in my eyes.[47]

But even for those who had not been there themselves—who were the children of refugees or who had arrived in Australia when they were too young to remember—empathy remained a powerful force. Some spoke in terms of "it *could* have been me" or "it *could* have been my family." Similarities in appearance, ancestry, faith, and language between themselves and those they perceived to suffer provided a way of imagining oneself in that person's situation. This came through particularly in the following conversation with members of the RDO I traveled to Indonesia with. Here, one young man explains his response to a woman he met:

> For me, there was this lady who has nobody there. She basically has no home. . . . So, what I did when I was there, I gave her some money, given her circumstances. I mean, I gave to others as well, but I especially focused on her. We also exchanged numbers to stay in contact. She is elderly—maybe sixty-five. She came to my hotel . . . and [for others] it was more about me saying [to them], "You know what? Life's not over yet, keep going. Things will get better and we're here for you." That did it for them. It didn't change their circumstances for them, but it gave them hope. But one that I couldn't was that lady . . . because she told me she has a kid . . . She said, "My kid's your age." You know what I mean? So, I can just imagine—that's my mother. Do you understand? Her kid's my age. . . . So, every time I speak to her, I want to help. (Adem)[48]

His colleague responds, "Yeah, I have a similar story. I have kids of my own, and one of the ladies said, 'I can't let my kids play outside.' She said, 'I can't even let them play inside.' They have to be quiet. These kids really need some help. They're just kids! Imagine your kids can't play inside the house, let alone outside? They've been like that for a year! . . . Imagine that! . . . I mean, that kills me" (Hassan).[49]

The ability to empathize with others' experiences was perhaps aided by a recognition of similarities between the participants in this study and those they were trying to help, as well as the capacity to draw on their own experiences and recollections of hardship. These were not abstract humans or distant *others* that they were empathizing with; they were familiar. They were brothers and mothers, and their pain was felt by many I interviewed, prompting them to help.

Guilt

Guilt can be understood as the cognitive or emotional experience that correlates with a realization or belief that one has acted in contravention of their own standards of conduct (moral codes). The "relational empathy" (Bornstein 2012) that resonated with many of my participants—that this was *family* who was suffering—also helps us understand reoccurring expressions of guilt. Many of my participants said they felt guilty for not doing enough, for being selfish, or for simply living a good life when those they felt connected to suffered. Some spoke of how they believed they were not fulfilling their obligations and felt guilty about living in Australia. For example:

> I have an enormous amount of guilt because I don't think I do enough, [and] that's not just a fall-on-your-sword kind of martyrdom thing. (Carmen)[50]

> The hardest thing [is] that selfish thinking of myself sometimes. Because we all have to go out and work and all that. You can't sometimes give a lot of time, but when you know that, it just hurts you. That's hard in your mind when you know that . . . the people are still there and stuck, and every day their lives are

> getting worse and worse. Thinking about that is very hard for all of us, I think. (Mohammed)[51]

> I'm very passionate about [helping] and I came from that background. I was once a refugee. I was once an asylum seeker. . . . There are lots of people who had the same situation but don't have the same fate that I have had. I feel obliged. It's a survival guilt. (Hamid)[52]

For those who expressed feelings of guilt, the sense of not fulfilling what they understood as their obligations caused them pain. This guilt was also present as an animating force in some people's explanation of why they continued to volunteer for RDOs, even when it felt hard. In some ways, then, we can see guilt as both a motivating and a sustaining force for volunteers involved in small organizations that perhaps, in other circumstances, may have ceased to exist.

Trauma

For a smaller number of interviewees, traumatic experiences in their past seemed to be an added dimension animating their involvement in RDOs. While I do not want to suggest that a trauma response was an overriding force for any of those involved in my research, there were some who clearly linked their personal commitment to helping with a way of healing and processing past traumatic experiences (see also Kira and Tummala-Narra 2015; van de Port 1999). For those living in Australia who had survived war, torture, and other deprivations, the murky experiences of their past informed their emotional response to the suffering of others and what they felt they could or should do about it. To illustrate this, take the following explanation given by Rosanna about why she tried to help:

> When they put me [in prison], I felt very lonely in the cell. . . . I felt I was going to be killed at that time. When I was behind the closed door, I was listening to what people were doing, because I was not able to see anything. The only time I could see them was when they hanged them or raped them. That is the kind of torture I have. Because of that, I promised myself and to the women that were killed that, if one day I come out, that I tell their story and be helpful to people.[53]

During fieldwork, I began to wonder how people within refugee diaspora communities responded to unfolding humanitarian crises, how this related to trauma responses, and whether, for those whose seeing or hearing about others' suffering brought about memories of past traumatic experiences, there was a more complex set of forces animating their actions. For example, during the period in which I was undertaking fieldwork (2014–2015), the security situation in both Iraq and Syria deteriorated, and millions of people were displaced. While both the Syrian and Iraqi diasporas in Australia mobilized to help, it seemed that the responses of Iraqis differed slightly from those of the Syrian diaspora at that time. Iraqi Australians I saw speaking at public forums during this period seemed to use a slightly different emotional register than their Syrian counterparts. The Syrian Australians I saw speak had not personally experienced violent conflict or forced displacement, unlike those from the Iraqi diaspora, who had arrived as refugees during previous waves of displacement. The Syrians were equally passionate but less emotional in their mobilization of supporters. Take the following narrative about why one woman founded an RDO in 2014 during the displacement of Iraqi Christians: "I remember when we had nothing. We were literally eating bread and drinking water for months. Sometimes we would get eggplant and that would be something special. We were sleeping on the floor. We went from being very well off and comfortable to sleeping on the floor. And that was a very difficult experience. I promised myself, if I get through this and have enough, I won't spend extra money on myself, I will spend it on others" (Carmen).[54]

Carmen's telling was emotional; she spoke with anger. But there was a similar expression of anger and a sensitivity to the injustices of the past that came through in other interviews. When I asked one man why he was involved in an RDO, he began his response with "I have a very sad story." He continued, "Back there I always felt like one of my legs was broken."[55] He framed his involvement in the RDO in his own painful experiences and his need to ensure that others did not suffer like he had. Barnett writes that compassion does not pulse evenly and steadily, "it surges at particular moments" (2011, 224). For some of my participants, it seems the surges in compassion in response to crises witnessed from afar ignited emotional responses that were rooted in a murky and traumatic past.

Pleasure

While I have so far written of more negatively experienced emotions—guilt, trauma, and empathy toward others' suffering—not all of the feelings conveyed by my participants were painful. An important affective force that was acknowledged by some participants was one of pleasure—it *felt good* to help people. Hadi describes the pleasure of helping people as "an addiction." He said, "If I can do something, why wouldn't I?"[56] Sabira said of her volunteering, "You feel that [there are] challenges and [it's] tiring, but there is joy. There is a joy that you're . . . part of making some differences."[57]

But perhaps the most prevalent pleasurable emotion that was described by participants was that of feeling satisfied. This satisfaction came from doing a good job or making a difference, even if only in small ways. One man said, "You know, I'm comparing my work with other organizations, and that's where the satisfaction comes."[58] One of Bornstein's insights into the experiences of wealthy Indians volunteering in orphanages is that the volunteers themselves obtained pleasure.

As she argues, this form of volunteering is "a gift of experience from the recipient to the donor" (Bornstein 2012), an idea that resonated with the experiences of some of the volunteers involved in RDOs in Australia.

Finally, there was the pleasure of sociality that seemed to also be part of what motivated some people to get involved in RDOs. I witnessed this when participating in a range of RDO-organized events in Australia. People danced, ate, and talked at RDO fundraising events (see fig. 3.1). Those who organized these events were congratulated for their contributions. They smiled. While the purpose of organizing a fundraising event in Sydney or Melbourne may have been to raise money for a project to help people in desperate situations, the actual event was talked about as having been both hard work and fun.

Power

As noted at the start of this chapter, there is growing recognition that configurations of power and politics are unavoidably present in humanitarian acts. Acknowledging that power dynamics are implicated in refugee diaspora humanitarianism should not diminish these acts as genuine attempts to do good or the fact that these actions do alleviate suffering. The two are not mutually exclusive. For the RDOs and individuals in this study, there was considerable variation in the undercurrents of power and politics that animated their actions. I suggest two that were of varying importance to different people: diaspora politics and homeland politics. A third expression of power was also apparent and relates more to the personal—how individuals saw helping as their *essence* and were motivated by their own capacity to bring about transformative change in the lives of others.

Diaspora Politics

I have described all the groups that participated in my research as refugee *diaspora* organizations, but there were some that oriented themselves to diaspora politics in Australia more than others. When writing about diaspora politics, I refer to the furthering of the interests of a group based on an assertion of a collective identity. Those motivated by diaspora politics tended to be involved in organizations that were formed to represent a group based on a diasporic identity first and foremost, rather than to provide humanitarian assistance. RDOs that were oriented more closely with diasporic identities were involved in mobilizing support for people outside Australia as part of a broader agenda of binding people together to preserve a collective identity tied to language, religious, social, and cultural practices (Tölölyan 2007). For instance, some had become involved in humanitarian work as a response to a crisis affecting their homeland or people. As Carmen says, "You see a crisis and [what is] under threat is the loss of our people. . . . Our lives and our heritage are at stake, quite frankly, so [getting involved in humanitarian activities] is a response to that."[59]

Figure 3.1 Raising funds, sharing food. Eritrean RDO fundraising dinner, Melbourne, 2015. Photo credit: EAHA.

Diaspora politics can be seen, in part, as identity politics. While there are some resources to be gained from establishing a diaspora organization in Australia (e.g., small amounts of funding), this is hardly lucrative. Instead, forming or supporting a diaspora organization seemed for some to be more about being visible and recognized as *a people* and of finding strength in belonging to a collective. Hassan describes his motivation as such: "I want to get to the point where, when someone asks and I say, 'I'm Oromo,' they say, 'I know.' . . . So there is obviously a political aspect to it. It's not in the way that you want to run for office or have any interest in politics, I'm just interested in making [people more aware of] who Oromos are."[60]

This sentiment was echoed by others who spoke in terms of their fear of losing their identity and of their need to come together to create a sense of belonging. One man said: "When you're in diaspora . . . you start to lose a part of yourself."[61] The antidote to *losing oneself*, then, could be asserting a distinctive identity and promoting your people so that those in Australia know who you are.[62] Diasporic identity and humanitarian action meet when people see acts of *doing good* as part of their desire to be viewed as *good people*. For example, when I asked one Afghan Australian man why he was involved in helping people in Australia and overseas, he replied, "I don't want other people to think my own community are not respectful [or] are not good people."[63]

Diaspora politics, like any kind of politics, involves struggle, conflict, and the negotiation of ideas and power between individuals or groups. The messiness of diaspora politics was apparent to me on several occasions during my fieldwork. During informal conversations, people expressed their frustrations about individuals jockeying for power, questioned the ideas or actions of those who were in positions of power within RDOs, or, more simply, talked about problems within their own community. Power struggles within diaspora communities seemed to play out in some organizations more than others—with breakaway organizations being formed, leadership turnover or challenges, and fluctuations in community support for RDO activities. One informant openly talked about why different RDOs had been formed within his small community. He said of the leaders of another RDO, "They have their own personal agenda. Some want to become famous. Some want to do something else. This is the dirty games of politics in every community, in every country around the world. Human beings are not perfect. As a result, I was compelled to split ways with them. I had to form a new organization."[64]

For some individuals, then, the desire to represent their community as the bearers of a distinctive identity and to show that they are good people may have been part of what motivated them to form or get involved in RDOs. This came through in two separate conversations I had with people who spoke in similar terms of the need to leave a legacy. The legacy that they envisioned was a demonstration that they—as individuals or as part of a group—had done something to further the interests of their people. Doing something to help alleviate suffering overseas enabled them to *do good* and *look good*. To some, their personal or collective identities, reputations, and status in Australia were at stake.

Homeland Politics

Much has been written about the long-distance politics of diasporas (see Bernal 2006; Betts and Jones 2016; Danforth 1995; Ghorashi and Boersma 2009; Wise 2004). While some of the RDOs in this study were directly and actively engaged in homeland politics alongside (or through) their humanitarian work, an equal number seemed explicitly concerned with *not* getting involved in homeland or diaspora politics. In terms of individuals involved in formal political action or whose organizational aims involved implicit or explicit support for political parties in their country of origin, their motivation to mobilize humanitarian efforts was tied to garnering support for political interests in their homeland. For example, one interviewee was involved in directly lobbying Australian members of parliament to support the ruling party in their country of origin. At least three of the RDOs in this study were aligned or affiliated with homeland opposition parties, some of which operated extensively from the diaspora. Others were not necessarily affiliated with a political group or party but were actively involved in opposing or challenging the actions of states, particularly on human rights issues. As one man forcefully argued about the government in his homeland, Myanmar: "Perpetrators [of human rights violations] should not go with impunity but should be brought to justice. . . . We're not only a socially, but also a politically active organization."[65]

That some people involved in RDOs expressed strong political views or are active in homeland political struggles should come as no surprise. These are people who, for all their differences, had a common commitment and belief in transformational change—and big *P* politics is one of the loci of change. However, a surprising number of interviewees seemed to express a frustration or disillusionment with formal political processes. For this subgroup, there was discernible suspicion of or openly expressed dislike for politicians. They did not see hope for change coming from political action, so they preferred to act in the margins. One interviewee described why he decided to set up an RDO after traveling overseas to participate in a political opposition meeting: "When I got there, what I found is that the opposition, they ignore that kind of help [i.e. the need for education] and they ignore [the refugees] there. I [had been] thinking one of the problems of [the] Eritrean people is the government. But when I went there I found out even the opposition, it's a problem. [And] the poor Eritrean people, they are getting it from both sides. . . . So, what can be done, even [at a] lower level? That's my thinking."[66]

This antipolitics sentiment was shared by other informants, who spoke about different contexts in which they felt their actions were more meaningful than the talk of politicians. They described themselves and their organizations as serving poor people, not political interests.

The views of those on the politics/antipolitics spectrum seemed to overlap when it came to the need to bring about change *for the people*, to pave the way for return. There were many who expressed a desire to return to their homeland and felt that these actions of RDOs were about contributing to the facilitation of return. A conversation with one man, John, highlighted this link between RDOs and the politics of return. John described his own journey to Australia, the process he had gone through to mobilize support to establish an RDO, and how in the future he wanted to develop educational opportunities in Myanmar. He spoke about the central importance of education to the future prosperity of his homeland and the need for those in the diaspora to prepare for return: "I always encourage my community members to go back. [Australia is] not my place, to be honest. I can be an Australian citizen by paper, but I have my own citizenship in Burma. . . . I have a land. I have a place. I have to go back there."[67]

But even those who had been in Australia for many years and did not personally see themselves leaving spoke about the need to help others to return. For example, this is how Anwar saw the long-term objectives of the RDO he helped to establish:

> I can't return. I'm Australian. . . . This is my second country, but it is the first country for my kid. So that link doesn't let me to separate from my kid. . . . So, for me, I'm Australian, and this organization is [an] Eritrean-Australian organization. . . . But, if the government [in Eritrea] becomes [a] democratic government, people [in] different countries—those who are in Saudi Arabia, in Sudan, Yemen, Ethiopia, all these countries—they will go back. And when these people go back, I can see still we're going to face problems there . . . because you are not going back to a country that is wealthy. So . . . at least we are going to ease that problem for the refugees who want to return.[68]

Bringing about change in a homeland so that *the people* (refugees, diasporas) could return was a central concern for many I spoke to. The question of how to bring about transformative change—through engagement with formal political processes or not—was less clear. A common thread that animated many people's involvement in RDOs was the desire to contribute in some way to paving the way for return.

The "Essence of Me"

One final theme that animated some of my informants concerned their own sense of power. One interviewee, Muzafar, drew my attention to this animating force. Muzafar was originally from Afghanistan and had been involved in establishing a refugee school in Indonesia and was now supporting this school from Australia. When I asked him why he was involved in this work, he began his explanation by describing his experience working for different humanitarian and human rights organizations in Afghanistan. He used an expression that resonated with what others told me about their histories of helping: "When I look back to those days [in Afghanistan], I think they were the essence of me."[69] Indeed, a history of helping was common to most of the people I interviewed, and I often heard participants talk about how they saw themselves essentially as helpers. These were not individuals who suddenly decided to become involved in establishing or running an RDO; they were people who had been helpers before, and many had become committed to transformational change early on in their lives. As Sabira explains, "I'm happy with hard work. Hard workers change things. I don't like slow things in life. I'm working from when I was seventeen or eighteen. I'm working for my community in this space from that time. . . . I don't think [about] things for myself. This is what I am."[70]

Being someone who wants to and can make things happen—who can create or lead an organization that has an impact on other people's lives—involves the accrual of skills, networks, and resources. The sense of power and satisfaction that came from being able to bring about change seemed to compel or, more accurately, sustain individuals to continue this work. These were people who had learned how to organize to help, and this meant they had a greater capacity to effect change. These were individuals who had developed networks with people in positions of power in Australia and internationally, who met with foreign ministers, and who were invited to and spoke at UN meetings. As one man, Raj, described: "It is some sort of continuation of what you have done initially."[71] Raj had started working in paid and unpaid roles as a community worker from the time he had been living in a refugee camp in Nepal, and he then applied the skills he had developed in Australia to undertake community work, both paid and unpaid.

Perhaps there is something more to be said about the personal interests and power that individuals gain from their involvement in RDOs in terms of recognizing their professionalism, capacity, and status in the Australian context. When some interviewees talked about their lives prior to living in Australia, I was struck by how the loss of status was acutely felt. These were individuals who had been politicians, teachers, journalists, activists, lawyers, artists, and successful businesspeople in the past. As is the common experience of many resettled refugees, the loss of occupational and social status in Australia was apparent for many of my participants (Olliff 2010). Getting involved in RDOs perhaps provided them with some sense of status regained. People came up and thanked them—or, as Sabira said, "They put you up high."[72] Another person said, "When I walk into my community, they always see me as someone who has done something for our community in the camp."[73] One man I interviewed showed me a chapter of a book titled *Unsung Heroes* that was written about him. For these people, their involvement in RDOs seemed to give them a sense of pride and achievement, but it also potentially offered status and recognition.

I do not wish to convey that these people were involved in RDOs because they were purely or even mainly motivated by self-interest and the pursuit of other people's gratitude and recognition. The people I met exhibited remarkable integrity, humility and wisdom, demonstrated through their actions and the significant personal sacrifices made. That they may have regained some sense of their own power and were recognized for their contributions should not diminish their acts. If anything, I make this point to comment on the migration context and on how—in a context like Australia, with its racialized hierarchies—RDOs provided a space in which people who are often sidelined can more readily assert their agency and apply their considerable skills to do good in the world.

SITUATED HUMANITARIANS

To understand what compels a person or a group of people to help a stranger in need, it is necessary to situate the helpers within their particular context, for helping is a complicated act. It requires someone perceiving another's suffering, feeling compelled to do something about it, and acting. Who we are as helpers, how we understand suffering, and what capacity we have to do something about it all matter. All humanitarian actors, whether individuals or institutions, are situated within specific histories and contexts that inform how suffering is recognized, the causes and solutions to this perceived suffering, and the actions that follow. For example, the people who were involved in the RDOs in this study were all situated in the Global North (Australia) and were exposed to some of the same opportunities to engage with dominant humanitarian actors as other Australians. Yet when I asked whether they would consider donating to, engaging with, or working for a larger institutional humanitarian organization, even one directly helping *their people*, the response from participants was almost uniformly *no*. These large humanitarian organizations—their messages and calls to action—did not seem to resonate with the people involved in RDOs. Instead, they painstakingly established their own voluntary organizations, which allowed them to help in ways that felt meaningful and important to them and aligned with their particular set of experiences, beliefs, and motivations.

This aversion to engaging with institutionalized humanitarian actors makes sense when you consider the recurring figures of suffering that refugee diaspora humanitarians evoke—that of a collective people who suffer, of ruptured social networks and people who suffer because they are alone or not able to fulfill their (expected) caring roles, and of refugees who are unheard, unhelped, and disenabled. To remedy this kind of suffering, one must focus on establishing and repairing social connections, listening deeply, and speaking up—things that a donation to Médecins Sans Frontières is unlikely to fulfill. It also makes sense in the context of the multiple forces—moral, affective, and involving dimensions of power—that compel refugee diaspora humanitarians to act. The moralities and motivations that animate this kind of helping reflect the distinct perspectives and positionality of the individuals behind RDOs—as diasporas, as survivors, as resettled refugees, and as people with a history of helping and being helped. Understanding *why* people act gives a better foundation for understanding *how* they go about organizing and *to what effect*, questions for which the remaining chapters are dedicated.

FOUR

MODALITIES

Governance and Economies

I BEGAN THIS BOOK WITH a vignette about a refugee school in Indonesia that was started with a US$200 donation and, five years later, was running a live online telethon that mobilized a global network of supporters to raise over US$55,000 in a few weeks. In reality, however, most of the refugee diaspora organizations (RDOs) that I engaged with had more modest budgets and fundraising strategies and successes. To convey some common RDO experiences when it comes to governance and finance, I start this chapter with another vignette, this time about Akademos Society, an organization that was initially established by a group of university students from the Hazara community in Australia. Akademos Society has been fundraising since 2013 to provide educational opportunities to disadvantaged students in Pakistan and Afghanistan.[1]

Akademos Society is governed by a small volunteer board that comprises early career professionals who are involved in overseeing projects, fostering partnerships, and raising funds. In 2020, the organization provided twelve scholarships to cover the costs of college-level education to students in Pakistan and funded a supplementary learning class and a "Kids off the Street" program that provides financial assistance to child laborers in Afghanistan to enable them to access educational opportunities. The organization's annual budget of around US$23,000 (2019–2020) is mostly raised from within the Hazara community in Australia through personal and community networks and online fundraising via social media. But the society's longevity is also tied to the contributions made by board members, who give their money (a yearly financial contribution), skills, and time to keep the initiative going. The governance structure, income, and expenditures of the organization are painstakingly accounted for in detail in annual reports that are circulated to all donors. The beneficiaries of scholarships are announced each year via social media and the Akademos website, along with an account of the selection process and video testimonies of scholarship recipients. Akademos Society may be a drop in the ocean when it comes to global refugee education needs, but it provides a means through which a small group of committed individuals with specialized knowledge and networks—who are compelled by many of the forces described in the previous chapter—can make a difference in the lives of *familiar strangers* living on the other side of the world.

The following chapter looks more closely at the *modalities* of refugee diaspora humanitarianism—that is, the implementation of actions that are situated in humanitarian moralities. In this, the concern is with *how* RDOs like Akademos Society are structured, what resources they mobilize, and how they account for and consider the effects of their actions. This chapter should be considered the first of two parts on the modalities of refugee diaspora humanitarianism. In this first part, the focus is on RDO governance and economies, both of which largely concern what happens within the host (Australian) context. The attendant chapter (chap. 5) looks more closely at transnational modalities—how RDOs work and move across time and place.

GOVERNANCE

Governance refers to the rules, norms, and actions that produce, sustain, regulate, and hold accountable a governing entity (Bevir 2013). How, then, are RDOs governed? One of the primary challenges in answering this question is the apparent diversity in the forms and activities of RDOs, as noted in chapter 2. While for some RDOs, it is much easier to talk about governance—they look much like small nongovernmental organizations (NGOs)—others were much looser in form, and the tools available to describe governance (e.g., principles, policies, guidelines) seem inadequate. This may be because much of what I observed involved ways of helping that appeared as happenstance. Actions came about through a confluence of factors: individual circumstances and abilities, and individuals and groups reacting to or seizing opportunities as they arose and with the resources that they could mobilize. The extent of preplanning within prevailing humanitarian frameworks and practices was, in most cases, limited. Moreover, the RDOs in this study were all formed and run by volunteers, and their investment in governance reflects the challenges and experiences of other voluntary organizations (see Brinkerhoff 2008). Many RDOs seem to exist only for a time and for as long as the people involved feel animated enough to invest their energies and resources into such an endeavor.

Having said this, it is still possible to talk about RDOs and governance. These organizations are involved in raising and transferring resources, their activities have implications for the lives of others, and, for the most part, they exist (or have existed) as legal entities. It is relevant to consider how decisions are made within these organizations, how they organize, and how they account for their actions. In discussing RDO governance, I focus on two key themes: their structure and accountability.

Structure

Of the participating RDOs in this study, roughly two-thirds (eighteen out of twenty-six) had a governance structure that appeared to be based on meeting the requirements of being an incorporated association. Incorporated associations are voluntary not-for-profit organizations or groups that have a specific legal status in Australia.[2] Incorporation requires an organization make explicit its rules, norms, and actions and to align these with an overarching governance framework determined by the relevant government authority.[3] For example, incorporated associations may be required to elect a committee of management, hold an annual general meeting, lodge an annual statement (including a financial report) with government authorities, and establish a set of rules for the association. Aligning oneself to the governance structure of an incorporated association—and therefore operating as a legal entity—allows organizations to be able to enter into contracts and to register as a charity for fundraising purposes.

The extent to which the rules of being an incorporated association were adhered to in practice varied considerably among RDOs that were or had been incorporated. Some RDOs operated with seemingly well-established committees of management, developing rules and an impressive governance structure, holding carefully planned elections at well-attended annual meetings, and complying with all reporting requirements. Others clearly struggled to meet these requirements, falling behind in submitting annual statements, providing incomplete financial reports, not adhering to the model rules that they had submitted, and holding annual meetings with limited participation. Indeed, while some RDOs on paper were incorporated associations, many were governed with a high degree of informality, as an excerpt from my field notes highlights:

> I am sitting in the community center waiting area. There are kids running around everywhere. People are wafting in and out, hoodies on, greeting each other, *As-salāmu ʿalaykum*! The Eritrean Community in Australia [a different organization from the RDO] has an ongoing agreement with the center to use the space on Saturday nights. Abdul and another man are sitting near me talking earnestly in Arabic, leaning into each other. It's freezing and dimly lit. My teeth are chattering. The meeting of the RDO committee was supposed to start at 6.30 p.m.; Mohammed sent a text message on Thursday as a reminder. At 7:00 p.m., no one had arrived. Anwar turned up at 7.30 p.m. in his work

clothes—fluorescent builder's fleece, paint-speckled pants and boots, his face tired, a small notebook in his hand. He had been working all day and said he had fallen asleep when he got home. Nobody else showed up.

The challenges of meeting the requirements of being an incorporated association were spoken about openly. Meeting financial reporting requirements was considered difficult because of the informality and invisibility of cash-based transactions overseas and concerns about drawing attention to the transnational nature of their work, often in conflict situations. For example, one man lamented the lack of a paper trail for a small project that provided a teacher at a refugee community-run school with a motorized wheelchair. The money for the wheelchair had been collected from a small number of women in Melbourne and given as cash to someone who was traveling to Sudan. The wheelchair was purchased in Sudan using this cash, which was converted into the local currency using a black-market currency-exchange service. The only evidence that this act took place was a handwritten receipt in Arabic from the purchase of the wheelchair and a short video that was taken of the teacher receiving the wheelchair and thanking the RDO and community members in Australia for their generosity. The fact that this act involved cash-based transactions with minimal written evidence (e.g., receipts to donors, bank statements, etc.) caused concern for those writing the annual statement required by local authorities. What would happen if the organization was audited? What would happen if the RDO was asked to prove that monies were *not* being transferred to a terrorist organization? Should they include this project in their annual statement at all?

While being an incorporated association gave some groups a sense of legitimacy, the legal obligations of incorporation also generated unease for groups that were primarily focused on helping people in humanitarian (conflict) situations. Only four of the RDOs in this study were registered as a charitable organization, a legal entity that would more appropriately reflect and enable their acts of helping. Being registered as a national charity allows organizations to apply for Deductible Gift Recipient status with the Australian Tax Office, increasing their fundraising potential, as some donors prefer giving to organizations that can provide a receipt that reduces their tax liability. Yet registering with the Australian Charities and Not-for-profits Commission (the government authority that regulates charitable organizations) and potentially applying for membership with the Australian Council for International Development (the peak body for international development organizations in Australia) and, if seeking government funding, with the Department of Foreign Affairs and Trade (the government department that oversees Australia's aid program) involves wading through a maze of legal documents, requirements, and forms. For small volunteer-run groups, this maze is almost impossible to understand and even harder to navigate. This is particularly so for the RDOs that are first establishing themselves or whose active members have more limited English or educational backgrounds.

In fact, about a third of the groups in this study had no legal status as organizations. To write about their governance, then, is to write about different governing rules, norms, and actions. These varied depending on the activities they were involved in and the networks drawn on. For example, two of the RDOs were coalitions involving different incorporated associations that united for a specific action and used their respective networks to mobilize resources to provide emergency relief in response to humanitarian crises. One of these coalitions was made up of Iraqi organizations, the other Eritrean. These coalitions effectively dissolved once the (humanitarian) project was finalized. Both coalitions came together prior to my fieldwork, so their decision-making processes could not be observed, yet interviewees spoke of those involved from the different coalition organizations meeting together, discussing what they would do and delegating responsibilities. Two other RDOs were associated with larger organizations—namely, churches. This did not mean that the church governance structures were necessarily involved in the decision-making and accountability of these groups, but rather that the members came together through association with these churches and mobilized support from within existing structures and networks.[4] Representatives of these RDOs spoke about ultimately moving to become incorporated associations once established (and indeed, one did register as an incorporated association in the following year), and both had begun implementing governance structures reflective of these legal requirements.

Finally, a handful of RDOs in this study could be described in much less certain governance terms, perhaps best characterized with reference to Dorothea Hilhorst and Bram Jansen's concept of "Non-Governmental Individuals" (NGIs). In describing the arrival of different humanitarian actors in the wake of the tsunami in Sri Lanka in 2004, Hilhorst and Jansen write of NGIs as people who "boarded a plane with relief supplies and money collected through their personal, neighbourhood, professional or church networks," who are characterized as sharing a dissatisfaction with established agencies, who are motivated by the idea of "humanity," and whose personal principles and practices share similarities with the codes of conduct of humanitarian NGOs (2010, 1131). Hilhorst and Jansen's description of the practices of NGIs resonates with descriptions given of the actions of individuals or small groups of friends within refugee diaspora communities. These individuals or groups were likewise dissatisfied with established aid agencies, and their decision-making and actions were highly individualized.[5] They collected money and goods from their networks, made decisions about the principles guiding their actions, and found ways to account for what they did. For example:

> Within the community, we have got individuals, they support families that have been referred to them by someone. They don't know them. They never saw them before. I come to you and I tell you, "Look, Louise, when I went to [this refugee camp], I saw a family with two orphaned kids. So, what we can do?" You tell me, "Look, I can help them. In a year, $500." If you want, I can connect you directly with them. Then you can deal with the money. You can send it to them person-to-person. Or, if you trust [me], you give it to me, and I will hand it to them. When I was in Sudan in 2013, I had a call from someone from [the] community. She's a woman. She's well-established here. She called me [and] said, "Look, could you please help me with finding five families? But the condition is they have to have kids underage and they have to be without husbands." . . . I provided her with ten families . . . and each one I did a small profile—like her name, her age, and her situation—and I sent it to the lady. She picked out five families from those, and she said she should help each family by [sending] $300 every year. And, until today, she is doing it.[6]

Other informants shared similar scenarios of individuals or small groups of friends supporting families in Syria, Jordan, Lebanon, and Eritrea. As Hilhorst and Jansen suggest, NGIs are often delegitimized by other humanitarian actors as "amateurs." Yet, as the above illustrates, the processes in which individuals or small groups identify needs, make principled decisions, and account for their actions seem to resonate with many formal agencies' principles and practices.

To summarize, most RDOs in this study were officially structured as incorporated associations. However, the extent to which the explicit rules, norms, and actions of an incorporated association were adhered to varied considerably, and almost a third of participating RDOs were not incorporated and operated as NGIs or informal networks. Whether incorporated or not, RDOs seem to operate with a high degree of informality. This means that decision-making processes are opaque to those not directly involved, and many seem to be governed by the (unwritten) rules of individuals and social networks.

Voluntary Failures

All of the RDOs in this study were volunteer-run, an important distinction between professionalized humanitarian organizations. RDO governance must be considered in terms of the fact that those who get involved do so voluntarily and on top of other work, study, social, and family commitments. Jennifer Brinkerhoff (2008) suggests that many diaspora organizations suffer from various forms of voluntary failure, categorized by Lester Salamon (1987) as: philanthropic insufficiency, rooted in an organization's limited scale and resources; philanthropic particularism, reflecting an organization's choice of clientele and projects; philanthropic paternalism, where those who control the most resources are able to control community priorities; and philanthropic amateurism. Shades of these failings were certainly evident in many of the experiences interviewees spoke about and in observing how RDOs scrambled to pull together resources to achieve organizational goals. As one woman, Leyla, lamented when asked what the biggest challenge was in being involved in an RDO: "Time! We're all still working, and we're doing this as volunteers. We don't have enough arms. Everybody wants something."[7] Another, Marama, said, "The challenge is you start from zero. When you establish an organization, decide to organize, you collect people from different areas. You bring them, you talk to them: 'Let us do something.' And then, when you do this, they have to sacrifice their time from [other commitments]. You have to convince all these people, 'If you have this amount of hours a week, can we just do something—like one hour? Can you commit?' So, you start from zero."[8]

It takes considerable time and resources to establish an organization and make it operational, with a sustainable governance structure where the burden of responsibility and work is shared. While some of these RDOs had received (limited) support to develop their organizational and governance structures, others described *learning by doing* and, as Marama went on to explain, spent years struggling to establish a viable organization.[9] Those that had persisted and grown had a noticeably greater number of people involved in the governance of the organization, with a devolution of responsibilities. One key informant working with RDOs described it thus:

> The reasons that [RDOs] don't get off the ground [is] because they can't keep a group together and they can't keep the momentum. The organizations are poorly constituted. They don't put the investment into actually setting up the organization that's needed . . . I mean, some of them can have a capacity to get money, and then they sort of cobble together an organization to be able to support that. And I think that has sustainability issues. But, some of them manage to . . . keep developing their organizations to the point where they can keep functioning. Others . . . just don't have the pulling power for the money and they don't have the organizational skills. Lack of money and lack of commitment to building an organization are the two deadly ways of just killing it in the bud.[10]

Indeed, many of those interviewed spoke about the enormous difficulty of creating and sustaining a voluntary organization and the history of failed organizations they had been involved in or heard about. As one woman, Elizabeth, said, "There's a lot of little organizations that would be like, 'Oh, yep, so we have . . . we just signed papers with the government and we're incorporated (supposedly). We're doing this, help us out.' Then people would go to help them, and after a couple of months, it just goes quiet; nothing comes back, nothing goes forth."[11] When asked why these organizations had disappeared or failed, most spoke of the lack of capacity to sustain or follow through, rather than a belief that there was a misappropriation of resources.

Those who had observed RDOs come and go over time noted that their effectiveness was linked to individual leadership capabilities, the relative strengths of an RDO's networks, and the availability of sufficient time and resources to see actions through. One interviewee framed differences in RDO effectiveness in terms of class:

> I think a lot of it is to do with education and ability to organize, and then ability to be able to speak the language of bureaucrats or the language of politicians and knowing how to do that. Communities that haven't had that experience—often they are the rural communities—find it much more difficult, whereas the Iraqis are well-educated people by and large. They know how to form associations. . . . When they meet, they can sit down and have a very clear strategy in terms of what they're trying to achieve. That will often take time. So, [it's] about levels of education and levels of spare time too. If you're working class—you're struggling to survive, get food on the table, you're working shift work or whatever—you don't have that time to give up hours of your day to represent your community. No matter how qualified or committed you are, those are the realities you face. Whereas people who have middle-class jobs, I'm not saying they don't work hard, but they tend to have [the] capacity to be able to do that volunteer work.[12]

This idea of class having implications for the effectiveness of diasporas' transnational engagements has been noted by Nicholas Van Hear and Robin Cohen, who suggest that "differences of wealth, resources, social capital and class shape the capacity and level of support which can be offered" (2017, 181). Although diasporas in Australia may have greater resources to draw on when compared with diasporas in less affluent parts of the world, there are clearly variations in capacity between communities in Australia linked to socioeconomic variables.

Voluntary Strengths

While it is easy to point to the challenges and limitations of volunteer-run organizations, a common theme that emerged from talking to people involved in RDOs was how they also saw the voluntary nature of these organizations as one of their core strengths. For some, *not* being paid was an important and valued distinction between RDOs and other humanitarian actors. It meant that all resources went directly to the people they were helping. Leyla, who founded an RDO, said of other humanitarian organizations: "We are doing the same thing. They've just been doing it a lot longer and they have the support of rich people. But they don't go deep into the community. . . . They need something local, and that's where we come in. We have that. And we also don't get paychecks. Every cent goes directly to people. We don't get anything. With the bigger NGOs, the people who work there don't have the passion to serve people. Our organization and people are driven by faith and passion."[13]

Indeed, the value some saw in being volunteer-run went beyond cost-effectiveness and was tied to convictions. Their commitment to *making a difference* was not, as many described it, sullied by personal gain. This was not a career or a profession, it was a calling. Anwar explains it this way: "When someone is doing things for money, it is different from someone who's doing things for a cause. . . . In Arabic, *iman*, it means 'conviction'; that's how my belief is. . . . And if that's the kind of belief you have, then I think you can always see success in front of you. . . . For me, every time I see [change for] someone—even only one person—I can see this as success. So money, it is nothing."[14]

This sentiment was echoed by Mohammed, who said:

> If I was hired by [the RDO], and my rent is paid and everything, and I'm here with [the RDO], all I care about would be my job. . . . Yes, I would care about those people, but they would be like my subjects—my clients, basically. That's how I would think of it. Whereas the way we have come and the way we're doing it, it doesn't matter how small or how big it is. Our link is continuous, direct, there's nothing in between, trying to impress some boss or get that commission or whatever. When you do anything from the heart, it's more powerful.[15]

The value and the limitations of RDOs being volunteer-run seem to be one of the paradoxes of this form of humanitarianism. Many RDOs struggle to establish viable and sustainable organizations because those involved have limited time, resources, and energy to invest in building the governance structure and capacity of their organization. Investing in governance potentially requires a (financial) investment in personnel, yet many spoke about the importance and value of *not* paying individuals, both to demonstrate accountability to donors that resources are going only to those they are serving and as evidence of their convictions. And yet, lack of governance capacity also undermines the effectiveness, sustainability, and impact of many RDOs. In this context, it seems unsurprising that RDOs emerge and fade with some frequency. It is also understandable that some individuals and small groups of friends may choose more direct person-to-person or informal ways of giving that circumvent the need for investment in organizational governance.

Accountability

Questions of accountability frequently arose in conversations during my fieldwork and seemed to have distinct dimensions for refugee diaspora humanitarianism and the governance of RDOs. In fact, the *lack of* accountability in humanitarian governance has been one of the criticisms that has been leveled at both institutional humanitarian actors (for their lack of accountability to affected populations in particular) and diasporas (for accountability to humanitarian principles or professionalism) (see Agier 2011; Barnett 2011; Harrell-Bond 2002; Hilhorst and Jansen 2010; Reid-Henry 2013). Yet how one understands these critiques depends on the position taken on fundamental questions: To *whom* is one accountable? *How* (through what means) are those in power being held to account? *For what* (which actions, and against which norms) is accountability being sought? (Goetz and Jenkins 2005, 3–4).

Michael Barnett asserts that the bias of international humanitarian agencies toward accountability to donors rather than recipients has led to a focus within humanitarian governance on measurable outcomes. Barnett argues—and I would agree—that this discourse of accountability masks "a drift in power to the donors at the expense of the recipients" (2011, 217). However, in the context of this research, what happens when the donors are not states or amorphous groups of individual donors in Western countries who give to large established organizations to help the needy *other*? What if both the donors and the organizations soliciting donations identify and relate in a different way with the recipients? What if the organization believed their actions involved a slightly different set of objectives to other humanitarian actors concerned with saving lives, such as preserving identity and homelands, of laying the ground for return, or of offering hope and fulfilling obligations to an (imagined) community? How are RDOs accountable in this context, to whom, and for what?

As the previous discussion on governance suggests, there is a high degree of informality in how RDOs organize. Yet the fact that many of these RDOs did not have well-functioning committees of management, annual meetings, and reporting mechanisms does not necessarily mean that they lacked accountability. The extent to which individuals and groups sought to account for their actions was, in some cases, considerable. As I will outline below, what is distinctive about RDOs is *who* they are accountable to, *how,* and *for what.*

Accountable to Whom?

Cindy Horst, Stephen Lubkemann and Robtel Neajai Pailey argue that diaspora organizations provide "high 'accountability' ratings for those who donate" and that "misappropriation is easily checked through trust-based networks" (2015, 226; see also Bornstein 2012). I would further this observation by arguing that the importance of trust-based networks to refugee diaspora humanitarianism means that accountability to donors and to recipients is closely connected. The relationship between donors and recipients in refugee diaspora humanitarianism appears much closer and more multifaceted than the donor-recipient relationship for larger humanitarian organizations, where the donor is a government, multilateral agency, or groups of individual (Western) benefactors who give to established charities. A significant proportion of RDO donors were, after all, on the receiving end of humanitarian assistance in the past. Many of the donors have strong personal ties with recipient populations and a deep understanding of the contexts in which RDOs are working. Having donors and recipients in direct communication means that checks and balances are oftentimes unmediated by RDOs themselves. In short, Barnett's assessment of the drift in power to donors over recipients in humanitarian practice appears less of a concern for RDOs because their donors have more direct lines of communication with recipients.

How Are RDOs Accountable?

Most of the RDOs in this study demonstrated a high degree of accountability to both recipients and donors but used a different suite of mechanisms to other (professional) aid organizations (see Horst et al. 2015). These mechanisms often involved donors and recipients being in direct communication—by phone, through social media, or face-to-face. One woman, Naj, spoke of how her RDO started off accounting to donors: "In the past, it [was] informal because the main sponsors [were] individuals. For example, there's a man who has a tiling business in Australia, he always donates every month, like $200. . . . Then I have [a family member] who has a very big business in Perth, and he does his own way of donation. And these people, if they see us basically sending them an email with pictures and reports, they [are] happy. But more importantly, when they also go overseas, they get to see [for themselves]."[16]

Many interviewees talked about reporting on the outcomes of their actions by asking community members from the diaspora to take videos and photos when they travel overseas to where the RDO is working. These people act as witnesses, reporting back to communities in Australia (i.e., to donors) and attesting to the trustworthiness of the RDO. For example, one Eritrean RDO organized a Skype video call with the principal of a school in Sudan at a fundraising event (see fig. 4.1). The principal spoke directly about needs and the impact of the RDO's work to the audience, many of whom had spent time as refugees in the town where the school was located. There was an opportunity for questions and comments from the audience, enabled by a shared language and understanding of the context. Yet this facilitation of direct communication also demonstrated accountability and transparency in a way that reduced the power differential and proximity between donors and recipients. The recipient was given space to speak. The principal could identify the needs and priorities he saw for his school and ask for assistance in a way that was relatively unmediated by the RDO.

Figure 4.1 RDO fundraising event, just prior to Skype call with school principal, whose image was projected on the screen. Photo credit: L. Olliff.

Of course, more conventional accountability mechanisms were also apparent. Some of the RDOs had websites, annual reports, and other forms of written documentation to account for the use of funds and their outcomes. This was the case for Akademos Society, mentioned at the start of this chapter. However, the detailed accounting of many RDOs seemed to go beyond anything that is remotely achieved through other humanitarian organizations' reporting mechanisms. By way of example, one RDO raised a modest amount of money (AU$9,000), mostly from within the diaspora community in Australia, to send to a refugee camp in the wake of a fire that destroyed many homes. After the money had been sent and distributed to beneficiaries, the RDO emailed donors a spreadsheet detailing who and how much was donated in each state and territory in Australia. A scanned document showing fingerprints of representatives of every household that received money in the camp and the amount they were given, as well as a letter of acknowledgment in English and Burmese from the refugee camp committee, were also sent.

Admittedly, this detailed accounting is largely possible because of the vastly different scale of operations between RDOs and other institutional actors.

Yet much of this onerous and detailed reporting also speaks to a hypervigilance by some RDOs to be seen as honest and transparent and, importantly, to demonstrate that no monies have been misappropriated or personally benefited those involved in the organizations. For example, in the case described earlier of community members purchasing a wheelchair for a teacher in Sudan, the video of the recipient thanking the donors also features the man holding the cash that was left over from this transaction and that was given directly to him; the wheelchair cost less than the monies raised, and instead of being used by the RDO, this money was given to the intended beneficiary. It is hard to imagine in which other aid organization such lengths would be taken to account for every dollar given and to show that it was given for exactly the purpose that the donors intended.

The importance of reputation and relationships of trust between donors and the RDO adds additional complexities and risks for diaspora humanitarians. The risk to the reputation of individuals involved in RDOs within their communities—both in Australia and where they are working—was spoken about by many. As Carmen describes, "You have people to be accountable [to]; those who are giving us their money. We know them. You're probably related to half these people in one way or another!"[17]

The risk to personal reputation within social networks also suggests a different dimension to RDO accountability. While trust is undoubtedly an important consideration for larger organizations' relationships with donors, for RDOs, losing or building trust involves much greater personal risk for the individuals involved.

Accountable for What?

Although humanitarian actors are not unified in their objectives—and therefore what they are accountable for—there are dominant models of humanitarian intervention that guide actions and priorities. The Sphere Project, for example, provides a humanitarian charter and minimum standards in humanitarian response that are used and referenced widely in humanitarian practice.[18] There is a very specific technical language and shorthand that is used to describe acceptable (and measurable) humanitarian actions. How RDOs prioritize and decide on their actions, on the other hand, seems to draw from a slightly different set of imperatives than "the right to life with dignity; the right to receive humanitarian assistance; and the right to protection and security" (The Sphere Project 2011, 21). The ways in which some RDO informants described what they were trying to achieve suggest objectives that sit uneasily in dominant humanitarian discourse because partisanship (as opposed to neutrality and independence) was clearly an undercurrent. As described in chapter 3, some RDOs saw their work as tied to political goals of creating or reshaping nations and of preserving identity. Their objectives were often couched in much bigger aspirations to see positive social change, but in ways that were historically and contextually informed and involved objectives that are hard to measure.

To illustrate this point, more than one of the RDOs in this study were providing emergency relief to roughly the same internally displaced population in Iraq. While their actions were clearly focused on meeting basic needs for a highly vulnerable population in an area where other humanitarian agencies had restricted access (i.e., providing food and shelter), there were other objectives that were articulated by these RDOs. Two interviewees spoke about the need to support the preservation of minority groups within Iraq, stressing the indigeneity of *their people*. They spoke about the imperative to support those who were internally displaced for fear that their people would be driven out of their homeland. In another example, one RDO was providing limited financial assistance to their target population, but informants spoke in detail about how a goal of their actions was to give their people hope that they were not forgotten. Their reasoning resonated with some of the nonquantifiable goals that Barnett (2011, 217) refers to: witnessing, being present, conferring dignity, and demonstrating solidarity.

In sum, RDOs are governed in ways that suggest a different orientation to (dominant) humanitarian organizations with regards to accountability. One interviewee, who provided training support to RDOs, described it so: "The way one lady said it [was] great. She said: 'I'm 40 percent Australian and the rest is Afghan, and so that's probably how I'll work. I'll be able to take 40 percent of all this accountability stuff. And even if it's just a spreadsheet so that I can show people that I haven't put things in my own account, I get that. But then I'm gonna do the 60 percent that I need to do to make it work, you know, back home.'"[19] What this quote implies is that there are different ways of demonstrating accountability, and what is expected in Australia (the spreadsheet to show "I haven't put things in my own account") and what works back home may involve different considerations as to whom, how, and what to account for. The direct connection between donors and recipients means that there is not always a separation between how RDOs account to both groups. The question of accountability *for what* also involves a more complex understanding of what could be considered as helping.

Without explicitly stated (or adhered to) rules, norms, and actions, the governance of many RDOs appears opaque. It is unsurprising that diaspora organizations have been delegitimized by institutional humanitarian actors because of their lack of observable or coherent governance structures (see also DEMAC 2016b; Horst 2013). It is hard for outside observers to understand who exactly RDOs are helping, whose interests are being served, what they are trying to achieve, and what impact they are having, particularly if these organizations are being held up to humanitarian frameworks that do not necessarily fit RDO objectives and practices. However, as the preceding discussion sought to highlight, the informality of RDO structures should not automatically be read as a lack of governance. In terms of answerability, there is much to be said for the hypervigilance with which many RDOs account to both donors and recipients. At the same time, it should be acknowledged that volunteer-run organizations face significant challenges in terms of capacity to make a difference at scale or in a sustained way. Being driven by passion and conviction may make funds donated to RDOs go further, but it also makes work more difficult for those who give their time to these endeavors.

ECONOMIES

Alongside governance, a second major theme relating to modalities of refugee diaspora humanitarianism and the Australian context concerns economies. What resources do RDOs mobilize and how do they make use of these resources? The following focuses on fundraising, one of the key activities that occupy RDOs in countries like Australia, as well as the other (nonmonetary) resources that RDOs draw on to "make do" in the context of enormous needs. I then look at the challenges small organizations face transferring funds to assist in humanitarian situations. Finally, the idea of *smallness* is discussed as an overarching theme that emerged when talking to both humanitarian professionals and diaspora humanitarians about the things RDOs do.

Fundraising

Over the course of fieldwork, I attended several RDO fundraising events that sought to mobilize resources to help displaced populations overseas. While there were some variations in fundraising strategies, most included community social events involving food, dance, presentations, and auctions. For example, the following is an excerpt from my field notes:

> I went to a fundraising dinner tonight—a women-only event. The event was held at a dimly lit and poorly heated reception center on Sydney Road in Brunswick. The center had a narrow entrance up steps into a large, long room with set tables on one side and a small stage on the other. A carpeted area in the middle was left for dancing. At the back of the room some women had set up tables selling jewelry, clothes, and Tupperware. Things got off to a slow start. The event was advertised to start at 7:00 p.m., but the room only started filling at 9:00 p.m. Before then, small groups of women came in dribs and drabs and sat shivering in dark corners, talking quietly. The organizers fretted about whether more people would turn up. Someone from the community had passed away, so it was thought that people would go to the wake instead of the fundraiser. In the end, the room filled with about 100 women, all Eritrean. They were dressed formally—in a combination of traditional "cultural"

> dress, colorful saris, and evening gowns. There were painted nails, elaborate hairstyles, high heels, and sparkling jewelry on display everywhere. At 9.30 p.m., three women gave short presentations in English, Tigrinya, and Arabic about the school in Sudan that the fundraiser was in aid of. Photos of the school and [the RDO's] activities were shown on TV screens. The final speaker spent time trying to drum up interest for someone to volunteer to organize the next women's event. I left at 10.30 p.m., and it seemed things were only starting to get going. The room was full of laughter and chatter, tables full of women and children eating. It felt warmer in every way. One of the organizers told me on my way out that they had raised over AU$6,000.

I attended other such fundraisers, where an RDO combined a community social gathering with an opportunity to raise funds. It seemed the amounts raised at such events depended on the strength of an RDO's networks, how frequently (or well) they were organized, and how emotive the call to give was. In most cases, the amounts raised were relatively modest—a few hundred or thousand dollars. When held in the wake of a humanitarian crisis that touched a community, however, it was apparent that these events could mobilize much greater resources. This was the case when the situation in Iraq and Syria deteriorated in 2013. The response from diaspora communities in Australia was significant, with reports of hundreds of thousands of dollars being given to community- and faith-based organizations. One Assyrian Australian woman said, "I think we had fundraisers last year where we raised, I don't know, up to $24,000 in a couple of hours."[20]

Anna, who had worked over many years with RDOs, marveled at the capacity within refugee diaspora communities to mobilize funds when needed or asked for: "It's a different value system. I would probably never be in that position. . . . We prioritize different things. People [from refugee diasporas] aren't necessarily focused on, you know, putting all their money into a home or this or that. They understand because they've gone through a situation how important it is to contribute and share that money, versus perhaps the goodwill of people who have not been in that situation."[21]

The generosity of individuals was something I observed many times. While at times you could see the performative nature of this giving—of people making a large donation publicly at a community event—there were other times when this giving was more private, as with the situation described earlier, when a community member decided to make a regular donation to five refugee women and their families, directly and without solicitation, receipts, or external recognition.[22] There were also occasions when $50 or $100 was given to someone from an RDO on the street or casually, and the person making the donation was noted as having little and giving a lot and asked for no acknowledgment. There were Hazara Australian women who each gave AU$150 (US$110) to buy computers for a library in Quetta. One man transferred his entire earnings from performing in a theater production to an RDO without letting anyone know. This money seemed to be given through trust-based social networks, without receipts or public display, but quietly and with the undercurrents of obligation, guilt, duty, or knowing from having been there woven through. Yet in terms of the governance issues described earlier, this form of giving also suited the informal structure of many RDOs.

While most funding for RDOs seemed to come from within diaspora communities—and most often through fundraising events—there were some that had managed to diversify their fundraising capabilities. For example, a few RDOs had set up membership systems where individuals (mostly from diaspora communities) paid a regular membership fee. There were others that had tried fundraising with a broader donor group in mind. One RDO had acquired a barbecue trailer through the support of a local rotary club and raised funds by selling sausages at public events. Two of the RDOs I engaged with had tried crowdfunding online. While RDOs, like other civil society groups and movements, have increasingly harnessed the potential of online crowdfunding and social media platforms to raise money, at the time of my fieldwork (2014–2015), most of the RDOs that I spoke to mobilized small amounts of money or goods largely offline and from within refugee diaspora networks in Australia.[23] Of note, none had successfully applied for or been granted money from any institutional donor.

While it is hard to generalize about RDOs because of their different objectives and activities, it is clear that most operate on a very small scale. It was hard for many RDOs to accurately estimate how much money they raised each year—and for some, this fluctuated considerably; only one RDO I spoke to had managed to raise over AU$200,000 (US$154,000) in a year. The majority operated with budgets closer to AU$10,000–AU$20,000 per annum, intimating the limitations of RDO fundraising strategies.

Money Transfer

One of the challenges faced by many RDOs in this study was related to transferring funds to the places where they were helping. Getting money from Australia to Iraq, Afghanistan, Syria, or to refugee camps in Thailand, Sudan, or Kenya presented difficulties for RDOs for several reasons. First, the informality and small scale of these organizations limit the avenues for transferring money. For many, the cost of using large banks or remittance companies was neither practical nor cost-effective. Some of these RDOs did not have their own bank accounts and had to use services that were available and accessible to their intended recipients (i.e., refugees). Instead, many preferred to use either *hawâla* (money transfer) services or to ask people from within their community networks who were traveling overseas to carry money with them.[24] Second, the insecure situations where money was being sent required RDOs to have strong trust-based networks and to know whom to transfer money to and how they could receive it with minimal risk. For example, one RDO spoke about how refugees are not legally entitled to open bank accounts where they are living, so they had to find people who had circumvented this domestic law and who were trusted and willing to withdraw money transferred into a personal bank account. Finally, due to institutional changes that have taken place over recent years within the international banking system to counter state concerns about remittances funding terrorism, larger banks have stopped offering money-transfer services to places where they cannot prove money will not end up in the hands of blacklisted groups. This has meant that even *hawâla* moneylenders have had to change their practices. As a result, RDOs trying to send money overseas face much riskier and more complicated processes, as the following fieldwork note highlights:

> I met A–– this afternoon in Footscray to help with transferring money to Sudan. To explain how convoluted, informal, and irregular this process is, let's start with what the money was for. The money was for the construction of three classrooms at a school at a refugee camp. The classrooms had been completed ten months prior to my meeting A–– in Footscray, and the builders had been partially paid by A–– while he was in Sudan. However, at the time he was there, the RDO did not have sufficient funds to pay the full AU$20,000 for the work. So, the RDO paid $10,000 and a local NGO paid the remainder, with A–– promising to send the balance to the NGO when he was back in Australia. Within months of A–– returning to Australia, the RDO had raised enough money to send the remaining $10,000. However, the exchange rate between Sudan and Australia was so bad that A–– negotiated with the NGO to hold off transferring the money until the dollar was stronger. He said that if he had transferred the money at that time, the RDO would have needed about $15,000.
>
> A–– called me on Friday last week to say that he had gone to the money transfer [*hawâla*] place in Footscray and the exchange rate looked good, so he had transferred the money owed and it had come to less than $10,000. However, as he hadn't had time to go to get cheques drawn up, countersigned, and cash withdrawn from the two banks where the RDO has accounts on Friday, the hawâla agent had transferred the money with an IOU—i.e., based on the exchange rate on Friday, and not charging extra. A–– said: "They know me and trust me."
>
> I met A–– at the hawâla agent in Footscray. The office is up an anonymous-looking stairway. There is no signage. To get to the office, you go behind the reception desk of a different business and through an entranceway with a "Staff only" sign stuck on the door. The office is a cramped room with [a] desk, chairs, and paper piled on every surface. An older man with a beard and kind eyes is sitting behind the desk. A–– and the man exchange greetings. I am

> accompanying A–– because I have agreed to transfer some of the money in my name. This is because I am told that regulations in Australia limit the amount that can be sent through these places to $1,000 per person per month. The RDO needs to send $10,000, which means ten people need to transfer $1,000 each. Moreover, the agent said we need different people to send this money to, as it would "look suspicious" if $10,000 was sent to the same person. So now we're involving twenty people (ten in Australia, ten in Sudan) to transfer money to pay for the construction of a school for refugee children. It seems ridiculous! When I say this to A––, he shrugs, saying: "And the people who are sending money for guns, they know how to get around these laws. It's not going to stop them sending money, but it makes it really hard for people like us."

Many of those I spoke to talked about the difficulty of sending money overseas. This did not stop money from being transferred; it just required RDOs to find ways of getting around restrictions. Many RDOs do this by finding individuals who will agree to mask collective remittances as their own. It requires people being willing to risk having suspicion cast on their actions and, of course, emphasizes the central importance of trust in the workings of RDOs. Sarah describes it thus: "[Transferring money], that's the problem. Before we didn't have the problem . . . but after what happened, we've been very careful how to send it, because they could be saying, 'You're supporting terrorists.' . . . Basically, what we do, [we've] got people here who've got connections in Syria or [somewhere]. We give them that money. We say, 'This is for this.' So, they take the money from us with a receipt and things, [and] then they, in their way, send it."[25]

It seems that the antiterrorism measures intended to inhibit those within diaspora communities from funding terrorist groups have also had a negative impact on those whose intentions are to help and not harm.

Making Do

In discussing the economies of RDOs, it would be misleading to talk only about fundraising and organizational budgets, for much of the resource input into these kinds of organizations is *not* accounted for. RDOs as volunteer-run and resource-poor organizations in many ways *make do* in the face of the enormous needs that they see and are responding to. Two ways in which RDOs make do are by relying on volunteer labor and by drawing on existing capacities within networks to decide on what to focus their energies on. In terms of this first point, one of the nonmonetary resources that RDOs draw heavily on (and do not account for) is people's time. If a comparison was made between the economies of institutional humanitarian actors (NGOs or multilateral organizations) and RDOs, one of the most notable differences would be how they account for labor costs. Unlike larger and professionalized humanitarian organizations, RDOs do not seem to include staffing costs in their operational budgets. As discussed earlier, many of those involved in RDOs saw their volunteerism as a demonstration of their convictions and what set them apart from humanitarian professionals. As one man described, "From what I can see . . . maybe 110 percent of what we get we are giving to them—110 percent. By saying that, [what I mean is] we give our time, our money too, and go there and do things."[26]

Indeed, it would be an interesting exercise to compare the dollar-for-dollar impact of an equivalent donation to an RDO and an established (professional) humanitarian organization, as it would make visible the contribution of skills and time given by diaspora humanitarians. One informant who works with both RDOs and larger international nongovernmental organizations (INGOs) made the following assessment: "I have no doubt that dollar-for-dollar, even including volunteer labor, . . . the diasporas are probably more effective. . . . Also, in terms of impact in a small area with the kinds of resources that they have, I'd put my money on diasporas. The thing about [INGOs], they've got access to such high levels of technical skill . . . I just don't think they do it well enough. You know, for the resources they've got, they're just not good enough. Whereas I think the diasporas would over-perform with the resources that they've got."[27]

One man attributed the efficiencies of RDOs to the fact that the small funds raised are so hard-won that using this money wisely is crucial. Anwar said: "To get that little money we [do] a lot of hard work. We want to see that money [go where we] are trying to help. On the other side, [for organizations that get] big sums of money, because it is easy money, they lose it easily."[28]

This is not to valorize the lack of resources or hidden labor costs of refugee diaspora humanitarianism. There is no doubt that having to make do is hard and, as discussed previously, is responsible for many of the shortcomings of voluntary organizations. I frequently heard people express frustration or exhaustion resulting from giving so much of their time trying to make something happen. I recall a conversation with Raj where he, mid-sentence, put his head on the table when we were discussing the work of his association. He was explaining how tired he was from all the work he was doing trying to help people overseas and those who were new to Australia. He winced and seemed to visibly shrink as he explained how, when he came home from work or studying and sat down with his wife and new baby, his phone would keep ringing. He said, "I just want to *not* answer. I want to say, 'Someone is being paid to help you, why can't you call them?'"[29]

It is clear from this that *making do* sometimes comes at significant personal cost. Yet if we understand the limited capacity of RDOs to mobilize money and the significance of volunteer labor to RDO economies, then the actions of these organizations also become clearer. Indeed, RDOs seem to look for and respond to humanitarian needs where they can draw on the skills, experiences, resources, and networks that they *do* have available. It becomes evident why RDOs send shipping containers of goods overseas, for instance, despite humanitarian professionals expressing frustration at the ineffectiveness of this practice (see Young 2016). If you have a strong social network that does not have significant amounts of money to donate but can easily mobilize donations of clothes, blankets, and toys, then shipping material aid seems an achievable goal.

There are other examples of how RDOs draw on the nonmonetary resources they have available. One woman, Naj, explained how her organization looked to provide psychosocial support to refugee women: "What we do is, we look at the needs and we don't worry about the funds. You know, initially, we knew we could help women with the torture and trauma they face in Afghanistan. [We thought], 'How are we going to educate one woman to become a psychologist? How can we do that in Afghanistan? Should we do scholarships for them to come to Malaysia to study?' A lot of things like that were very costly. But then we realized [there's a way that is] less costly, and we can find it."[30] In this case, some of the women involved with the RDO had trained as social workers, psychologists, and torture and trauma counselors in Australia. They went through different options for trying to provide psychosocial support to Afghan women and ultimately decided to explore setting up a Skype counseling service. While this initiative had yet to come to fruition during my fieldwork period, the process was illustrative of how those in the diaspora think about needs and what they *can* do with small amounts of money and an appreciation of how to best make use of the nonmonetary resources they have access to—time, skills, and networks.

The Value of Small Things

During my fieldwork, I talked to several people who were working or had worked for large humanitarian organizations. When I explained my research, many of them initially reacted with a combination of interest and acknowledgment that they knew little about what refugee diaspora communities did to help in displacement contexts. However, when I went on to explain the types of activities and the small scale of RDO projects, a common response was *What difference can it make?* Indeed, at times I also wondered about these small acts—of organizations helping a few hundred people with a few thousand dollars—in the context of the international humanitarian system with a budget in the billions and of a world with over one hundred million people displaced. Yet for those involved in RDOs, there seemed to be an acknowledgment of the importance of doing small things. As one interviewee, Ladan, noted, "It wasn't a lot. I think it was about $3,000 that we raised. And this school, it's not very big, [but] it's better than being under a tree."[31] Indeed, *smallness* was a recurring theme in how people talked about their ways of helping; of small acts making a big difference and their frustration at only being able to do small things in the face of overwhelming need.

Several of my informants spoke about how being small had its advantages: RDOs can sometimes do things quickly, as they operate with greater flexibility and without the slow machinery of larger, more bureaucratic organizations. For example, money raised in Australia could be sent directly to a recipient without an intermediary because an RDO may not be dealing with a large population but with a single family in need. Nobody sees RDOs as powerful, and this allows these organizations to act without the same kinds of expectations or demands that are made of large INGOs. As one man said of being allowed to move into an area that local police had prevented larger NGOs from operating in, "There are big advantages in being small."[32] He noted that if he had been working for a big NGO, the local authorities would have felt compelled to intervene because the government's policy was to restrict cross-border movement. As he was representing a small, informal group, they turned a blind eye.

There was a sense among some refugee diaspora humanitarians that small acts could be powerful. This was often spoken about by drawing on personal experience in which small acts of care that someone experienced when they were a refugee were remembered and mattered. One man, who had spent many years living as a refugee in Kenya, said, "You shouldn't underestimate how important small things can be. When I was living in that camp, we got soap that had 'Germany' stamped on it, twice a year. I still remember that and [how] we were so thankful. I supported Germany in the World Cup because I still remember that soap!"[33]

Some interviewees spoke about how gestures that may seem small from the perspective of someone looking at the wider humanitarian system do not seem small to the recipients of these acts. Remarkably, three of the people I interviewed told a variation of the starfish story (Eiseley 1978). In this story, a person is on a beach throwing starfish back into the ocean. The beach is covered as far as the eye can see with starfish that have washed up after a storm. Another person walking along the beach stops to ask them why they are bothering to throw these few starfish back in, because it will not make a difference to the thousands that are dying. The person responds, "It matters to the ones that I save." Small things may not make a dent in the sea of unmet needs, but it means something to those whose lives are impacted. Iterations of this theme were conveyed by many different people when asked about why they were involved as volunteers in RDOs. I asked one man what gave him the greatest satisfaction, after he had explained the long and arduous process he had been involved in to support the resettlement of a small group of Palestinian refugees. He said,

"The fact that they have arrived. That I made a difference to more than two hundred people's lives. To see them here working and studying and contributing and [living] their life and buying cars and selling property... *khalas* (that's it)!"[34]

Another example was provided by Raj. He said that when someone in a refugee camp in Nepal has a chronic health issue, there is very little support to be found. In these situations, families turn to the community to pay for treatment for serious illnesses or conditions or for burial costs if a person dies outside the refugee camp. In these cases, the individual matters. While large aid organizations look at the resources they have available and consider health care from a broader perspective, small RDOs can work at an individual level, and, for the individuals and families they help, this matters.

Finally, some people involved in RDOs spoke about small things in relation to the big things they did not have the power to change. As they saw it, acting in small ways is better than doing nothing; for example, building a small school is surely better than having children learn under a tree. Yet some also spoke of enormous frustration and feeling powerless for *not* being able to address the injustices they see underlying the need for humanitarian action, which they described in terms of structural problems and political systems. Hassan, for example, described the hardest thing about traveling to Indonesia to help a group of asylum seekers: "For me, the hardest thing is being unable to help. You know, there was this mother by herself who has seven kids. She's sick. She has no support. Being unable to help is the hardest thing for me. I wish I could just lift them up to somewhere where she can get treatment. The hardest thing is actually hearing, knowing, but being unable to do anything about it. Because supporting them financially, you can only do so much."[35]

Moreover, many people I spoke to wanted to help in much bigger ways. As Mae Sie explained of his organization helping people on the Thai-Burma border: "It's very important to me to help people who need help. Of course, I want to help everyone in the world, but it's not possible. So, I do what I can."[36] Another man said, "Give me one million [dollars], and I'll show you how big [a] difference we can make!"[37]

A DROP IN THE OCEAN

Humanitarian assistance provided by refugee diaspora communities through small, volunteer-run organizations is a drop in the ocean when it comes to meeting the needs of displaced populations globally. RDOs' voluntary nature can be seen paradoxically as both a strength and a weakness—a strength because it allows those involved to demonstrate their convictions and commitment to the people they are helping and enables more resources to go toward project costs, and a weakness because these organizations commonly struggle to effect change and sustain their activities. While many RDOs seem to mirror, at least on paper, the bureaucratized, democratic structures of incorporated associations, in practice they operate with a high degree of informality. This does not mean there are no rules and norms governing these types of organizations, but rather that the (legal) structures they seek to adhere to do not necessarily fit with how they are able to organize and the activities they engage in.

In describing the distinct ways in which RDOs organize, it is apparent that there is a need for RDO governance to be understood on its own terms and not held up against the rules, norms, and actions of other types of institutional actors, particularly larger humanitarian agencies. Indeed, if we take one aspect of governance—accountability—we can see that many RDOs demonstrate a high degree of accountability to both donors and recipients, and in ways that reflect their distinct characteristics, capacities, and objectives. Thus, it is hard to imagine how accountability measures deployed by larger humanitarian actors would be useful to RDOs, in the same way that it is hard to imagine how the hypervigilance to accountability and transparency exhibited by some RDOs would be practical for organizations working at a much larger scale.

How small of a scale RDO work is when held up to the overwhelming needs and systemic humanitarian responses was most apparent when I was undertaking fieldwork in Geneva, surrounded by representatives of organizations talking about their beneficiaries in more abstract terms and with budgets in the millions. The resources RDOs mobilize seem infinitesimal when compared to this wider humanitarian system. The smallness and informality of RDO governance structures and economies present a range of practical challenges. At the same time, resourcefulness shapes the actions of RDOs and, in many ways, makes these types of organizations extremely efficient in turning a donation into an outcome. RDOs doing *small things* and *making do* can be seen, then, as a modality of necessity that has its advantages. Furthermore, RDOs' contributions within the broader humanitarian context should not be dismissed simply because of their small size (Foulkes 2015). From the perspective of refugee diaspora humanitarians, if only a few starfish can be saved on a beach where there are thousands of stranded starfish, surely it is still worth bending down, picking one up, and throwing it back in.

FIVE

MODALITIES

Mobility, (In)Visibility, Knowledge, and Networks

AS WE HAVE SEEN IN previous chapters, there is considerable variation in what refugee diaspora organizations (RDOs) do to try to help in refugee situations. At the same time, there are discernible parallels in how these kinds of organizations go about their helping. This chapter draws out four overlapping themes that relate to the transnational practices characteristic of refugee diaspora humanitarianism: mobility, (in)visibility, knowledge, and networks. These themes emerged from fieldwork and interviews and took shape as I began to note similarities in practices and ideas that connected RDOs working in disparate contexts. In discussing each of these themes, we further see the distinct ways in which RDOs use their positionality and capacities to help familiar strangers.

MOBILITY

A central theme relating to RDO modalities that emerged from this research concerned how refugee diaspora humanitarians move and organize both within and outside Australia and how mobility enables and shapes how they help. When discussing mobility, I refer here not only to the physical movement of people but also to their ability to travel virtually and communicate and connect across dispersed space (Urry 2007). The fact that mobility emerged as a theme should come as no surprise. As Nina Glick Schiller and Noel Salazar point out, "movement and interconnection are fundamental to the human condition—past, present and future," and studies that focus on movement and transnationalism as "novel and transgressive" somehow (incorrectly) reinforce the notion of stasis as the norm (2013, 186). Yet what these authors recognize—as I hope to also—is the need to "simultaneously normalize an array of forms of mobility but not minimize the ways in which legal status, as well as global racializing categories, can make a world of difference in terms of ease of travel, the repercussions of trying to move, and whether or not the traveler gains or loses status from being from elsewhere" (Glick Schiller and Salazar 2013, 188).

With this understanding in mind, I argue that there are three dimensions of mobility that are significant in shaping refugee diaspora humanitarianism: differential regimes of mobility for members of RDOs; people moving and working transnationally (physical mobility); and people working and organizing across dispersed space (virtual mobility).

Regimes of Mobility

Before discussing physical and virtual mobilities, it is important to contextualize these in terms of power and the "regimes of mobility" (Glick Schiller and Salazar 2013) that diaspora humanitarians are constrained or enabled by. As many mobilities and transnationalism scholars have argued, not everyone has the same relationship to mobility (Bauman 2000; Hannam et al. 2006; Massey 1993; Sheller and Urry 2006; Urry 2007). For instance, those from the Global North tend to have the potential to move across state borders in ways that reflect their privileged status (Isotalo 2009; Monsutti 2008; Redfield 2012; Schapendonk 2012). As Peter Redfield writes: "One of the starkest divides falls between people who travel easily and people who do not. At the most literal level, those equipped with funds and the right documents pass lightly over borders, whereas the poor and undocumented incite security concerns" (2012, 358).

Yet mobility goes beyond moving across international borders. The regimes of mobility at play in the movement of refugee diasporas can be broken down at different institutional levels—international (refugee regime), nation-state (immigration policies), and individual (how individuals are constrained/enabled or inclined/disinclined to travel)—all of which are shaped by the intersections of class, gender, race, disability, age, and sexual orientation. Glick Schiller and Salazar describe these institutional and personal dimensions as such: "[There] are *regimes* of mobility that confront both the theorist and the traveler. The term 'regime' calls attention to the role both of individual states and of changing international regulatory and surveillance administrations that affect individual mobility. At the same time, the term reflects a notion of governmentality and hegemony in which there are constant struggles to understand, query, embody, celebrate and transform categories of similarity, difference, belonging and strangeness" (2013, 189).

In the case of institutional dimensions, it is evident that the legal status of those involved in RDOs—whether they are Australian citizens or permanent residents—makes some difference to how they travel and engage in humanitarian work.[1] Although none of the individuals involved in this research were on temporary visas, it can be assumed that those without permanent legal status who share similar experiences, motivations, and connections to displaced populations overseas have incapacitating restrictions placed on their mobility. Of note, those on temporary humanitarian or bridging visas who travel overseas cannot easily return to Australia, as their temporary visa would be invalidated upon exiting Australia unless prior dispensation to travel is sought.

How people felt about traveling to help was discussed in interviews, and this was influenced by "governmentality" (Foucault 1977; 2010) linked to institutional regulation and surveillance (Agier 2011). For example, several interviewees spoke about how they perceived the suspicion of Australian authorities about movement to certain places—countries such as Somalia, Iraq, and Afghanistan—being associated with terrorism and how they had to be willing to contend with scrutiny if they were to travel. One man who traveled to Iraq to facilitate the distribution of donated goods spoke about being detained and questioned by immigration officials for hours upon return about what he had been doing. Others simply spoke about the impossibility of travel, even when there were no apparent institutional reasons why they could not depart and return to Australia. Traveling was considered impossible because of risk assessments that factored in what the Australian government and the government of the country they sought to enter would or could do. For example, one interviewee told of how someone he knew had traveled to their country of origin and, upon arrival, had seen the airport immigration official check his (Australian) passport against a list of names. This list of names was understood to include those who were *personae non grata* and presumably people who were active in the wider diaspora.

This experience of feeling—and indeed, being—under suspicion was apparent when I traveled to and from Indonesia with members of an Oromo RDO, as the following excerpt from field notes illustrates:

> We arrived back in Melbourne just before 7:00 a.m. There were five of us traveling from Bali—Youssef, Hassan, Germa, Adem, and myself. Hassan and Youssef were first to come through immigration after me, and we stood around talking, waiting for our bags to appear. Hassan was dressed like he'd been at a resort—long shorts, casual polo, and sandals. Youssef was still in his suit. As we were waiting, a stern woman wearing an Australian Border Force (ABF) uniform came and asked to see our customs declarations. She circled the question that said "Have you brought drugs into the country?" We laughed at this. We were all tired and in good spirits. Germa and Adem then arrived at the baggage carousel. They also looked like they'd come from a relaxing resort holiday. As soon as they joined us, the ABF woman came and asked for their customs declarations. So now we all had the "drugs" question circled on all

our forms. As we collected our bags and put them onto trollies, more officers gathered and one asked if we were traveling together. Hassan said that we were, and we were asked for our passports and told to follow them.

We were each taken to separate areas in a quiet part of the customs hall and questioned. After some time, the woman questioning me started relaxing (she had been very officious at first). It was clear that she had no idea who "the Oromo people" were and what the situation of asylum seekers in Indonesia might be. She asked if we were "trying to help them to get to Australia." I told her we knew there was no chance of that; we were just helping them to have food to eat. She frowned when I said this.

Things slowed down when the woman searching Hassan's bags found a pile of visa application forms. Hassan looked uncomfortable when she found these. I had no idea he had them; I thought he knew the people we met in Jakarta wouldn't be eligible to apply for a visa without refugee status. (Later he said he knew this but took the forms people gave him anyway.) The ABF woman made a phone call about the forms. I said I was happy to explain what these forms meant if it was unclear, but she said she just wanted to check if "there were any persons of interest in these documents." We laughed about this later, as if a "person of interest" would fill in a thirty-six-page visa application form.

After forty-five minutes of being searched and questioned, we were finally told we could go. One of the friendlier officials—an older man with a kind face—shook his head and said, "We would never have picked this story." Which made me think *What story would you have picked?* Adem and Germa spoke angrily as we were leaving about how we had been treated. They had also been detained and questioned by ABF officials on their way to Indonesia. Youssef said, "They're just doing their job."

How people understand their own personal safety and risks enables or constrains their mobility. Naj spoke about the decision for her organization—a women's group—to work in Iran and Pakistan, not their country of origin: "Unfortunately . . . it has been very difficult to have a closer connection with my own country, and that's because I still do not feel secure. I still have memories which [are] giving me fear to step in. And I think this is the case with many other refugees [in] Australia. . . . Afghanistan [is] still not safe for women and girls. It is very difficult to step in and to do something [there]."

In sum, not all those involved in RDOs have the same ability to travel to and from Australia to help others, and much depends on their legal status and related *motility*. Motility here refers to the "potential for mobility" (Hannam et al. 2006, 3). As Mekonnen Tesfahuney argues, "differential mobility empowerments reflect structures and hierarchies of power and position by race, gender, age and class, ranging from the local to the global" (1998, 501). Those who have Australian citizenship (passports) have the greatest potential to travel to different places and, of importance, to subsequently return. But institutional regulations are not the only factors enabling or inhibiting mobility. A person's disposition to travel is also impacted by how they perceive risks and possibilities for mobility or how they believe others perceive their mobility. This is particularly so for those who are helping in places that the Global North casts in a suspicious and undesirable light as places associated with terrorism, illegality, and irregularity.

Physical Mobility

Many refugee diaspora humanitarians that I interviewed spoke about traveling within or outside Australia to facilitate the work of RDOs. However, it quickly became apparent that traveling to help people was not the only—and often not the primary—reason for their travel. Many conversations about facilitating RDO projects overseas included a description of traveling to spend time with family and friends, to create new family connections (i.e., to marry), or for business. For example, three members of one Eritrean RDO traveled to Sudan and married in recent years. One man spent a year in Sudan with his new wife and baby, providing an opportunity for him to oversee and facilitate the RDO's activities there. Indeed, the need to travel to visit, care for, reunite with, and create new families was a theme evident in most of the conversations I had about RDO travel, reinforcing the important research that has focused on transnational families in forced displacement contexts (see Al-Sharmani 2010; Horst 2008b; Johnson and Stoll 2008; Monsutti 2004; Soh-Leong 2009).

While undertaking humanitarian work is often not the primary reason RDO members travel overseas, their mobility certainly *enables* humanitarian action in several ways. It provides opportunities for those in Australia to better understand the current situation for those they are trying to help, it helps with needs identification and project planning, it allows RDO members to oversee or participate in the implementation of RDO activities, it has the potential to strengthen networks of trust with people or local organizations in the places they are working, and it enables monitoring and accountability.

With regard to the first point, one man who frequently travels overseas for business and family reasons spoke about the importance of visiting refugees wherever he went so to better understand their situation. He gave the following example:

> With [temporary protection visas], Phillip Ruddock—the former Immigration Minister—[suggested using] the Swedish model of detention centers for illegal arrivals to Sweden. So I went and I visited the detention centers in Sweden. I had relatives there also. I asked, "What is the procedure? How does it work?" That gives me enough information and knowledge for when I talk to officials, government people, or people like you about the situation. So if you ask me

> what is the situation in Iran, I know. I know the situation of all the refugee or migrant countries. Even countries you never thought about, there are Iraqis there. (Hadi)[2]

The importance of traveling to meet with and hear directly from refugees was echoed by others and links to the second point about mobility enabling needs identification and project planning. For example, as the situation deteriorated for refugees in Turkey, Jordan, and Lebanon in 2016, I became aware of members of three RDOs traveling to this region to meet with people from their respective communities (Mandaean, Syrian, and Afghan). They returned armed with information and ideas for projects and advocacy. Sabira, a Hazara-Australian woman, described visiting Pakistan and how this enabled needs identification and project planning:

> Last time I was in Pakistan, I went shopping and I saw a board saying "Library." I went into that library. It was underground. I saw there is a good space, good books over there, and some boys and girls are studying. . . . I was astonished. I said, "How [did] you manage to establish this library?" . . . The manager said it was because of some help from abroad. "They send us money and we've established this library. Now we have attracted students here. They are coming here for tuition . . . and for help." [The members of their group] were trying to do something good for Hazaras. . . . I was very happy to see them working. . . . When I came [back to Australia], I said, "Let's do something." . . . The girls [from the RDO] came, and we did henna in the shopping center plaza in Melbourne city [and other places]. We collected $800. Then I went to ladies [from] my community. I said, "For $150, you can buy a computer for [this] many girls and boys." Some of the ladies [gave money for one computer each]. I sent money to them. They bought computers. They did some work [inside] the library. Now they're happy, and we are in touch via internet. They [are] asking for some more projects. I said, "Let's talk via Skype. I will see what projects. We can work together."[3]

Some of the people I spoke to traveled overseas not only to identify needs and plan responses but also to get involved in project implementation. This included activities such as transporting funds, overseeing or facilitating the purchase and distribution of goods, recruiting and training local people, and using their own skills and labor as in-kind contributions to reduce overall project costs. For example, one RDO set up four shops in Iran as social enterprises involving and benefiting refugee women. This entailed the RDO collecting clothes in Australia and shipping them to Iran. Members of the RDO traveled to Iran on different occasions to recruit and support the establishment of small women's collectives that could oversee these enterprises. So, rather than working with locally established organizations, this RDO worked directly with the intended recipients.

The benefit of traveling to implement projects links to the fourth point about mobility strengthening the transnational social networks that sustain humanitarian work. This was most clearly articulated by Anwar, who worked in the building industry in Australia and who traveled to Sudan on separate occasions and utilized his own skills and labor in the construction and repair of school buildings and a health center. Like others, Anwar did not travel only to undertake RDO activities, but also to visit family. However, the benefit of spending months visiting family was that Anwar had the time to recruit and work alongside locals to achieve the RDO's objectives (see fig. 5.1). Importantly, not only did this reduce the amount of funding needed for the project but it also had what he described as the added benefit of encouraging locals to contribute their labor: "The bigger projects we are doing, we [always] make sure someone goes there and [does] it. And sometimes this is beneficial because when you go and do it, you know the place, you know the country, you know things, and even you can do it yourself. You can ask a plumber, you can hire a carpenter, and you work together with [them] or involve your friends or relatives. [This] contributes in the expenses . . . and I think [when] someone goes from [Australia] and they see them working, everyone is welcome to help."[4]

A final point regarding physical mobility and refugee diaspora humanitarianism is that many involved in RDOs also spoke about traveling *within* Australia to organize and mobilize supporters. Indeed, some of the RDOs in this study involved committees of management whose members lived in different parts of Australia. One South Sudanese RDO, for example, had committee members in each state and territory. This was an intentional strategy to both unify and expand the organization's potential supporter base. In this case, fundraising activities could be held in eight different cities instead of one. At the same time, this sort of dispersed governance, which was also evident for other RDOs, presented logistical challenges in terms of organizing and consolidating working relationships. These challenges were overcome by committee members physically traveling to meet one another or connecting online.

Virtual Mobility

It is not only physical mobility that is significant to how RDOs work but also *virtual* mobility. The transnational engagements of RDOs highlight the intersection of new technologies, mobilities, and social relations. The ways in which people move and organize across time and space show the complexity of mobility systems and the "inter-relational dynamics between physical, informational, virtual and imaginative forms of mobility" (Hannam et al. 2006, 15). In particular, the development of information and communication technologies (ICTs) has

Figure 5.1 Local construction workers employed by an Eritrean RDO work alongside an RDO representative from Australia (left) to build a retaining wall at a refugee community school in Kassala, Sudan, in 2011. Photo credit: EAHA.

allowed new forms of coordination of people, meetings, and events to emerge (Sheller and Urry 2006). These technologies are key to mobilizing, facilitating, and sustaining refugee diaspora humanitarianism. Far from being virtual, ICT allows very real social contact between people at a (geographical) distance. It enables, as Cindy Horst (2006b) suggests, the direct involvement of members of a diaspora in each other's lives. In the following, two aspects of RDOs' virtual mobility are discussed: how ICT connects people and is used to mobilize support for RDOs and how RDOs organize with no fixed address.

Earlier I suggested that regimes of mobility have implications for the physical mobility of different individuals within refugee diaspora communities and their capacities to help. Virtual mobilities, then, are important for understanding the work of refugee diaspora humanitarianism, particularly where physical mobility is constrained. Virtual mobility allows people to travel in and out of places—to connect with and, importantly, *imagine* people at a distance. Developments in ICT have created more accessible ways for dispersed groups of people to connect. The example given in the previous chapter of a teacher in Sudan speaking via Skype at a fundraising event in Melbourne is but one example of the virtual mobility of RDOs.[5]

During the time I spent with RDOs, it was apparent that an array of ICT is used to connect people in Australia and those they are working with overseas. Without exception, those involved in RDOs used smartphones and computers to connect through such virtual interfaces as (at the time) Viber, Paltalk, Yahoo Groups, Skype, Twitter, WhatsApp, Google Groups, YouTube, text messaging, Facebook, digital radio, and online news and discussion groups. The information, images, and ideas that are shared through these interfaces create webs of interrelations. For example, one day I met with Youssef, the chairperson of an RDO in Melbourne, to discuss advocacy for refugees he was in touch with in Egypt who were experiencing significant hardship due to their legal status. As soon as we met, Youssef pulled out his smartphone and told me, "It is better if you discuss direct." He used Viber to call a contact in Cairo—a woman I will call Aya, who was working as an interpreter for nongovernmental organizations (NGOs) and had established a local community-based organization (CBO). I could see Aya's small image on the phone. Passing the phone between us—with Youssef and Aya switching between languages—we discussed concerns that she had and what advocacy could be done from Australia. While we were talking, Aya sent scanned images of documents relevant to the discussion, and Youssef was busy on my computer forwarding emails. Different senses were engaged in this exchange. I could hear the traffic outside the hospital in Cairo where Aya was standing; it gave the surreal sensation of being both in an office in Melbourne, Australia, and somewhere else. It made me think about how the immediacy of virtual technologies has the potential to draw a person in. It also made me think that if you felt deeply connected to a place or obligated to the person who is asking for help—as many of those involved in RDOs clearly do—such technologies make the imperative to act more acute. Youssef told me on several occasions how he was contacted by people from his community all over the world asking for help, day and night. "Anyone, they can call you," he said.

More than person-to-person communication, virtual interfaces are used by RDOs to simulate the experience of travel—to show the need for, and impact of, an RDO's activities. For example, videos taken on smartphones when someone traveled overseas were edited and set to music and then posted on Facebook or projected at diaspora community events in Australia. During my fieldwork, a YouTube video was circulated through social media about the Eritrean diasporas' use of ICT to "be the voice" for those inside Eritrea, one of the most heavily media-controlled countries in the world (VICE News 2016). This video included footage taken on mobile phones in detention camps in Eritrea for military deserters. The video also shows some Eritreans, who had recently crossed into Ethiopia, with their heads down as they concentrated on their phones and spoke about accessing Facebook for the first time. The wonky frames and mundanity of the scenes—of gaunt young men being served watery soup and sitting in somber groups—provided a virtual window into a place where physical access for those in the diaspora is almost impossible. This sort of virtual mobility, one could argue, is essential for creating purpose and mobilizing support for humanitarian action.

These evocations of place (and need/impact/connection) are created by both RDOs and the people they are helping. I observed CBOs reaching out to refugee diaspora communities in Australia through ICT in creative ways, sustaining connections to—and presumably support for—their own work. One refugee-led organization I visited in Indonesia, for example, regularly posted photos and videos and livestreamed events on Facebook and Twitter, tagging individuals within the wider diaspora to share with their networks. After returning to Australia, I remained connected to this organization through social media. I was struck by the immediacy of being invited via Facebook to a farewell celebration for one of the organization's founding members, a young Hazara refugee who was being resettled in America and who I had met in Indonesia. The celebration was in many ways an intimate gathering for those connected but living far apart. Those at a distance could interact virtually, in real time. These unseen participants (myself included) could watch, comment, and read other people's comments. They could share greetings, express gratitude, reminisce, and offer well-wishes for the young man whose departure was being honored. We could see the changing expressions on familiar faces. There were times when nothing of interest was happening, just as there are when one is physically present at an event. This was not a curated representation of something that had taken place in the past; those taking part were there, but not there. For those in the wider diaspora with connections to different humanitarian contexts, virtual mobility means being able to (re)visit people and places in ways that create a sense of immediacy and connection. This virtual mobility, one could hypothesize, is key to mobilizing diaspora communities to support and sustain connections with *their people* living in other parts of the world.

It is important to note that even though the use of virtual technologies seemed instrumental to the work of RDOs in this study, access to ICT is not uniform or universal. There are notable exceptions to the virtual connectivity of refugee diaspora communities. For example, in the refugee camp I visited in Thailand, mobile phone coverage was only accessible by climbing to the top of a hill, and physical mobility outside the refugee camp, where mobile network connectivity was much higher, was officially restricted by Thai authorities. For those with limited computer or literacy skills, the ease with which virtual technologies can be employed is also compromised.

While virtual mobility creates connections between people at a distance, it also enables RDOs to operate in Australia with no fixed address. Very few of the RDOs in this study had access to offices or meeting spaces, such that interviews and meetings I participated in were conducted in spaces that in no way resembled an office. We met in people's houses, in cramped storage rooms above restaurants, in family-owned businesses, in cafés inside shopping centers, in the foyers of recreation centers, and in the margins of meetings organized by bigger NGOs. Yet I marveled at the connectivity of RDOs and how they managed to organize despite this lack of (physical) infrastructure. As Muzafar said of his involvement with an organization that operated both in Australia and Indonesia, "[I am] co-project manager for this school. [My friend] is mostly responsible for taking care of the issues within Australia. I am mostly liaising with my team in [Indonesia], with the school. [I] talk to them regularly, and we attend weekly meetings . . . through Skype and Viber."[6]

This ability to organize and work across dispersed locations was apparent with another project that involved a refugee-led organization in Thailand and different groups in Australia and the United States. The president of an RDO in Australia described how he had cofounded a technical college in a refugee camp in Thailand and been heavily involved in its development before being resettled. After arriving in Australia, he continued to act as a representative of the college because he had well-established relationships with its international donors. From Australia, he collated information sent from the camp and sent funding acquittal reports. While he may have physically relocated to a different continent, he was able to send the donors regular information in the same format, as if he was still there in Thailand and not building a new life in Melbourne.

In sum, understanding differential mobilities is key to grasping the modalities of refugee diaspora humanitarianism. Not everyone involved in RDOs has either the capacity or desire to travel overseas to undertake humanitarian work, and much depends on their legal status and related *motility*. Physical mobility is also linked to governmentality and how people perceive and internalize their own motility. For those who travel overseas to help, their reasons for traveling are multifold. Most travel to visit, care for, or reunite with family and friends, suggesting that refugee diaspora humanitarianism and the ways in which transnational families connect exist side by side. And finally, the virtual mobilities apparent in refugee diaspora humanitarianism are striking. ICT has provided possibilities for RDOs to organize across dispersed locations and to mobilize and sustain support for humanitarian work by creating or sustaining affective connections between people who are living worlds apart.

(IN)VISIBILITY

Another notable characteristic of refugee diaspora humanitarianism that became apparent during my fieldwork relates to how RDOs and the people involved use their visibility or invisibility to different effect, depending on context. *Visibility* refers to the ways in which others can see or not see refugee diasporas as humanitarian actors and their "otherness" in the Australian context or "sameness" within humanitarian spaces (Hall 1997). Indeed (in)visibility is key to how RDOs work and to their distinctiveness as humanitarian actors. The following explores three dimensions of visibility: RDO visibility in comfortable humanitarian spaces, RDO invisibility in liminal humanitarian spaces, and the invisibility of refugee diasporas within humanitarian response systems more broadly.

Visibility

How groups define themselves in relation to others is a well-worn area of anthropological inquiry (for example Barth 1969; Goffman 1959; Hall 1997; Okolie 2003; Said 1978). As Andrew Okolie notes, "Social identities are relational; groups typically define themselves in relation to others. This is because identity has little meaning without the 'other.' So, by defining itself a group defines *others*. Identity is rarely claimed or assigned for its own sake. These definitions of self and others have purposes and consequences. They are tied to rewards and punishment, which may be material or symbolic. . . . This is why identities are contested. Power is implicated here, and because groups do not have equal powers to define both *self* and the *other*, the consequences reflect these power differentials" (2003, 2).

For refugee diaspora humanitarians, being *othered*—as refugees and (mostly) nonwhite, as "vulnerable" or "in need of help" (Malkki 1996)—is familiar territory. While much can and has been said about *othering* in white Australia (see Hage 2012), what is notable in the case of refugee diaspora humanitarianism is how identity is used symbolically and strategically for effect. In particular, there are common ways in which these organizations and individuals self-identify in comfortable humanitarian spaces—in Australia or in the offices of humanitarian organizations in Geneva and New York—to be *seen* to represent the people who they are trying to help. This requires making visible the otherness that is imposed in alternate contexts. Without wishing to suggest that this self-othering creates a significant shift in power dynamics, within the sphere of garnering scarce humanitarian resources, being visible as *the other* adds some legitimacy and authority to what RDOs are advocating for or doing and for which group they are understood to represent.

As Okolie suggests, definitions or presentation of *self* have purpose and consequence (see also Goffman 1959). The importance of being seen to represent a group that needs help—not as an Australian but as a refugee—was apparent in much of the RDO advocacy and resource mobilization I observed. In short, it brings rewards. The following interview excerpts illustrate this purposeful visibility:

> People would respect when organizations like us talk about Ogaden because we would know exactly what's going on and what's happening and can explain that to people. And people like to hear exactly what's happening and have that evidence base. That somebody within the community was tortured, was raped, actually expressing what happened, then that will make a difference. (Ladan)[7]

> At the [fundraising] event, we explained what [the RDO] is about, why we want to do it. We provided Sudanese food. We had performances from the Sudanese community. All the women, they sang. Our church group, they sang. Then we had testimonies from people. One was my Auntie, who could recall her memories from the 1991 civil war. Another person [recently] came back from South Sudan. He worked in the government. He could explain what the fight was about. Another person was there when the war broke out, so he explained (Elizabeth).[8]

The use of testimony and performance (singing, dancing, wearing of traditional dress) to demonstrate group belonging was evident in several RDO fundraising events I attended, particularly those reaching out to a nondiaspora audience. Self-identification was often described in terms of being *a refugee*—a representation that emphasized victimhood and suffering (Malkki 1996). This self-identification was used not only to compel giving (fundraising) but also to advocate for systemic change. In figure 5.2, for example, we see two RDO members addressing a UN meeting on indigenous rights in New York on behalf of Assyrians in Iraq. While both women live in Australia, their legitimacy in speaking about displacement and the rights of *a people* is arguably heightened by their visibility as Assyrians, performed to an audience (the United Nations) by the wearing of a distinctive traditional dress.

The point about the visibility of refugee diasporas as *the other* in comfortable humanitarian spaces is not to suggest that the individuals involved are not part of, or do not feel they belong to, the groups they are representing. The connection between those involved in RDOs in Australia and those they are helping does not exist as a simple humanitarian/beneficiary binary. There are many other relational configurations—as families, friends, coreligionists, coworkers, former colleagues, classmates, neighbors, and so on. However, being visible as *a refugee*—a label that most have previously worn or had conferred on them—has symbolic and signifying effect. To use the example of the photo at the UN meeting, the woman speaking could equally highlight her legitimacy by speaking from her expertise as a lawyer. But there is some power in being visible as the Other in the

Figure 5.2 Two members of Assyrian Aid Society-Australia address a United Nations meeting on indigenous issues in New York, May 17, 2014.
UN Web TV, screenshot, accessed July 26, 2016, http://webtv.un.org/meetings-events/index.php/watch/3rd-meeting-permanent-forum-on-indigenous-issues-thirteenth-session-12-23-may-2014/3563929570001#full-text.

world of humanitarianism, at least in comfortable humanitarian spaces like New York, Geneva, or Sydney. This visibility communicates the idea that the person speaking knows the situation because they have been or are a refugee, and this is a perspective that is hard to refute.[9]

Invisibility

We now move to less comfortable humanitarian spaces—displacement or conflict situations—where the visibility of RDOs can be seen in a very different light. Contrasting the performance of otherness in Australia and elsewhere, many of those involved in RDOs spoke about how they used their *in*visibility to do things that may be difficult or carry greater risks for humanitarian actors who are easily identifiable (who are *visible*). For example, some RDOs have members who are willing and able to move in and out of conflict zones to facilitate projects or deliver material aid to hard-to-reach populations. They can do so without being identified as an international aid worker—an identity that brings with it signifiers of power, privilege, and foreignness and the associated risks and benefits (see Barnett and Weiss 2011, 32–34; Fassin 2010c). For example, during my fieldwork, several RDO members traveled to areas within Iraq and Syria to try to help (see also Sezgin 2015).[10]

For some refugee diaspora humanitarians, being seen (or not seen) as *a refugee*—a person with no power or resources—meant being able to help more effectively. These individuals described how their understanding and willingness to negotiate with local systems of power allowed projects to be implemented in cost-effective and efficient ways. For example, they could use their ability to blend in with a local refugee population to avoid the inflation or red tape that can otherwise hinder or escalate the cost of humanitarian interventions by more easily identifiable international actors. Being *not seen* in humanitarian contexts, then, has its advantages.

The value of invisibility was apparent when my fieldwork took me to visit CBOs on the Thai-Burma border. I asked CBO representatives what they would like those in the wider diaspora to do to support them in the future. Several people responded by saying they wanted those who had resettled to return to the camps as teachers and to share the skills and experience they had gained overseas. I asked if this would be practical—could those associated with RDOs easily work in the camps, considering Thai government restrictions on people and organizations accessing these spaces? Their responses seemed to suggest that if someone looked like and spoke the language of those in the camp (i.e., they were not visible as foreigners), then it was possible for them to move in informal, unofficial ways. Jordan explained this as the advantage of being "ordinary": "You know, maybe if you are a member of parliament . . . you can't get through [into the refugee camp]. But I can go through. . . . I will be [seen as] an ordinary person and can get in there."[11]

Being visible or invisible, then, can bring material and symbolic rewards for RDOs, depending on the context. In comfortable humanitarian spaces—in advocating for change within the international humanitarian system in Geneva or New York or in raising awareness and mobilizing resources in Australia—being visible as a refugee can add weight to words and solicit empathy from those who may otherwise feel no connection to a distant suffering *Other*. In contrast, blending in (being invisible) has purpose and effect in more liminal spaces. Being (not) seen as "ordinary" can mean being able to move in and out of areas where access is restricted or where being identifiable as a humanitarian worker may involve greater risks, costs, and red tape.

The Invisibility of Refugee Diaspora Humanitarianism

A final dimension of (in)visibility concerns how the work of RDOs is seen or not seen within the humanitarian arena, where different actors vie for access, legitimacy, and resources (Hilhorst and Jansen 2010). Without wishing to dwell on a point to be discussed in more detail in the following chapter, it is worth noting here that the *lack* of engagement between RDOs and more powerful actors renders their work largely invisible within the humanitarian arena. This is tied to what is noted above about purposeful invisibility enabling refugee diaspora humanitarianism—that making oneself invisible as a humanitarian worker can be useful in liminal spaces. At the same time, this invisibility renders the actions of refugee diasporas as invisible or inconsequential to broader response systems.

I return here to the Eritrean Australian Humanitarian Aid (EAHA) case study from chapter 2 to illustrate this point about invisibility within systems. EAHA was started in 2009 with the purpose of supporting education and health projects for Eritrean refugees. One of EAHA's projects around 2013–2014 was to raise funds to construct a school building in a refugee camp in Sudan. The school had been operating for some time on the site without a permanent structure, limiting its ability to hold classes during the rainy season. As the Sudanese authorities responsible for camp management restricted access to this space, the RDO worked with a local (Sudanese) NGO that was already active in the camp to arrange the purchase of materials and employ construction workers.[12] The money raised in Australia was given directly to construction workers by an RDO member, who traveled to Sudan and negotiated with the different stakeholders. While the result was that a six-room school building was completed, the role of RDOs in this outcome remained largely invisible to the camp management and to other humanitarian actors working in this space.[13] There was no signage on the school with the RDO logos branding their involvement for all to see. If someone were to ask who had funded and built the school, the most likely answer would be that it was the Sudanese NGO that had facilitated the RDO's access to the camp.

Many other initiatives I heard about also spoke of this quiet, invisible work of RDOs. I heard about life-saving operations being funded by RDOs that had facilitated connections between individual donors in Australia and people in desperate need in Jordan and Kenya, a medical center built by and for internally displaced persons (IDPs) in Myanmar through direct RDO funding, and money being raised by an RDO in Australia and sent through church networks to fund an agricultural project in South Sudan. None of these initiatives could easily be seen by others working with these populations.

While the invisibility of RDOs within the humanitarian arena may not have concerned many of those involved, others saw the lack of recognition of diaspora contributions as problematic. At the Diasporas and Afghanistan forum, the founder and president of Hazara Women of Australia, Najeeba Wazefadost, lamented, "There is a lot of work [that is] being done by the Afghan diaspora themselves all around the world, but there is [a] problem: documentation. We do not have enough recognition from the international aid agencies [of] what diasporas themselves are already doing."[14]

The implication of refugee diaspora humanitarianism being invisible within the international refugee regime and humanitarian system will be revisited in chapter 6. What should be noted here is that there is a paradox of invisibility in refugee diaspora humanitarianism. On the one hand, there are practical advantages to being *invisible* or *ordinary* in terms of accessing people and spaces in humanitarian contexts. Yet this invisibility also means there is little appreciation within the humanitarian arena about how the actions of refugee diaspora communities and organizations have consequence. Taking this argument even further, we can also see that refugee diasporas' invisibility as humanitarian actors contributes to the perpetuation of the symbolic othering of refugees as suffering victims/people in need, and not as people with agency and capacities to help.

KNOWLEDGE

How any actor goes about helping a stranger in need will be based on their understanding of a situation, what they believe needs to be done, and what they think the best course of action is. Humanitarian responses in refugee situations are undeniably messy equations. Humanitarian emergency contexts are defined by their fluidity; they are "states of exception" (Agamben 2005). As such, knowing how to best assist requires dominant humanitarian actors to draw from frameworks and practices that have been developed and refined over decades of experience (Barnett 2011). It is safe to say that the knowledge (justified true belief) that volunteer-run RDOs in Australia draw on to decide how to help differs markedly from that of professionalized humanitarian organizations. Bertrand Russell (1997) makes a useful distinction between "knowledge by acquaintance" and "knowledge by description," with the former being a unique form of knowledge "where the subject has direct, unmediated, and non-inferential access to what is known," whereas knowledge by description is knowledge that is "indirect, mediated, and inferential" (Russell, referenced by DePoe, n.d.). Using these distinctions, we can see that RDOs—particularly those involving people who have experienced life as a refugee and have been on the receiving end of humanitarian interventions—base their decisions on both types of knowledge, leading them to act in particular ways.

In the following, three aspects of knowledge are explored as they relate to modalities of refugee diaspora humanitarianism: how RDOs draw on descriptive/acquainted knowledge to understand humanitarian contexts, needs, and solutions; how those involved in this study spoke about their own and others' knowledge gaps (what they *don't* know); and how distinctions are made and values placed on *expert* versus *local* knowledge.

Knowing

One question I asked RDO representatives in interviews and informal discussions was: *How do you go about identifying the need for your project/s?* This question sought to understand the knowledge that informed an RDO's choice of activities. Interviewees generally responded to this question in one of two ways: either they spoke about how needs were identified directly by the people they were trying to help or they spoke about how they knew because they had essentially been in the same situation as the people they were targeting. The following exemplifies this first type of response: "I think it's definitely the grassroots approach; being able to identify what they need and working with what they've requested. Not coming in and being like, 'Oh well, so yeah, it looks like you don't have enough food. Here you go,' and walking out. Letting them tell us what they need and working with that" (Elizabeth).[15]

This approach can be described as basing action on *local* knowledge. Of course, it is a somewhat problematic simplification to say local knowledge is an unambiguous, uncontested field. Obviously, who one seeks knowledge from will color their understanding of needs. A young single mother with a sick child asked to identify needs will likely give a different response than an older man with a large family who has nowhere to sleep at night, although both would identify needs that could invite a humanitarian response. Yet what was interesting in how RDO representatives talked about locals identifying needs was their acknowledgment of their own limited resources and capacity. They were not seeking to identify the needs of the whole affected population; they were looking for the most effective and achievable way to meet someone's needs, however small, and with what they realistically could do.

The identification of needs is clearly shaped by what RDOs perceive as possible, and this is influenced by the capacities of the individuals involved in these organizations. While some had a broader sense of what needs they could or should respond to, others clearly saw their own knowledge and skill sets as guiding the direction of their needs-identification process and subsequent actions. For example, a group of Iraqi Australian doctors trying to help those besieged by fighting in Iraq clearly looked for medical needs to respond to. An Afghan Australian woman with a PhD in science sought to develop a scientific education program for women in Afghanistan. Former journalists from Ethiopia established a human rights advocacy organization to document abuses. An Arabic language teacher set up an organization to help a group of refugees with visa applications that required translating a significant number of documents from Arabic to English. As Alaa said, "I can do the language. I can prepare the legal [documents] through my network. So, I thought, it's possible."[16] In all these cases, what was possible with regard to the knowledge, skills, and capacity of RDO members shaped how needs were identified and the actions that followed.

While *what is possible* seemed to direct RDOs' identification of which needs to address, their subsequent actions were also clearly informed by the acquainted knowledge (cultural, language, social norms) of those involved. One of the advantages of having acquainted (insider) knowledge of the local contexts in which RDOs are helping—which many professed to have—is that it provides a nuanced way of interpreting needs and appropriate responses. As Hadi said of the advantages of diaspora humanitarians over other actors in identifying and prioritizing who is most vulnerable, "It's the knowledge of culture, language, and mindset.... As a community we know the ground, we know the language, we can differentiate between which one is which. That's a very hard process [for others]."[17]

This links to the second type of response to my question about identifying needs. Many involved in RDOs spoke of their own experiences and how they *knew* what was needed because they had been in the same place or in a similar situation. They spoke about how this knowledge went beyond what people said to an understanding of what this telling meant. Jordan, for example, spoke about the gaps in knowledge of other humanitarian actors because their understanding is filtered by what refugees choose to say or show. He described it as the difference between someone who knows what is inside a person's house because they are "in there" and a neighbor who can only see what is on the outside and makes assumptions about what is inside: "They're not right in there, so they don't know much."[18]

Contrasting this, representatives from different RDOs conveyed how they were "right in there." Anwar described his knowledge based on experience as such: "Because I [was] in that school a long time ago, I know exactly what's needed there.... I know because I'm from that environment and I have been in that situation."[19]

A key informant who works closely with RDOs saw this insider knowledge and ability to read situations as one of the natural advantages of diasporas over other types of humanitarian actors. As she described, international agencies come in and identify needs according to what they see and what the people they talk to say, whereas diasporas "go from under the line." She added, "They can tell who are the poorest people in the village, which are the groups that most need attention, which are the areas out of this geographical area, which one needs a primary school. They know. And they know immediately, and it's accurate.... So they've got those kinds of natural advantages."[20]

So, while dominant humanitarian organizations draw from descriptive knowledge based on a breadth of experience from different contexts and over time, refugee diaspora humanitarians draw from knowledge that is highly context-specific, the strength of which is their ability to read the local situation (needs and appropriate responses), rather than apply frameworks that are general and which may take some time to translate into a local context.

Not Knowing

Two criticisms leveled at diaspora humanitarians relate to a perceived *lack* of knowledge: that RDOs have lower levels of technical expertise and engagement with the wider humanitarian system and that, contrary to the evidence above, there is a disconnect between diasporas' and local communities' understandings of a situation (see DEMAC 2016b; Sezgin 2015).

A heated exchange I observed illustrates this first critique. The exchange happened at the Diasporas and Afghanistan forum held in Melbourne in 2015, which involved representatives from both RDOs and larger humanitarian INGOs. A man and a woman, both originally from Afghanistan, were participating in a discussion group. The man worked for a large INGO, and the woman was involved in a small, recently established RDO. The group was discussing how diasporas identified and responded to needs in humanitarian contexts. The man was visibly agitated as the woman spoke about fundraising to support a school in Afghanistan. At one point, the man interjected in an exasperated tone: "See, this is the problem!" He then drew a line on a piece of paper with a circle on either side. He pointed to one circle and said, "Someone has family in this village, and they build a school, but they don't see that there is a village on the other side of this mountain that needs a school more! They just help here. It's not based on need; people who have family and friends overseas get more help."

Equally exasperated, the woman responded, "But we have to start somewhere! We only have small money. We are taking money from our own pocket. If I know someone, I can do something more easily."

What this exchange highlights are the different capacities for knowing and acting between RDOs and larger institutional humanitarian actors. For the man, working for a large INGO presumably means he has—or has access to—technical expertise and resources to identify needs in a more comprehensive way. The identification of needs by INGOs is based on data that covers a wider geographical area and is informed by humanitarian principles and practice guidelines.[21] Contrast this to the decision-making of the woman from the RDO, who may *know* a lot about the needs in the village where she has connections but *not know* about needs in villages in the rest of Afghanistan. The man can "see" both villages, and the organization he works for has the resources to base its decisions on this broader understanding of need. The larger humanitarian actor may also have knowledge of what others are doing or planning to do within a greater geographic area because they are engaged in humanitarian coordination systems. Of course, this is not to say that the RDO in this scenario is *not* responding to an identified need; the RDO's knowledge of the context and its ability to respond are much more localized and not necessarily coordinated with others who are acting within a wider response system. From this wider perspective, the knowledge and actions of RDOs may indeed appear fragmented and, for institutional actors—more problematically—partisan.

The second weakness in knowledge that diaspora humanitarians have been criticized for is the disconnect between diasporas' and local communities' understanding of a situation (see DEMAC 2016b). This is, of course, contrary to what many of the people I spoke to thought about their knowledge and connections to those they were trying to support. Yet it did seem from observing RDOs that some have stronger and broader channels of communication with people overseas. As highlighted in the discussion on virtual mobility, many RDOs are well connected with those they are trying to help, and information and ideas move easily and in real time. For example, I asked Sabira whether diasporas in Australia had up-to-date information about humanitarian situations. She replied: "It's never, never old knowledge! You can have breaking news always from your country. Viber, Facebook, anything. We are very close now. When I post something, I get [comments] straight away from Bahrain, from Kabul, from Quetta, London . . . America. Really, the world is very, very connected in that way. It's good for good things and bad for bad things."[22]

Another woman I spoke to, Ladan, acknowledged that those within her organization (an Ogaden RDO) had varied understandings of the situation for those they were trying to help and that knowledge depends on how long someone has been in Australia and how often they travel overseas. Yet in recognizing this knowledge gap, this RDO intentionally recruited committee members who were more recently arrived. She said of them: "They know what's going on. . . . It's more like we learn from them. They have current information."[23]

The disconnect between a diaspora's and a local community's knowledge of a situation can also run both ways. Some RDO members spoke about *not knowing* being an issue for the people they were supporting, leading to misunderstandings about what diaspora communities in countries like Australia were able or expected to do. Naj said: "They have a glorious picture [of] this part of the world, which also needs to become [clearer]. Afghan women in Australia [made a video to show] how we are coming together and working. We took the video to Iran [and showed it]. You know, they didn't expect my office, for example, to be that [basic]. They said, 'Oh, is it your office?' . . . So, it [is] sharing both ways."[24]

These kinds of misperceptions of how the expectations of those they were trying to help did not match the reality of their situation in Australia were spoken about by others. This makes sense if we consider that it is easier to imagine, empathize with, or understand the experiences of another if you have been in a similar situation. It follows that it would be harder for someone currently living as a refugee to deeply understand the perspectives and possibilities of those who have been resettled or are living in the wider diaspora. Many involved in RDOs carry the knowledge of having experienced both contexts.

Humanitarian Knowledge

Discussions about knowledge and humanitarian practice frequently place a distinction between *expert* and *local* knowledge. Michael Barnett argues that these distinctions can be traced to the transformation of humanitarianism in the 1990s: "The field was becoming rationalized, aspiring to develop: methodologies for calculating results, abstract rules to guide standardized responses, and procedures to improve efficiency and identify the best means to achieve specified ends. Humanitarian organizations were also becoming bureaucratized, developing spheres of competence, and rules to standardize responses and to drive means-ends calculations. Professionalism followed, with demands for actors who had specific knowledge, vocational qualifications that derived from specialized training, and the ability to follow fixed doctrine" (2005, 729).

Within this evolving field and in the context of fierce competition for resources, organizations with specialist knowledge have the advantage. Barnett argues that expert knowledge is "the trump card" that is given precedence over local knowledge and that what constitutes valuable knowledge within the humanitarian field is very much shaped by professional actors (2011, 235; see also Horst et al. 2015, 221). In highlighting the vested interests of dominant humanitarian actors, Barnett and others have suggested that there is potential for broadening humanitarian knowledge in ways that challenge the expert/local distinction (Barnett 2011; Hilhorst and Jansen 2010; Horst et al. 2015; Pacitto and Fiddian-Qasmiyeh 2013). Indeed, I suggest that RDOs draw on sources of knowledge that have the potential to bridge these distinctions. This is particularly so in the case of those who have both technical expertise (relevant training, skills, or descriptive knowledge that makes provision of assistance more effective) and local knowledge (language, culture, social networks, or acquainted knowledge). Hamid described the vantage of diaspora professionals as such: "Let's say there are [two] professionals: one with no Rohingya background, one with Rohingya background. There is this difference between them, in that the Rohingya one can identify the problem just like that. The other guy will have to wander around a lot."[25]

This ability to understand a situation and how to respond from multiple perspectives—from the perspective of the person at the receiving end as well as of those who are intervening—was discussed by other respondents as one of the strengths of refugee diaspora humanitarianism and as an area that needed further development. For example, when asked how they could be more effective in their helping work, some RDO representatives spoke about wanting to have greater knowledge of how to plan and implement activities more professionally.

Yet the inherent value of professionalized ways of working should not go unquestioned. Professionalization within the humanitarian sector has, after all, created distance and distinctions between helpers and those being helped. Acting professionally leads to ways of working that may not be the only, or even the best, approach. As Barnett laments:

> As professionals relying on expert, objective, and generalized knowledge, they had less need to learn about nuances of the local conditions before developing and implementing their policies. Professionalism, observed Rony Brauman, had the effect of reducing proximity to technique and creating greater distance between the giver and the receiver. As one [Médecins Sans Frontières] MSF worker reflected about the noticeable lack of informal interactions with local populations, "We have less time to drink tea. Most of us avoid interacting on a one-to-one basis with the people. We don't have time. We like being on the internet. We don't think that much can be gained that will help us do our job." (2011, 218)

Contrast this to what I observed while in Indonesia with members of one RDO. Five people from Melbourne traveled to Jakarta because a group of Oromo asylum seekers in Indonesia had asked for help. In trying to find out what they could do, the RDO organized a series of meetings with Indonesia-based Oromo community members. More than one hundred people turned up at these meetings—almost everyone in Indonesia who was Oromo except those in immigration detention centers. A significant amount of time spent at these gatherings involved individuals standing and talking about their journeys, their difficulties, and their needs. The stories were harrowing and were told with tears and expressions of desperation. The RDO members listened, asked questions, and took notes. Along with these formal meetings, informal meetings began taking place at the hotel where we stayed. Every time I entered the lobby, I saw Indonesia-based Oromo community members sitting at tables, eating, and talking with their Australian compatriots. Over the six days we were in Indonesia, the Oromo Australians disappeared for various periods of time. When asked where they had gone, they said they were visiting people from the community. They traveled to

Figure 5.3 Indonesia-based Oromo refugees and asylum seekers meeting with Oromo-Australian RDO members in Jakarta. Photo credit: L. Olliff.

their houses and listened to what they wanted to tell them. They "drank tea." Countless photos and videos of these interactions were taken, and Facebook connections were made (see fig. 5.3). On reflection, much of what the members of this RDO did by traveling to Indonesia seemed to be about bearing witness. The time spent at gatherings and the close proximity between the helpers and those who were asking for help created space for a deeper understanding of the particular situation facing this small group of individuals seeking asylum in Indonesia.

To conclude, people involved in RDOs who have experienced life as a refugee and been on the receiving end of humanitarian assistance have the possibility of drawing on both descriptive and acquainted knowledge to inform their actions. While RDOs have their blind spots—particularly when it comes to working within a wider humanitarian system and in cases where there is a disconnect between diaspora and local community understandings of a situation—they also have some natural advantages. Refugee diaspora humanitarians have the advantage of being able to read situations and interpret nuances by virtue of their insider status. But perhaps the greatest distinction between the knowledge of refugee diaspora and other humanitarian actors is the proximity between the helpers and those they are helping. The ability of refugee diaspora humanitarians to communicate and listen—and to take the time to do this—points to a slightly different emphasis in diaspora approaches to understanding a situation and determining what is needed and how to respond.

NETWORKS

Social networks are an undeniably important feature of how RDOs go about their helping work. Local networks within Australia and transnational networks with people living in displacement contexts and among the wider diaspora are all influential in shaping refugee diaspora humanitarianism. In the following section, RDO networks are conceptualized in terms of transnational social fields and rhizomatic networks. The significance of trust to these networks is explored, along with how the strength of RDOs' local and transnational networks enables effectiveness.

Transnational Social Fields and Rhizomatic Networks

As Glick Schiller holds, "transnational social fields" are composed of observable social relationships and transactions: "Multiple actors, with very different kinds of power and locations of power, interact across borders to create and sustain this field of relationships. As networks of interpersonal connections that stretch across borders, transnational social fields are people-to-people relationships through which information, resources, goods, services, and ideas are exchanged" (2004, 455).

The use of the term *transnational* to describe these observable social relationships and transactions speaks to the way in which the nation-state shapes—but does not contain—such linkages and movements (see also Basch et al. 1994; Glick Schiller 2004; 2012). For this reason, the subsequent discussion of RDO networks is organized with reference to their location within states—within Australia, between countries of refuge (humanitarian contexts), and between states where the "wider diaspora" (Van Hear 2006; 2009) reside. The unequal power and resources held by people within a transnational network are influenced by their relationship to nation-states in each of these different sites and thus warrant separate consideration.

Before turning to what RDO networks do, it is useful to first conceptualize these networks in terms of "decentralized, distributed patterns of human organizations" (Ghorashi and Boersma 2009, 670) or rhizomatic networks (Deleuze and Guttari 1987). Gilles Deleuze and Félix Guttari write that "unlike trees or their roots, the rhizome connects any point to any other point, and its traits are not necessarily linked to traits of the same nature; it brings into play very different regimes of signs, and even non-sign states. . . . It is composed not of units but of dimensions, or rather directions in motion . . . the tree is filiation but the rhizome is alliance . . . the fabric of the rhizome is the conjunction" (1987, 21, 25).

Rhizomatic networks within transnational social fields are not neutral phenomena. These networks involve people with differential power, resources, and social capital. As Halleh Ghorashi and Kees Boersma conclude: "Social capital is the sum of resources, actual or virtual, that increases if an individual becomes connected to networks of more or less institutionalized (durable) relationships . . . In this way, social capital is linked to one's identity, not so much in terms of one's roots but in terms of one's rhizomatic, networked connections" (2009, 670).

Bringing together these ideas of rhizomatic networks within transnational social fields, we can begin to see how refugee diaspora humanitarianism is enabled by the (moving) connections between people in different places, whose conjunction is found in a shared—or the perception of a shared—identity. These networks involve transactions of information, resources, goods, services, and ideas. They involve actions and have effect.

Trust

What binds social networks together is both *transactional* (an exchange of goods, information, services, and ideas) and involves *affect*. Much of the discussion I had about the different people or networks RDOs draw on in their helping work involved considerations of who is and is not to be trusted (see also Bornstein 2012, chap. 2). Trust is crucial for getting things done. As people-to-people helping often involving organizations with informal governance structures, it is not hard to see how important trust-based relationships are to refugee diaspora humanitarianism. An assessment of trustworthiness is important in the relationships among people based in Australia and with those they are working with in other countries. Trust bridges the distance between helpers and those they are helping, particularly when the implementation of projects or carriage of funds is through individuals in distant, and often highly insecure, places. But trust was also spoken about as crucial in mobilizing communities *within* Australia to get behind an RDO and as a significant factor in both the successes and challenges of diaspora humanitarianism.

For RDOs in Australia, trust seems to come from personally knowing someone, being able to verify a person or local group's trustworthiness from different sources, or being able to see for themselves that a person or group is trustworthy. For example, one RDO responded to internal displacement within Iraq by raising funds and sending part of this money to a trusted person—a family relation of the RDO's chairperson. Only part of the money was sent in the first instance because the RDO wanted to ensure that the person receiving the money did what they said they would. After verifying from multiple sources that the funds had been used as directed, the RDO then sent a second installment. Other RDOs used established networks to verify information from sources they did not have an existing or strong connection to. As Sarah explained, when a person contacted her organization and asked for help, "We [have] our people we trust there who can tell us if this [person] is really in need. [They can say], 'No, they [have] some support from overseas. They [have] cousins or friends or whoever. They can send them [money].' So, we can check."[26]

Knowing who and what information to trust runs both ways within refugee diaspora transnational networks. In other words, with relationships of trust come expectations. Intended recipients of RDO activities make their own assessments about an organization's trustworthiness and whether to engage. Conversations with people working for CBOs or NGOs in Indonesia, Thailand, and South Sudan, for example, revealed different views on the trustworthiness or reliability of those in the wider diaspora. While they talked generally about a willingness to engage with RDOs, several of the people I spoke to expressed a desire to understand how to work with RDOs better to ensure that what was promised was acted on.

However, by far the greatest focus of discussions about trust concerned social networks within Australia, particularly within diaspora communities. As one key informant supporting RDOs in Australia said of why some organizations succeed while others fail, "I think that [it is about] being able to create trust within the community [that is] actually going to give you money [to] do things. So, it's that—being able [to] prove yourself trustworthy."[27]

This sentiment was echoed by others from RDOs when talking about the challenges they faced in mobilizing support within Australia. Naj said, "For my association to run successfully, it was very important for me to build my reputation first."[28] Another person spoke of the long process of rebuilding trust within a community where previous RDOs had failed to do what they said they would and noted that the feeling of mistrust of community-initiated humanitarian endeavor was reportedly high: "My role first is [to] get that trust back [from] people. [To show that] there are people who can do things. We are like selling ourselves: 'Trust us. We'll do a lot.'"[29]

RDO Networks

The following details how RDOs' networks in Australia, in humanitarian contexts and in the wider diaspora, enable or facilitate acts of helping.

Australia

RDO social networks in Australia enable refugee diaspora humanitarianism in two main ways: by identifying needs through people who have personal ties to an affected population overseas and by mobilizing support for the work of RDOs. To return to Glick Schiller's description of transnational social fields as "people-to-people relationships through which information, resources, goods, services, and ideas are exchanged" (2004, 455), the first of these areas involves a transaction of information or ideas, and the second involves the transaction of goods, resources, and services.

To illustrate how social networks are instrumental in conveying information and ideas that guide RDOs activities, consider the following account from my fieldwork notes of how the decision was made for members of an RDO to travel to Indonesia to assist a group of asylum seekers:

> In explaining why they decided to travel to Indonesia, Hassan said it wasn't the first time community members from Australia have done this sort of thing. He previously went to Kenya to do similar advocacy. He said these visits were often reactive. He further explained how they came to know about the issues facing Oromo asylum seekers in Indonesia. He said his wife's brother was among this group and had traveled to Indonesia from Djibouti six months ago. His brother-in-law had called his sister (Hassan's wife) to ask for help. Before this call, they had not known that his brother-in-law was intending to fly to Indonesia. Hassan said that he did not consider they could do much when he first called. It was only when someone from the Oromo-Australian community accompanied his wife on a business trip to Indonesia and incidentally came across a group of Oromo asylum seekers standing outside the United Nations High Commissioner for Refugees (UNHCR) office in Jakarta, and then came back to Australia with stories and photos of the terrible situation they were in, that Hassan mobilized others from the community in Australia to act.

So many of the descriptions of how needs were identified by RDOs seemed to involve an element of chance; someone traveled and saw someone who needed help, then mobilized support from within diaspora networks to respond. Earlier I wrote about how the actions of RDOs seemed to come about through happenstance. Yet we can also see that this is not just chance. Social networks are key to the exchange of information and ideas that are then acted upon, and the strength of these networks is significant to how and what information is shared. To use another example, one Sydney-based woman who cofounded an RDO spoke about how the idea had come about. Elizabeth said that a friend in Darwin had called her to talk about the unfolding displacement crisis in their homeland, South Sudan. Her friend said, "I think you know quite a few people, let's try and do something." They then contacted "like-minded friends" across Australia and established an RDO with committee members and fundraising capacity in each state and territory.

The identification of needs is, of course, only part of the story of how social networks in Australia shape refugee diaspora humanitarianism. The relative strength of an RDO's social networks—both in terms of bonding and bridging social capital (Putnam 2000)—is significant. While many people within refugee diaspora communities have (transnational) social networks to be able to identify needs, not everyone has the social capital to take information or ideas and translate these into effective action. In the above example, what was key to the success of these two people in establishing a South Sudanese RDO was not only that they were able to identify needs and have an idea about how to respond but also that they were able to mobilize a network of supporters to make something happen. It may not have been chance that Elizabeth was also the daughter of a well-respected, long-serving, and active community advocate in Australia and could presumably draw on these networks, skills, and experiences when trying to turn an idea into effective action.

Social networks are particularly instrumental for RDOs in mobilizing financial and human resources, with organizations drawing on the relative strength of their networks within diaspora communities. In almost all cases, the biggest financial contributors to the RDOs in this study were from diaspora communities. The same can be said for the human capital that enables RDO activities. The RDOs in this study were mostly run by people who were active in diaspora communities and who could draw on these social networks to identify other people who could help. As the following account of one community's response to a conflict-induced displacement crisis illustrates, those with strong social networks have the potential to mobilize a significant volunteer base and in-kind support:

> "We announced [our project] through our community media—the internet and emails and through mosque and through word-of-mouth—but the response was really, really good. We sent two containers, but what we received is maybe six containers. [We] had people that worked on [sorting out donations] as, you know, it is not an easy job. [We] put things in different places and with different guys, and we [had] people come and organize it. . . . With all our groups, our clubs, we have teams to do this work" (Iraqi RDO).[30]

Although it was less common, there were some RDOs in this study with much stronger bridging social capital that had managed to mobilize support from wider (nondiaspora) networks. For example, two RDOs were directly associated with churches that had diverse congregations, one had strong links with a local rotary club, and a number were led by people with well-established professional networks (e.g., university, business) that provided an avenue for mobilizing both financial and human capital.

One RDO that seemed to have both strong bridging and bonding networks is illustrative of the capacity of different networks to turn ideas into action. The RDO was started by a former refugee from Myanmar, Jordan, who was closely associated with a church in Melbourne. Before starting the RDO, Jordan invited members of his church to join him in visiting the refugee camp on the Thai-Burma border where he had lived and still had connections. Six members of the congregation—of whom only Jordan was a former refugee—took up the invitation. These individuals became key to mobilizing other supporters from within the church community and brought with them different skills and social networks. Jordan spoke about the importance of building wider support networks thus:

> I think some people [from my community] would [have] a different view. [Some leaders] would say, "This is [our community]. We should stick together. We should call [on] our own community or work through our problem." But for me, I see that [it needs to be] a little bit wider. . . . I knew from experience as well. In 1994, when I first came, [we could only] start with a small prayer group. We would collect money and raise $1,000, $1,200, $1,300. . . . That's all we can do. Other than that, we pray. . . . But if we go with a wider group—with the church and other people—we can get [more] support, [because other] people have a lot of connections.[31]

What can be surmised from Jordan's and others' experiences is that bonding social capital is instrumental in getting RDO ideas off the ground, as diaspora networks seem to be more readily mobilized to help. However, RDOs that are able to draw on wider (bridging) social networks might also be able to sustain or expand their capacity to help over the longer term.

Humanitarian Contexts

As with social networks within Australia, RDO networks with people in humanitarian contexts are key for exchanging ideas and information and for getting things done. These networks are particularly important in spaces that are harder for those perceived as outsiders to access. In 2013, Médecins Sans Frontières reported that diaspora organizations were able to deliver aid to civilian populations inside Syria that were inaccessible to other aid organizations through their "well-established networks" (Sezgin 2015, 245). If we consider what these well-established networks look like, what seems to matter most is that they involve trusted relationships with (local) people who are in positions of authority or have the necessary skills and networks to be able to exchange information, ideas, goods, and services with their contacts in the wider diaspora. More often, the people who can do these things are involved with or represent local CBOs that implement activities on behalf of RDOs. And, in almost all of the examples I heard about, the strength of relationships depends on who knows who and how well.

The following description of the process that led to an Eritrean RDO funding the construction of a school building in a refugee camp gives a flavor to how transnational social networks are deployed: "[We knew] someone who was a friend of ours [when] we were teaching back in the '80s in Sudan. [He] heard about us, that we had come there, and [now] he's a principal of one school. [He asked us to come and visit.] He told [us] the story about the school, his school, and Berhan went there to just see."[32]

What we see here is the importance of the relationship between the principal of a school and two members of an RDO. The relationship between these individuals existed prior to the RDO coming into existence, but the fact that the man was now a school principal meant that he was in a position to provide information and ideas to the RDO members about needs and to facilitate the implementation of the response on the ground. Indeed, in this case, the principal was key to negotiating the outcome—the construction of a school building on an existing site in a refugee camp—with camp authorities, a local NGO, and RDOs in Australia.

It is important to note that the networks that RDOs have with people in humanitarian contexts are not always well established, and some interviewees talked about the challenges of building or maintaining relationships with people outside Australia. Relationships that were identified as problematic tended to be those involving people whose trustworthiness had yet to be tested and were based on connections that were newly established. For example, Naj identified monitoring as a challenge facing her organization because "the people that we've chosen in those countries we have had very limited relationships [with], face-to-face." In this case, the RDO sought to strengthen these relationships by having its members travel from Australia to offer training to the women they had engaged locally. Part of the rationale of offering face-to-face training was that it would strengthen the relationships of the RDO with their locally engaged counterparts and, importantly, build trust.

The Wider Diaspora

We move now to RDO networks with counterparts in the wider diaspora—in more affluent countries in the Global North. I was surprised by the number of people I spoke to whose organization was in direct communication, and at times coordinated, with RDOs in other countries. Take the following exchange, for example:

> LOUISE: Are you associated with Ogaden community groups in different countries?
>
> LADAN: Yes, there's an Ogaden community in Minnesota, Washington, Dallas, and the same with Europe—we've got London, Sweden, Norway [and so on].

LOUISE: Are you regularly in contact with them?

LADAN: Yes, [we] regularly have conferences over the phone or Skype.

LOUISE: To discuss issues happening in the Ogaden region or in the diaspora?

Ladan: To discuss issues in Ogaden and also the issues for the refugees in Kenya and how we can support them.

LOUISE: Have you done any work as an international network to support refugees in Kenya, or do you usually work as national or local groups?

LADAN: It's a bit of both. There is the umbrella. [We] have the Ogaden Orphan organization. That's basically around the world. The head office is in Kenya. So, each country helps out. Each country organizes fundraisers to help the kids buy books.[33]

There were other examples of coordination or collaboration between RDOs in the wider diaspora, where relationships forged while people lived as refugees were maintained or reinvigorated after individuals were resettled to different countries. Again, the strength of preexisting trust-based relationships is key to how dynamic or significant these transnational networks are to those in the wider diaspora.

In sum, refugee diaspora humanitarianism is enabled by transnational social networks. These networks are built on trust-based relationships between people in different parts of the world—in Australia, in humanitarian contexts, and in the wider diaspora—and involve transactions of information, resources, goods, services, and ideas. Moreover, these are rhizomatic networks—or networks in motion—as connections are made or transformed in response to events (crises) and mobility (resettlement, travel). The relative strength of an RDO's social networks plays a key role in what they decide to do and how effective they are in following ideas through to fruition.

DISTINCT MODALITIES

The four themes explored in this chapter illuminate the ways in which refugee diaspora humanitarianism can be understood as a practice with common characteristics and modalities. While there may be considerable variation in the populations and contexts in which RDOs are working, there are also many parallels in how mobility, visibility, knowledge, and networks shape what is possible and practicable in terms of diaspora helping. Examining the modalities of RDOs more closely reveals the distinct strengths and capabilities of these kinds of organizations as actors engaged in displacement contexts. Having a permanent legal status in a country like Australia, for example, allows individuals who have deep insights and trust-based social networks with people in refugee situations to move in and out of liminal humanitarian spaces for the purposes (although not the sole purpose) of providing assistance. Having both descriptive and acquainted knowledge of needs and solutions as well as the flexibility to respond to direct (even person-to-person) requests for help makes refugee diaspora humanitarians and their organizations important actors in contexts of scarcity, insecurity, and vast unmet need.

As I noted in the previous chapter, refugee diaspora humanitarianism also faces distinct challenges, not least of which is the capacity of RDOs to turn their strengths into effective actions. There are also risks that refugee diaspora humanitarians face that reflect their positionality. The flip side of having greater motility and being able to access liminal humanitarian spaces by being treated as though you are invisible, for example, is that you also face the same dangers and risks that ordinary people face. Unlike for people working for larger, established humanitarian organizations, there are fewer safety nets for refugee diaspora humanitarians, who are both insiders and outsiders in these spaces. Diaspora humanitarians also face risks to reputation and to social networks built on trust that must be delicately managed and can have significant personal ramifications. For many, the fact that helping is so deeply tied to personal histories, past experiences, and existing social relationships is both a blessing and a curse.

SIX

IMPLICATIONS AND IMAGININGS

THE PRECEDING CHAPTERS DESCRIBED THE ecology, motivations, and modalities of refugee diaspora humanitarianism, framed as collective acts of caring for forcibly displaced people (familiar strangers) who suffer in the context, and as a consequence, of the shortcomings of global governance regimes. I have argued that refugee diaspora organizations (RDOs) are distinct humanitarian actors with modalities and motivations that reflect the positionality of refugees who are resettled in countries like Australia. This chapter turns now to the implications of these findings and the future possibilities for refugee diaspora humanitarianism. We will revisit the intersections between humanitarianism and the international refugee regime, this time exploring how the actions of RDOs fit within or challenge understandings and practices of refugee protection and humanitarian intervention.

This chapter is divided into three broad and overlapping areas where refugee diaspora humanitarianism has implications: for strengthening refugee protection, for diversifying understandings and practices of humanitarianism, and for challenging public discourse in resettlement countries that frame refugees as either victims or threats. As this chapter is concerned with both implications and possibilities, this discussion draws in policy debates as well as the perspectives of humanitarian professionals interviewed as part of this study. In many ways, what follows is intended to be both practical and an imagining of what could be if refugee diaspora humanitarianism was better realized and recognized.

STRENGTHENING REFUGEE PROTECTION

As described in chapter 1, the international refugee regime can be understood as a dominant structure governing global responses to particular situations of forced displacement. The lack of effectiveness in realizing the durable solutions espoused by this regime has resulted in two notable trends: a steady rise in the number of people living in protracted refugee situations and the increasing irregularity and onward movement of people seeking protection and failing to find it, resulting in more people living precariously in the "margins of the world" (Agier 2008). Refugees often rely on or seek help from humanitarian actors who govern in the spaces that states have ceded or abandoned (Ferguson and Gupta 2002). At the same time, the professionalized, bureaucratized, and rationalized world of dominant humanitarianism has been criticized as an arena whereby resources, legitimacy, and status are contested, where governance is asymmetrical and hierarchical, and where accountability to the people that humanitarians serve is often superseded by other interests.

Yet even those who are critical of dominant forms of humanitarianism see the importance of helping those who are distant from us, particularly where there is such inequity, injustice, and suffering in the world, and the awareness of suffering and the possibility to do something about it are enabled by "new mobilities" (Sheller and Urry 2006). Indeed, responses to forced displacement are constantly being challenged from within and have evolved through considerable soul-searching and introspection by dominant actors themselves (Barnett 2011). Some of those providing the most critical perspectives have worked within humanitarian organizations. For example, Hugo Slim was former head of policy for the International Committee of the Red Cross (ICRC), Didier Fassin and Michel Agier both worked for Médecins Sans Frontières (MSF), Jeff Crisp and Kristin Bergtora Sandvik for the United Nations High Commissioner for Refugees (UNHCR), and Miriam Ticktin for various human rights organizations. Many leaders within the international refugee regime have also openly acknowledged the inherent shortcomings of traditional approaches to meeting the protection needs of refugees and have argued for better ways of doing things (see Türk 2011, 2019; Türk and Garlick 2016). To use the parlance of the humanitarian aid industry, the need to "innovate" has never been greater.[1]

THE CHANGING LANDSCAPE OF REFUGEE PROTECTION

There have been several trends in refugee protection policy and practice in response to the shortcomings of the international refugee regime to realize timely and durable solutions to displacement, and the limited capacity of humanitarian actors to mobilize sufficient resources to meet the needs of all who require international protection. There have been attempts to draw in nontraditional humanitarian actors, including development agencies and the private sector, as well as a drive toward innovation in how programs are designed and implemented with the aim of creating greater efficiencies. There has been a growing recognition of the significance of local actors in ensuring refugees can live in dignity and safety and a push toward the localization of humanitarian responses (discussed below). And finally, there has been a growing recognition of the agency of forcibly displaced people and a move toward humanitarian actors working to strengthen existing community support structures. It is the latter of these trends—seen in the rise of community-based protection (CBP) and self-reliance discourses (for example, see *The Nation* 2017)—that I focus on here.[2]

Community-Based Protection

That refugees are active participants in finding solutions to the protection challenges they face is hardly a groundbreaking idea.[3] Though displaced persons are frequently represented in public discourse as voiceless, vulnerable, and passive victims (Malkki 1996), their agency in negotiating their own solutions has been described in detail by many scholars (see Bakewell 2008; De Montclos 2008; Harley and Hobbs 2020; Harrell-Bond 2002; Harrell-Bond and Voutira 2007; Hilhorst and Jansen 2010; Horst 2006a; Monsutti 2008; Sandvik 2009; Uehling 1998; Zetter and Long 2012). As Erica Bornstein and Peter Redfield remind us, "acts of care" within communities go on in times of disaster just as they do in everyday life (2010, 252). Yet much of what this research on refugee agency has shown is how people deploy their own individual or group strategies to survive, sometimes despite or against the actions, policies, or objectives of humanitarian actors.[4] Less well interrogated is how humanitarian actors—and particularly those with the greatest power over the lives of refugees—engage refugee populations through participatory processes.

While there is less scholarly research on refugee participation in humanitarian governance, references to participatory approaches are frequently found in policy discourses. In parallel with the development industry, humanitarian actors have increasingly talked about refugee participation, even where critics point to the limitations of the participatory approaches deployed (see Barnett 2005; Benner et al. 2008). In an article titled "Neglect of Refugee Participation," Marie Theres Benner and colleagues argue that "the participation of affected populations in planning or implementation of humanitarian aid in conflict or post-conflict situations has too often been neglected" (2008, 25). These authors contend that participatory approaches have been "reduced to providing staff for health and education services and food distribution—to the administration of activities rather than the design and planning of programmes" (Benner et al. 2008, 25) and that participatory approaches have reinforced inequalities between humanitarian professionals and affected communities through hierarchies in divisions of labor.

Michael Barnett is particularly scathing in his analysis of the distance between affected populations and humanitarian workers: "In the typical humanitarian case, the ruling class is made up of well-to-do foreigners, and local populations largely provide security, support, and menial labor in a way that is reminiscent of earlier empires. In fact, aid agencies have even developed a 'remote control' system that allows headquarters to direct field operations carried out by locals. . . . In the pursuit of effectiveness, humanitarian governance has become more professionalized and bureaucratic, probably improving its efficiency but potentially at the cost of expanding local participation" (2011, 222).

The concept of CBP has been a more recent iteration of participatory approaches in refugee policy and humanitarian governance. While the rise of CBP may have a longer history, UNHCR only released its Protection Policy Paper, *Understanding Community-Based Protection*, to clarify its approach in 2013. This paper lays out twelve key lessons of CBP for UNHCR staff, including: CBP "is a *process*, not a project" (lesson 1); community counterparts should be selected with care (lesson 2); "communities are well placed to identify protection challenges but external partners also have an important role" (lesson 3); and "communities already employ protection measures" (lesson 5) (UNHCR 2013).

Although more clearly articulated than the amorphous concept of *refugee participation*, CBP still assumes a central relationship (and division) between affected communities and external actors. A document developed by the Humanitarian Practice Network is illustrative of this. It states that CBP requires "a reorientation of operational protection frameworks that reflects the right, capacity and desire of crisis-affected communities to engage, and be engaged, in *international humanitarian efforts* to enhance their protection" (Berry and Reddy 2010, 1, emphasis added). Reorientation still assumes the centrality of external efforts and differs only in terms of how those implementing CBP approaches are more directly focused on engaging people from affected communities in planning and implementation. In short, the CBP agenda can be seen as an acknowledgment of both the existent capacity within affected populations and the need to retain the expertise of humanitarian professionals who can carefully guide, enable, or watch over community processes so that they align with what are accepted protection practices.

One of the potentials of CBP models is the possibility of shifting decision-making power and resources from institutionalized actors to affected populations. This was something that Barbara Harrell-Bond argued many years ago when she cynically suggested that "self-distribution is . . . unlikely to be any more arbitrary than what actually happens when organizations distribute aid" (2002, 57).

Bornstein and Redfield offer a similar analysis of the international response to the Haitian earthquake in 2010: "With bare hands and minimal tools Haitians rescued far more of their own than any of the specialized teams with their elaborate equipment" (2010, 252). Yet this is a potentiality that requires some radical reconfiguration on the part of dominant humanitarian actors, as it involves the (possible) relinquishing of power and resources and leaves open the possibility of a diversification of ideas about what *protection* is and how to go about it. This is a significant change, as refugee protection—like other forms of humanitarian response—has been highly professionalized and rationalized into widely accepted and replicated frameworks; there are easy-to-remember acronyms like AGD (age, gender, diversity) and industry shorthand like the protection "egg model."[5] If affected communities were enabled in ways that developed or supported their own models of protection—if it was community-*led* protection rather than community-*based* protection—things could look quite different.

One of the challenges of CBP is how to bring together the knowledge and perspectives of affected communities on an equal footing with the knowledge and perspectives of humanitarian professionals. This would require a significant shift, as suggested by some of my informants, who narrated suffering in terms of the disabling and disempowering experiences of seeking help. Even in the documentation and discussions about CBP, a distinction between *professionals* and *communities* is made quite clear. Take, for example, the following case study from UNHCR's CBP Policy Paper:

> When the 2004 tsunami struck one community in north eastern Sri Lanka, people helped one another from being swept away without considering whether the person at risk was Tamil, Muslim or Sinhalese. People at a community level had always turned to others in the community for support, and helpers continued to play this expected role after the tsunami hit. Within a few weeks, however, international [nongovernmental organizations] NGOs entered the area with large sums of money, hired most of the natural helpers, and paid people for their work. This had the effect of dismantling community support structures and monetized helping behaviour. Within six weeks of the tsunami, most people had stopped helping each other spontaneously and expected to be paid for doing tasks that previously they would have done without charge. Local people referred to the destruction of their helping system as the "Golden Tsunami." (UNHCR 2013, 36)

This story, indicated by its title—"Financial Interventions, if Poorly Planned, Can Distort Well-Intentioned Responses under Certain Circumstances"—warns against monetizing helping behavior within communities. It suggests making sure that local people continue to help each other, even if that means they are not paid in ways that "outsiders" (aid workers) presumably are.[6] References such as these—and particularly the recurrence of the term *sustainability* and the repeated focus on the challenges of directly resourcing community-led initiatives—hint at how the CBP agenda is also partly about reducing costs while retaining the need for, and expertise of, humanitarian professionals.

At the same time, it is important not to be overly critical of the cautious approach evident in discussions about CBP. The possibility of shifting power, resources, and decision-making from humanitarian professionals to affected communities is not straightforward and presents complex challenges. This is particularly the case in emergency situations, where social networks are disrupted and people have not had time to regroup. How, for example, does decision-making happen when a group of people are brought together potentially under traumatic circumstances and may not be characterized as a community at all?

The messiness of creating community connections in a displacement context was evident during my fieldwork in Indonesia, where I observed the coming together of a group of Oromo asylum seekers to form an association. This could be considered a community-*led* initiative, with no external actor involved in instigating the association. It was also a fraught process. The association was being formed to represent and support a group of two hundred mostly unrelated people of varying demographics (university students in their early twenties alongside older women with children) who had arrived in Indonesia over a two-year period and had not found a space or way to meet prior to the visit of the RDO in 2015. Knowing who was who among this group in Indonesia, who the natural leaders were, how they would ensure the needs of the diverse community were identified and represented, and how to support those who were particularly vulnerable—those in remote detention centers, unaccompanied minors, the elderly and sick—presented complex challenges. Yet these were challenges that were being actively discussed and negotiated. The difficulties this group faced establishing a community association highlighted the importance of creating spaces for people to come together to develop their own support networks and of identifying external actors who could support the strengthening of these networks and mediate when needed. This experience also highlighted the potential role of RDOs in CBP initiatives that could act as both *insiders* and *outsiders*.

Refugee Diasporas and Community-Based Protection

From a critical standpoint, CBP and the localization agenda can be understood as part of a broader trend of shifting responsibility for refugee protection from the international to the local and from states to civil society. These trends are echoed in many other spheres of governance and have been linked to "neoliberalization" (Harvey 2005) and its "demands for self-sufficiency and its attempts to shunt the burden of caring for the unfortunate onto the unfortunate themselves" (Dunn

2014, 193; see also Ferguson 2009). Even so, these shifts also present the possibility of redistributing some power and resources to people who have hitherto been the objects of humanitarian assistance, albeit in modest ways. Such a possibility is dependent on how concepts like *the local* and *communities* are understood and translated from policy into practice. What, for example, constitutes *a community,* and what do *local actors* look like? What can local actors do that is distinct from their international counterparts? Does localization mean different models of protection or just differently funded providers? In short, how are lines drawn around *communities, the local,* and *the international* in spaces that are dynamic, mobile, and contested?

CBP and localization are both relatively recent and evolving debates within policy and practitioner circles, but the mobility, dynamism, and contestation of *the local* and what constitutes *community* has been understated in some discussions. For example, communities are often discussed in geographically bound terms, despite the obvious and evident mobility and fluidity of refugee populations.[7] Likewise, the term *local actors* as a distinct category from *international actors* appears insufficiently or superficially understood in geographically bound or state-centric ways. There are, of course, more nuanced ways of understanding both *the local* and *communities* that embrace the dynamism inherent in these terms, but nuance and policymaking that requires clear lines for decision-making are not always compatible. Even so, pushing the boundaries of these terms creates possibilities and spaces for diverse actors—including RDOs—to be more fully understood and incorporated in efforts to strengthen refugee protection.

Transnational Communities, (Trans)Local Actors

How communities are perceived has practical implications for who is engaged in discussions on protection risks, priorities, and responses. On a more abstract level, communities can be characterized in various ways. They can be grouped by common interests (e.g., a scientific community or the NGO community), a common ecology and locality (e.g., the highlands community or a school community), or a common social system or structure (e.g., the Canadian community, the Muslim community). It is widely accepted that people exist within multiple overlapping communities that are contested and dynamic. This concept, however, does not translate easily into policy and organizational practices that require delineation and categorization. When it comes to CBP policy, references to *a community* as a static entity abound. What is meant by *a community* frequently relates to people (refugees) who share a common locality—to the population of a refugee camp or urban area, for example, or to people from the same country of origin living in a geographical area (e.g., the Syrian refugee community in Lebanon).

CBP is most often framed, and perhaps rightly so, in terms of geographically proximate communities—of the practices of local host populations into whose space refugees enter and reside, and the community structures that are formed within place-based refugee populations.

Yet forcibly displaced people are also, quite obviously, part of transnational communities. Refugees must cross at least one state border to be recognized as such, and most maintain active connections with people in their homelands as well as other parts of the world. It should come as no surprise that the connections that people draw on for support in difficult times are not only those that are geographically proximate. But perhaps a better way of thinking about communities of support in the context of forced displacement is not as transnational, but as *translocal*. As Arjun Appadurai (1996) has argued, translocality describes the ways in which emplaced communities become extended via the geographical mobility of their inhabitants across sending and destination contexts. This concept foregrounds the significance of locality without restricting the understanding of locality to that within the nation-state (see also Conradson and McKay 2007). This idea of translocality is useful because it also incorporates the experience of internal displacement; of people who may not cross an international border but are forced to move from one locality to another in search of safety. Moreover, the term *translocal communities* usefully describes the social networks integral to refugee diaspora humanitarianism. They are emplaced but also mobile and connected.

It is not hard to find evidence of translocal support networks that forcibly displaced people draw on to strengthen their ability to live in safety and dignity. This has long been recognized by those highlighting the significance of remittance-sending practices to refugee protection (see Barnett and Weiss 2011, 26; DEMAC 2016b; Monsutti 2004).[8] But translocal communities do more than send money. Translocal CBP, as this research has shown, takes many forms. Collective remittances, information, ideas, and other acts of solidarity that flow between people who are geographically distant but who connect as a community are significant. The RDO in Australia that provides direct funding to Hazara community-based organizations (CBOs) in Pakistan, for example, enhances protection by strengthening capacity and leadership within refugee communities. So too is protection strengthened when those in the wider diaspora share information about the potential risks and dangers of journeys in search of protection or advocate for and mobilize resources to help people find safer places to live, such as the Palestinian RDO (ASPIRE) profiled in chapter 2.

Understanding refugees as part of translocal communities means seeing the potential for enhanced protection but also how these communities can be implicated in undermining protection. During my fieldwork, when the security situation in Iraq and Syria deteriorated significantly, I became aware of many people in Australia not only sending remittances but also actively supporting strategies to help family members, friends, and others from their community find safer places to live. Some of these strategies seemed misinformed or ineffective. For example, some people were paying migration agents exorbitant fees to facilitate resettlement, even though these agents could not influence a visa outcome, thus reducing the financial resources of people already living in precarious situations. Yet the strategies that were employed by institutional humanitarian actors at this time to address the exploitation of refugees by unscrupulous agents did not appear to see the wider diaspora as part of the community that needed to be engaged. This was despite evidence that a significant amount of the money to pay agents was coming from countries like Australia, Canada, and the United States and that misinformation about the effectiveness of these strategies was being fueled by some within the wider diaspora.

The idea and practices of CBP—of strengthening the social networks of support that displaced people are able to draw on to find safety and security—warrant further consideration and development. They acknowledge that people do not stop helping one another in times of crisis and that social networks can be vitally important resources. At the same time, *communities* need to be conceptualized more dynamically than in ways that privilege geographical proximity. In the case of refugees living in places from where there has been resettlement, it is unlikely that the connections between those who are resettled and those who remain will cease at the point of departure. Where trans*local* communities emerge—including through the mobilization of RDOs in resettlement countries—there is the potential to enhance protection for those who are not resettled. As this research has shown, those in the wider diaspora (former refugees) have distinct capacities to help. And while refugee diaspora humanitarianism is not an inevitability, this research has shown that it is a common experience for resettled refugees to find ways to support *their people* from afar. In seeing refugees as part of translocal communities, then, community support networks (and CBP) should also be viewed with a wider lens. Translocal communities are able to draw on potentially more diverse resources, ideas, and information than more narrowly place-based communities, and this has the potential to both undermine and strengthen refugee protection. What effect the wider diaspora has on strengthening refugee protection very much depends on whether or how they are considered or included in discussions about CBP.

DIVERSIFYING HUMANITARIANISM

There are many overlaps in imagining how RDOs could further strengthen protection practices and how these kinds of organizations could play a role in diversifying understandings and practices of humanitarianism. To return to the discussion in chapter 1, how can spaces be created for strengthening *diverse* humanitarian responses? Is the localization agenda that came out of the 2016 World Humanitarian Summit an opportunity for RDOs to bridge the local and the international? And how can the perspectives of refugee diasporas inform ideas about suffering and responses to suffering?

Spaces for Diverse Humanitarianisms

In many ways, the time is ripe for diversification within the humanitarian arena. Although there are still only a relatively small number of dominant humanitarian actors, these same actors are actively seeking new partners, sources of funding, and ways of doing things. The World Humanitarian Summit in 2016 was illustrative of the transformations taking place in this field, although there are critics who have suggested that the pace and scope of reform is too modest or misdirected (see Bennett and Foley 2016; Parker 2016). Yet alongside discussions about the diversification of humanitarianism, there are tensions and debate about "new" humanitarian actors, including questions about how these actors adhere to humanitarian principles and what actions should be labeled *humanitarian* in the first instance.

A main area of contestation when it comes to the diversification of ideas and practices is how different humanitarian actors are identified and given legitimacy to act because of their adherence (or otherwise) to humanitarian principles of neutrality, impartiality, and independence. Even though it has been argued that these principles are aspirational and have been imperfectly applied in the messiness of humanitarian contexts (see Barnett 2005; Fassin and Pandolfi 2010), they have also been instrumental in allowing identifiable humanitarian actors—and particularly multilateral agencies, the Red Cross and Crescent movement, and international nongovernmental organizations (INGOs)—access to populations in desperate need of assistance. There is therefore understandable anxiety about how the diversification of actors will water down the hard-fought-for humanitarian identity of more established actors, potentially undermining their capacity to create safe spaces to deliver life-saving assistance in times of conflict.

On the other hand, Christina Bennett and Matthew Foley suggest that the legitimacy of humanitarian actors—particularly those who wear a Western face—has already been too sullied and that "despite a decade of system-wide reforms, the sector still falls short in the world's most enduring crisis responses, and perceptions of humanitarian work in recent crises suggest that the formal, Western 'system' is not doing a good job in the eyes of the people it aims to help" (2016, 68). The consequences of this crisis of legitimacy have been evident in conflicts such as that in Syria, where neither the Syrian regime nor armed groups have recognized international humanitarian actors in the apolitical terms in which they wish to be seen (DEMAC 2016b). The same can be said for the war in Ukraine (Slim 2022). Indeed, the *lack* of diversity among dominant humanitarian actors may have contributed more to this distrust than the emergence of new actors.

As described in chapter 1, the humanitarian arena has hitherto been dominated by a small number of larger organizations with remarkably similar genealogies. One of the key criticisms leveled at these actors is that they have evolved to reinforce an order with asymmetrical power, both in terms of organizational actors—with multilateral and larger international organizations at the top and local organizations at the bottom—and between humanitarian workers and the people that they serve. The influence of a small number of organizations within this order has created dominant practices that are perpetuated by professionalization, rationalization, and bureaucratization within the field. Barnett explains this by drawing from sociological institutionalism, a branch of organizational theory that emphasizes the "socially constructed normative worlds in which organizations exist and how the social rules, standards of appropriateness, and models of legitimacy will constitute the organization" (2005, 729). Barnett writes that "because organizations are rewarded for conforming to rules and legitimization principles, and punished if they do not, they tend to model themselves after organizational forms that have legitimacy" (2005, 729).

This idea of legitimization is an important one, particularly for future diversification of humanitarianism. Dorothea Hilhorst and Bram Jansen argue that conceptualizing humanitarianism as an arena recognizes that humanitarian action is based on a range of driving forces, including "organizational politics—the desire to continue operations and retain staff—or as a form of legitimization politics—showing the public that the agency is doing good work" (2010, 1122). Moreover, vying for space, resources, and legitimacy within this arena may mean crowding out or delegitimizing other actors, including by questioning their adherence to the humanitarian principles whose moral force carries this quality of "untouchability" (Fassin 2010d). Indeed, this process of legitimization and delegitimization could be seen unfolding during the World Humanitarian Summit, where diasporas featured more and more in discussions (DEMAC 2016b, 2016a). The legitimacy of diasporas as humanitarian actors has been questioned on the grounds of a lack of perceived adherence to humanitarian principles and their (perceived or actual) involvement in taking sides in a conflict. But other questions have been raised of a more mundane, technical manner: Are smaller RDOs efficient and effective humanitarian responders? How do these kinds of organizations connect or coordinate with others? Do they have the resources or institutional capacity to implement sustainable and larger-scale interventions? As this research has confirmed, these are important and valid questions.

Yet, regardless of whether the wider humanitarian system recognizes or chooses to engage with RDOs or not, these organizations will continue to act when and where *their people* suffer. The forces that compel diaspora humanitarians are considerable, particularly as mobilities enable both an awareness of suffering and the injustices of living in a vastly unequal world and the capacity for people to connect and to act translocally. This was apparent when I asked participants from RDOs whether they would consider either donating directly to, or working for, a more established humanitarian organization. Many were quick to respond that they would not, as they believed their own organizations helped in more direct, effective ways. More so, many felt an obligation to help directly—and in solidarity. This obligation could not be fulfilled by channeling support through a professional aid organization, even one assisting their own people.

The disconnect between the ideologies and foundations underlying refugee diaspora and other dominant forms of humanitarianism was evident when I conversed with professionals working in the field. Mingo, who works for a large humanitarian organization, spoke about how the INGO she worked for and RDOs differed:

> For organizations like [mine] it's all about at least attempting to uphold principles of neutrality and independence and—[while] most will debate whether anybody can be truly neutral and independent—[we] work very hard to strive for [this]. So, a diaspora organization working within, let's say, the Syrian opposition movement, will still reach out to people in need but it does so on the base of [not] being neutral and independent, but on behalf of a political siding with one group or the other. It is a completely different universe that diasporas work [in] compared to professional aid organizations. . . . We work in different paradigms [and it raises the question of] how we ever could cooperate, because [it's] a very strong ideological clash.[9]

This research raises the idea that refugee diaspora humanitarianism could complement and strengthen international responses to humanitarian crises while at the same time acknowledging the various paradigms in which different actors operate. For the most part, RDOs work parallel to other actors, with opportunities missed for constructive collaboration, mutual learning, and coordination. An earlier illustration about humanitarian knowledge—the Afghan RDO that worked to support a school in one village where they had connections but were unaware of what other organizations were doing or planning to do—highlighted this. They simply had no way of finding out how their own activities corresponded with those being planned or undertaken by others and vice versa.

For Mingo, larger international humanitarian agencies and smaller diaspora organizations have different strengths and perspectives that can be complementary.

In our interview, she started off by commenting on how larger organizations have advantages in being able to engage more easily with institutional actors such as government authorities. On the other hand, she said:

> There is a lot that smaller volunteer organizations can do that large organizations cannot do. They have better networks with people on the ground and firsthand information of what the real needs are. . . . And sometimes it helps when you are out of a situation to look at it from that angle and see what can be done. And I think that's the advantage [diasporas] have. [Rather than] just supporting because of a passion to support, they have firsthand experience of what it means to be in that situation and what difference it makes to respond in a particular way.[10]

Jacinta O'Hagan and Miwa Hirono argue that there is a need to cultivate a "cohesive yet pluralist" international humanitarian order through the development of mechanisms of cooperation and coordination "that provide common premises for action while allowing for and respecting a diversity of approaches" (2014, 414; see also Bennett and Foley 2016). Although these authors may have had other (non-Western) states in mind when writing about diverse approaches, it is possible to think of ways in which refugee diasporas could also be part of pluralist coordination and response mechanisms. For example, refugee diaspora engagement in humanitarian responses does and could include the philanthropy and initiatives of RDOs evidenced in this book, remittances sent by family and friends during crises, and professionals from within diaspora communities being employed by humanitarian organizations to bring both technical skills and contextual knowledge to their work (see also Horst et al. 2015). These are significant contributions, yet until very recently there has been little recognition of these various engagements in humanitarian response systems.[11] Creating a voice for these engagements in discussions on humanitarian responses would be a practical first step.

But beyond a space at the table, there are also important implications to consider about how to strengthen refugee diaspora humanitarianism in and of itself and what could work to make RDOs more effective. This is not about instrumentalizing diasporas to fill gaps in a flawed system, but acknowledging that, like all who try to help, these actors have both strengths and weaknesses. Leah, a humanitarian professional who had worked for a large INGO in the Kakuma refugee camp in Kenya for eight years, described her experiences with diaspora helping as such:

> During the recent conflict in South Sudan, we had a lot of former refugee residents in Kakuma who were settled in the diaspora seeking to know [how] they can help. These were very ad hoc and not structured in any particular way. I think that the communities in the diaspora can contribute a lot [in these]

> situations. . . . It would be better if these [diaspora] organizations looked at ways of working in partnership with organizations that are already there or looked at the coordination mechanisms and structures that are in place. . . . I think that would be a good practice.[12]

As this quote suggests, those in the wider diaspora may be ready to contribute to humanitarian crisis responses, but in the absence of any facilitating structures, this desire to help can pose challenges for effective coordination. As an early report from the Diaspora Emergency Action and Coordination (DEMAC 2016b) project suggests, "Diaspora relief, if not sufficiently resourced and coordinated, can also be too ad-hoc, sporadic and fractured to be sustainable" (2016b, 8). Having said this, there are many practical ways that these challenges can be addressed, including by developing diaspora coordination platforms, creating opportunities for diaspora contributions to be channeled through larger diaspora organizations or networks, and finding ways to ensure information about response planning is disseminated and accessible to diaspora organizations so as to inform their own knowledge of needs and gaps. To be clear, finding ways to include diasporas in coordination planning is not just about resourcing; it is about creating spaces for knowledge and ideas to be exchanged and recognizing refugee diasporas as legitimate actors in pluralist humanitarian ecosystems.

Diaspora Humanitarianism and the Localization Agenda

Earlier I described RDOs as trans*local* actors that create people-to-people connections across international borders. This raises a question about how RDOs fit within the localization agenda that has commanded so much attention in the lead-up and aftermath of the 2016 World Humanitarian Summit. Briefly, the humanitarian aid localization agenda can be understood as the push for more resources to go directly to national or local rather than international actors. This push has been spearheaded by some of the leading humanitarian donors and aid agencies through the *Grand Bargain* and the *Charter for Change*. The thirty donors and agencies that signed the *Grand Bargain* committed to achieving "by 2020 a global, aggregated target of at least 25 per cent of humanitarian funding to local and national responders" (Agenda for Humanity 2016, 5). The *Charter for Change* involved eight commitments that INGOs voluntarily agreed to implement by May 2018. These included commitments to increase direct funding so that 20 percent of INGO funding for humanitarian action is transferred to Southern-based NGOs, increase transparency around resource transfers to Southern-based national and local NGOs, and provide support to build local humanitarian capacity

(Charter4Change 2016). The fact that only 3.1 percent of humanitarian funding *was* actually channeled through either local or national actors in 2018 (Development Initiatives 2019, 64) suggests that efforts to realize these ambitious commitments have been less than forthcoming.

Part of the difficulty of localization is that what *the local* means was poorly elaborated in the first place. What is meant by *local* in this agenda, and what, exactly, is being localized? For example, does localization mean decisions are made closer to the ground, including with people who are affected by disaster and conflict? Is it more about resource allocation and efficiencies, reducing the amount of budget spent on expensive international staff, and setting up parallel systems? Is localization about changing the humanitarian response system more broadly or just changing who is paid within this system? What makes an organization a local actor, and what else must they do or represent in order to be considered more effective than international actors in their response? There are many grappling with these sorts of questions, especially within humanitarian organizations, highlighting that the implementation of ideas that require fundamental shifts within complex systems is rarely straightforward.

Trying to place RDOs within this localization agenda illustrates the challenges of shaping a system based on actor type or location. Where, for example, would an RDO that sought funding from international donors be considered in this schema of international versus national or local? Where, indeed, would refugee-led organizations be placed if *local* is understood in more territorialized terms (i.e., as nationals or citizens of the state in which an intervention takes place)? If we see local actors in a refugee situation as those most closely connected to affected populations, then refugee-led organizations—and even RDOs working translocally—may well see the benefits of the push toward localization. That only 0.1 percent of humanitarian funding went to local NGOs in 2018 (Development Initiatives 2019, 64), and funding to refugee-led organizations is even rarer (Ealom 2021), suggests that there is still a long way to go before funding is distributed directly to organizations led by affected populations. With regard to refugee diaspora humanitarianism more specifically, it is not hard to imagine how the localization agenda will make RDOs even more invisible or marginal in humanitarian coordination and response systems, as international actors work toward shifting resources to more identifiable local agencies and avoiding partnerships with actors that cannot easily be accounted for in a schema of local/national/international.

Diversifying Ideas about Suffering and Caring

Barnett has argued that "humanitarianism is nothing less than a revolution in the ethics of care" that has been carried out in the name of "the international community"—a community that is "not as universal, transcendental, and cosmopolitan as its leaders presumed" (2011, 18). Barnett and other humanitarianism scholars have critiqued the rise of a dominant form of humanitarianism for depoliticizing structural problems of inequality and domination. Yet even these critics acknowledge that humanitarianism operates like a field in the Bourdieuian sense, with its actors "committed to competing definitions of the issues involved in humanitarianism and the best way to meet them" (Fassin 2010a, 279). In other words, this is a field of contestation not only of actors but also of ideas. Refugee diaspora humanitarianism, envisioned and practiced by RDOs in countries like Australia, involves a distinct type of actor and brings with it different ideas about suffering and the practices of caring.

To start with, refugee diaspora humanitarianism is a practice of solidarity that is characterized by a less asymmetrical relationship between those who help and those who suffer. Refugee diaspora humanitarians, like other humanitarians, are removed from the situation of displacement (suffering), but this disconnect is of a different nature. For individuals or groups who self-identify with the affected population—or who have recently lived in a similar situation—the line between helpers and helped can be blurrier. In the previous chapter, this was illustrated in describing how RDO members move in and out of humanitarian contexts in ways that other outsiders cannot, drawing on their distinct capacities: mobility, (in)visibility, knowledge, and networks. The small scale and informal people-to-people helping of refugee diaspora humanitarianism allow ideas to be generated through an ongoing dialogue between those in displacement contexts and those living in the wider diaspora. These are conversations that do not begin at the point of an RDO forming or deciding to do something; there is a longer and potentially messier history. For observers, the things that RDOs do can seem, as Leah described, "ad hoc." But perhaps this is because these acts are not meant to be models that can be replicated or scaled up; they are highly contextualized, localized, and temporal. RDOs are not confined to replicating models that seem to have worked more or less in other similar situations. What matters for RDOs is that they do something for *these people*, in *this place*, at *this time*. Indeed, Leah went on to speak about this when she reflected on the potential for refugee diasporas' knowledge to inform practices of bigger actors: "I think [diasporas] could actually have a lot of valuable input even to the way programming is done by these large organizations, because sometimes we are caught up in a system that does things almost without thinking too much about it."[13]

In terms of diversifying ideas about what it is to care for strangers in need (humanitarianism), RDOs offer context-specific understandings of suffering and how to respond, and they grasp the importance of helping in ways that are nonquantifiable. It is worth restating Barnett's lament about "the neglect of non-quantifiable goals such as witnessing, being present, conferring dignity, and demonstrating solidarity" as institutional humanitarianism focuses on what is measurable (2011, 216). Barnett asks: "If these activities and their impacts cannot be operationalized, will they be left outside of the model? And, if so, will humanitarian agencies privilege those activities and outcomes that can be measured, thus altering the basic ethical calculations that underpin their interventions?" (2011, 216).

Refugee diaspora humanitarianism seems to offer much by way of nonquantifiable acts of caring—of standing in solidarity, of bearing witness and amplifying the voices of those who are displaced. There is no accounting, for instance, for what a small group of Oromo-Australians achieved by traveling to Indonesia to meet with a group of asylum seekers there. This act was as much a demonstration of solidarity and community building as it was a transfer of modest resources to a small number of people trying to survive in extremely difficult circumstances. As another of my interviewees, Rosanna, said, "It is not always [about] sending the money. You also have to send the message."[14] As to what the message is that refugee diaspora humanitarians send, perhaps it is that refugees have not been forgotten, that they have a voice, that there is a community that is scattered around the world and that can be called on. Importantly, refugee diaspora humanitarians who identify with an affected population perceive and recognize the suffering of displacement in its collective form, not only through a lens of individual suffering but also through the lens of suffering that is brought about by the rupturing of social fabric. Their responses, then, should be seen in terms of the nonquantifiable and complex process of reconfiguring, recreating, and supporting existing social networks in contexts of forced displacement.

In many ways, refugee diaspora humanitarianism is complementary to other humanitarianisms. RDOs do what other (larger) actors cannot or do not have the capacity to do. There are many examples of this that came through in my research. For example, Raj spoke about the lack of care for Bhutanese refugees in camps who are "too sick" or "not sick enough." He said: "If you are not that sick, you don't get treatment because you are not too sick. And if you are chronically ill, you don't get treatment because it costs too much for the aid agencies; you have to be in between to get treatment."[15] And so, members of the Bhutanese diaspora help on either side of the "in between"—sending collective remittances to care for the chronically ill and for dignified burials, and individual remittances for families with members not sick enough but still needing care.

The same can be said for the many examples of RDO education projects that I came across. While there is widespread acknowledgment of the need for refugees to be able to access education, the provision of postprimary education is often not prioritized (or possible) within underresourced humanitarian budgets. When RDOs fund postprimary education projects, they are supporting something that other humanitarian actors would undoubtedly endorse if they had the capacity themselves to respond. In many ways, RDOs have much greater flexibility to identify and respond to gaps and to try out new ideas. They are not looking at a situation with specific frameworks, budgets, and time frames in mind and making decisions based on this; they are talking to people within an affected population about what is needed and what is possible in their particular situation and then trying to make it happen.

There is much to be said in favor of creating a less asymmetrical, more diverse humanitarian response system. While larger humanitarian actors remain important, particularly in coordinating large-scale and rapid responses to sudden-onset emergencies, responses to various displacement contexts could be made stronger through the diversification of actors and ideas. This is not about making new actors fit into existing models, but about creating spaces for the coordination, collaboration, and recognition of the various strengths and capacities of different actors, big and small. In this space, RDOs could be recognized as legitimate and distinct actors that tap into potentially strong translocal social networks and have the ability and willingness to mobilize resources and support for populations in need. At the same time, what RDOs do is likely to be highly variable and context-specific. The paradigm in which diaspora humanitarians work (being connected to and compelled to help a particular group of people in a particular situation) may not lend itself to being instrumentalized or scaled up to fill gaps. However, the ways in which RDOs help could complement the wider system if better channels existed for engagement and exchange.

Opening up space in humanitarian dialogue for smaller actors like RDOs may also allow for the diversification of ideas about what constitutes acts of caring in responses to forced displacement. Refugee diaspora humanitarians offer a unique perspective, gained through lived experience and the capacity of individuals to reflect on this from the privileged spaces of countries where they now hold a passport or residency. The insights of those in the wider diaspora who have been past recipients of humanitarian assistance or who have embedded understanding of local contexts could well inform other humanitarian actors as they design, implement, and evaluate responses. Perhaps refugee diaspora engagement in the broader field of humanitarianism could lead to international responses that more fully recognize collective forms of suffering alongside the physical suffering of individual bodies and the power and significance of community-led responses that recreate or strengthen social networks of care.

ENABLING REFUGEE DIASPORA TRANSNATIONALISM IN RESETTLEMENT STATES

The final implication of refugee diaspora humanitarianism I will touch on here relates to what these actors and actions could potentially mean for countries where refugees resettle. While this section focuses specifically on Australia, there are likely similar observations to be made about other resettlement states—the United States, Canada, New Zealand, and in Europe. Indeed, many of my participants referred to organizations similar to theirs in other countries where wider diasporas reside, suggesting structural dimensions underlying refugee diaspora humanitarianism. It was not within the scope of this research to compare how wider diasporas mobilize in different contexts, although this would be an interesting question for future comparative research. What is important to note here is that, although this book highlights the transnational, mobile, and dynamic practices of RDOs, the significance of place should not be underplayed. Although there are likely to be similarities in experiences of refugee diaspora mobilization in other parts of the world, there are also specificities of history, society, institutions, place, and so on that will color how refugee diasporas mobilize and act in different contexts. In other words, to understand the movement of people, ideas, and practices across space, it is important to consider forces including, but not confined to, the policies of states (see Gamlen 2019 for an excellent comparative study of state diaspora engagement policies).

The findings from this research about diverse refugee diaspora groups mobilizing for the purposes of helping suggest that there is an enabling environment that allows these types of organizations to form in Australia. At the same time and evidenced in previous chapters, RDOs face common challenges that suggest there are also forces within the Australian context that inhibit transnational practices of caring, including policies that limit remittance sending, the lack of resources available to support the governance capacities (sustainability) of RDOs, and institutional restrictions that limit the mobility for some groups of refugees. The remainder of this chapter focuses on these challenges and possibilities, first by looking at current understandings of refugees, diasporas, mobility, and transnationalism in Australian government policy and then by imagining spaces where refugee diaspora humanitarianism could be more clearly envisioned and enabled.

Diaspora Transnationalism from Australia

To understand how refugee diaspora humanitarianism is enabled or inhibited within the Australian context, we must consider how RDOs as actors are envisaged in policy and practice. If one looks at evidence within current government policy, the answer seems to be that diaspora humanitarianism is not seen at all. There is no obvious reference to diaspora organizations helping in humanitarian situations. Having said this, diaspora transnationalism is starting to attract attention in Australian research, policy, and practice discussions, with the inaugural Diasporas in Action: Working Together for Peace, Development and Humanitarian Response conference taking place in Melbourne in 2016, funded by the

Australian government and opened by the Minister for International Development and the Pacific (Diaspora Learning Network 2016). A second Diasporas in Action conference was held in 2018. More broadly, and following the growing interest internationally in the "migration-development nexus" (Fullilove 2008; Gropas 2013; Nyberg-Sørensen et al. 2002), there is emergent interest in Australia in diasporas as development actors, in their engagements in conflict situations (with a focus on diasporas' negative engagements as foreign fighters or as sources of funding for terrorism rather than as humanitarian actors), and in humanitarian responses to climate-induced disasters in the Pacific, a region that is geopolitically significant to Australia. In 2020, the Foreign Affairs, Defence and Trade References Committee in the Australian Senate held an inquiry into issues facing diaspora communities in Australia.

While at the time of writing there was no evidence of specific Australian government policy pertaining to diasporas and humanitarian responses in refugee situations, it could be argued that government policy is generally enabling in several important ways.[16] First, the mobility and potential that are enabled by being granted permanent residency status or citizenship in Australia—of being able to leave, return to, and live in a place where basic rights are afforded—should not be understated. In addition, Australia's official policy of multiculturalism, whatever its recognized and real shortcomings, and the country's historically robust policies toward civil society organizations allow for associational forms like RDOs to be recognized as legal entities. As outlined in chapter 4, it is not hard to create and register an incorporated association, for whatever this is worth. Likewise, the formation of an incorporated association based on a diasporic identity is supported by both government policies (multiculturalism) and a context in which there is a long history of migrant groups self-organizing for mutual support.

But alongside these enabling factors, there are also challenges that the Australian context presents for refugee diaspora humanitarianism. These relate to specific policy omissions, such as the lack of articulated policies, funding, or program support to enable diaspora organizations to work more effectively in humanitarian contexts. There are also broader socioenvironmental factors—including racism, socioeconomic marginalization, and structural disadvantage linked to migration and integration—that undermine the capacity of would-be diaspora humanitarians. For refugee and humanitarian entrants, there is an added dimension relating to the symbolism of being labeled a *refugee* and what this enables or, more likely, *dis*enables. The structuring experience of forced displacement and engagement with the international refugee regime is one that does not end when someone is resettled and becomes an Australian permanent resident or even citizen. Being labeled a refugee has symbolic effects that do not automatically change once someone legally becomes "an Australian." Indeed, the symbolic effect of being labeled a refugee, laden with notions of victimhood, vulnerability, voicelessness, and, more recently, latent or potential threat, is one the bearer may have no choice but to wear; it is a label that is conferred.

The recent merging of public discourses about refugees and securitization/ threat is one that presents challenges for refugee diaspora humanitarianism, particularly when former refugees try to assist people in conflict situations. This is evidenced in the public statements made sporadically, but not infrequently, by elected parliamentarians and in the media about the cost of refugees coming to Australia and about their lack of capacity, their neediness, or their dangerous *otherness*. Again, this is not unique to the Australian context. In the public imaginary, refugees are mired by a dubious history of conflict, violence, and suffering. In November 2016, for example, the then Immigration Minister, Peter Dutton, publicly commented on "the mistake" made by previous administrations of allowing Lebanese Muslim refugees to resettle because a small number of second- or third-generation Lebanese Australians had been charged with terrorism-related offenses (Belot 2016).[17] In this case, the refugee label is conferred not only on the children but also on the grandchildren of those who arrived in Australia as refugees, and a link is made between refugees and security threats.[18] Within this context of refugees being framed as victims or threats, it is less surprising that refugee diaspora humanitarianism is rendered invisible. Perhaps this is also because the actions of RDOs are small and are seen as of little significance when cast against stark figures of global displacement and humanitarian budgets in their billions. But perhaps the invisibility of diaspora humanitarianism, and particularly acts of helping where the actors are identified as refugees, has more to do with the incompatibility of public discourses that portray humanitarians as moral heroes and refugees as victims or threats.

Beyond Victims or Threat

While refugee diaspora humanitarianism may be made invisible or disabled through public discourses and a lack of engagement by policy makers, at least in the Australian context, this research suggests there are alternative ways of framing refugees in public narratives besides as voiceless victims and latent threats. There is little space in public narratives for the humanitarian label to be applied to refugees other than as a trope to describe paying back the gift of resettlement. Bringing the terms *refugee* and *humanitarian* together entails a dissonance that speaks volumes about the assumptions and stereotypes contained within both terms. Yet the profoundly generous and effective ways in which refugee diaspora communities organize and go about helping those in need, quietly and invisibly, hold great potential significance. Just imagine, for example, if the story of young Hazara Australians providing higher education scholarships to refugees in Pakistan was more widely known—with the alumni from this scholarship program becoming future leaders in Afghanistan—and not just accounts of Hazaras as "illegal" maritime arrivals (threats) or the victims of genocide. What sorts of possibilities would be enabled if diaspora transnationalism was envisaged beyond its development potential (rendered in terms of cost-benefit economics) and the involvement of diasporas in homeland politics (rendered as either peacemakers or the fuel to conflicts) toward diasporas as innovative humanitarians?

Of course, diversifying narratives about refugee diasporas to include their role in humanitarian crises overseas is not about replacing the generalizing tropes that currently exist with another. Not every refugee who is resettled will identify in a diasporic way, become involved in an RDO, or engage in acts of helping. At the same time, there *is* something structuring in the experience of forced migration and third-country resettlement that makes refugee diaspora humanitarianism a predictable outcome. People who have lived as refugees, been the recipients of past humanitarian assistance, and gone through the process of third-country resettlement may represent a significantly diverse population, but they also occupy a particular perspective and space. There will be many former refugees with motivations and capacities to help in humanitarian situations and to act in ways that are structured by their past experiences and positionality.

Moreover, there is the possibility for a much wider engagement with the world than is currently envisaged in government policy, in Australia or elsewhere. To explore these possibilities would mean a deeper and broader understanding of diasporic transnational engagements. For example, there is potential for recognizing the distinct skills, knowledge, and networks that resettled refugees offer, not just to the country in which they are resettled or to their countries of origin inhibited but also to the places of asylum or refuge where many remain actively connected. This implies moving discussions about diaspora transnationalism away from the limiting binary of *homeland* and *hostland* and appreciating that diasporas represent people-to-people networks that, in the context of forced displacement, may connect people across many different countries and contexts.

Creating a more enabling environment for refugee diaspora humanitarianism means looking more closely at the *dis*enabling policies that currently exist. For example, antiterrorism regulations disenable transnational flows of money to places and people that are perceived as security threats (de Koker 2014). But these regulations also disenable transnational flows of money to places and people in desperate need of assistance, for whom individual and collective remittances from diaspora communities could amount to much-needed and life-saving help.

When diasporic transnational engagements are looked at primarily through a lens of risk, the potential for protective and positive engagements can be unwittingly undermined. The examples given in chapter 4 of the challenges faced by RDOs transferring money overseas is suggestive of this. So too are discussions within international humanitarian dialogue about how to enable remittance-sending practices in displacement contexts as potentially a greater and more effective contribution to protecting vulnerable populations than other forms of aid (see also DEMAC 2016b; Monsutti 2008).

In terms of strengthening refugee diaspora humanitarianism, there are enabling policies and practices that have been implemented in other contexts that could be explored in other resettlement states, including Australia. For example, the US government has recognized the flow of remittances from diasporas living within their borders as part of their official development assistance since 2002 (Brinkerhoff 2011, 39), the Danish government has pioneered support for conflict-affected diasporas to undertake development projects by funding the Danish Refugee Council's Diaspora Programme since 2012, and the European Union's Humanitarian Aid and Civil Protection department has contributed to strengthening diasporas' humanitarian responses through its 2015 DEMAC project involving Syrian-German, Sierra Leonean–British, and Somali-Danish diasporas. While these models may not be easily replicated in other countries, they do suggest that there is potential to explore how states enable community helping practices and recognize the contribution of refugee diasporas in humanitarian responses as a form of civic participation (Sinatti and Horst 2014). The establishment of the Diaspora Learning Network (DLN) in Australia in 2016 is significant in this regard and is a potential space for increasing understanding and engagement within Australia to further develop policy and practice (Diaspora Action Australia, n.d.).[19]

Refugees, Resettlement, and Mobility

Australia is considered a key resettlement country within the international refugee regime. For many years it was consistently one of the top three resettlement states along with the United States and Canada.[20] Australia is also recognized as a leader in resettlement practice, with well-established policies and programs in place for those who are granted visas through the offshore component of the Humanitarian Program. Yet Australia's resettlement program—and perhaps resettlement more broadly—is designed to be the end of the story of forced displacement. Once refugees are granted a permanent visa to resettle, they are technically no longer refugees, even though, as highlighted above, they may carry the symbolic label for many years (or generations). Their engagement with the international refugee regime officially ceases with the attainment of a "durable solution." However, what this research has shown is that the engagement of resettled refugees with populations of concern to the international refugee regime does not end in Australia, Canada, or Europe. Indeed, there is potential for Australia and other resettlement states to articulate resettlement as a point in a journey and highlight and strengthen, among other things, the loop of refugee diaspora humanitarianism that connects those who are resettled with those in host countries and those who choose to return home.

This research has highlighted how resettlement changes the motility of refugees and is often the precursor to new forms of mobility and transnationalism. Third-country resettlement does not just give someone a safe(r) place to live; it also gives them the power to move and act in new ways. Alessandro Monsutti's study of Hazara migratory strategies has similarly illustrated the potential of mobility to sustain communities whose livelihoods have been disrupted by conflict and displacement. Monsutti shows how social relations are maintained transnationally through remittances and the considerable impact this has on refugee populations, arguing that remittances "are considerably larger, and much better distributed, than the total sum of humanitarian aid" (2008, 71). Further, he suggests—and I concur—that dispersion and mobility "may be seen as an asset with a social, economic and political dimension" (2008, 71; see also Brees 2010; Horst 2008a). In contrast to the enhanced motility of resettled refugees, the reduced motility of refugees on temporary or insecure visas in Australia and elsewhere can be viewed as a policy of disablement. Those on temporary visas are unable to connect with and support those they left behind in the ways that former refugees with permanent visas can, which means a loss of capacity to care, sustain, and protect. For refugee policy in Australia, then, enabling the mobility and transnationalism of refugee and humanitarian entrants is an area that warrants much greater consideration.

CREATING BETTER RESPONSES TO FORCED DISPLACEMENT

This chapter has focused on three broad areas where refugee diaspora humanitarianism has potential implications for realizing better responses to forced displacement. There is potential, for example, to strengthen CBP by understanding refugee communities in more transnational/local, fluid, and interconnected ways. Refugee diaspora humanitarianism has the potential to diversify the field of humanitarianism in terms of both actors and ideas, opening the door for new collaborations, innovations, and understandings of how to respond to the suffering of those who are forcibly displaced. Refugee diaspora humanitarianism also invites us to imagine and understand former refugees in new ways, beyond the disempowering or othering tropes of refugees as victims or refugees as threats. Indeed, a more robust appreciation of refugee diaspora humanitarianism by institutional actors—governments, NGOs, and multilateral organizations—has, I believe, the potential to contribute to redressing the significant failings of the international refugee regime and humanitarian responses to forced displacement, not least by calling into question the "neediness" and power differentials between *helper* and *helped*.

However, the implications of refugee diaspora humanitarianism go well beyond refugee, humanitarian, or migration policy and its potential to address institutional and systemic failings. Refugee diaspora humanitarianism should not be understood only in relation to the structure of the international refugee regime and institutional responses to forced displacement. The imaginings that RDOs invite have less policy-relevant implications, deepening our understanding of the lived experience of forced displacement and of the structuring effect of third-country resettlement on both individuals and groups. Indeed, the collective acts of caring described in this book may pale to insignificance when cast against the sheer scale of global forced displacement and the international refugee regime as a structural response to human mobility, but these small acts are significant for our understanding of everyday humanitarianisms and how people try to "do good" in the world. They also help us to see the transformation of social networks of care as a consequence of human mobility, all of which will be explored in the final chapter.

SEVEN

HELPING FAMILIAR STRANGERS

THE WAYS IN WHICH REFUGEE diaspora communities in countries like Australia mobilize to help their people displaced in other parts of the world have received scant attention in scholarly inquiry. I began this research by seeking to answer three key questions: What do refugee diaspora organizations (RDOs) in Australia do to help displaced people overseas? What if anything is distinct about refugee diaspora humanitarianism? What role does or can the wider refugee diaspora play in the international refugee regime? I started out wanting to make visible those acts of helping that have largely gone unnoticed in research as well as in policy and practice, because I wanted to think through how *doing good* could be done better.

Through embarking on this journey, I have come to understand refugee diaspora humanitarianism as a distinct transnational practice. The mobilization of RDOs to help in refugee situations—as grassroots transnational social networks of care—can partly be understood as a response to the significant shortcomings of more powerful institutions and structures to ensure forcibly displaced people are able to live in safety and dignity. But these acts should not be held up or examined only in relation to what they say about the failings of states and global governance systems. The genealogy of refugee diaspora humanitarianism lies within much older and more diverse everyday practices of helping strangers in need and speaks to the vitality and dynamism of social networks of care in a globalized and mobile world.

REFUGEE DIASPORA HUMANITARIANISM AS DISTINCT TRANSNATIONAL PRACTICE

There were many times throughout my fieldwork when I wondered whether I was imagining this phenomenon—that I, as an activist-researcher, somehow wanted to find these organizations and people who were *doing good* and draw a circle around them. I would doubt myself. How can I draw connections between such disparate groups of people and activities? But then I would receive a call while working for the Refugee Council of Australia from someone representing an RDO I had never heard of (in this case, a Rohingya group in Melbourne), and they would ask for something simple (Can I help them to find a room to organize a fundraising event?); in talking, I would find that they had raised AU$20,000 from their community networks the previous weekend to send to those being targeted by violence and fleeing Myanmar, and I would think *These actions* are *remarkable*. Moreover, I could see a pattern in their response and the responses I had heard about from other RDOs responding to very different situations. I am confident now in saying that refugee diaspora humanitarianism *is* a distinct transnational practice, and, moreover, it is a practice that needs to be understood on its own terms.

While there is obvious diversity in the structure, activities, and contexts in which RDOs act (see chap. 2), refugee diaspora humanitarianism is describable as a practice because of the commonalities in *how* and *why* groups of people come together to help. As Australia has had a well-established refugee resettlement program with an annual intake since the 1970s, there are significant and diverse diaspora communities across the country with members who have experienced life as a refugee elsewhere in the world. Within these communities, it is common for small organizations or groups—what I have termed *refugee diaspora organizations*—to mobilize with the objective of helping their people overseas. While these organizations are not the only way that refugee diasporas help in situations of forced displacement—individual or household remittance-sending practices, for example, can also be considered acts of solidarity and assistance—these collective or associational forms fall within the realm of humanitarianism in that the people these groups seek to help are strangers, not kin. However, it is also apparent that the recipients of refugee diaspora humanitarianism tend to be individuals who RDOs self-identify with as *their people*. While they may not be family or friends, they are familiar strangers.

At first glance, who and where RDOs help and the activities they engage in seem considerably varied. The humanitarian contexts in which RDOs are working include the full spectrum: from complex humanitarian emergencies to protracted refugee situations, from refugee camps to urban settings, and targeting internally displaced populations, refugees, and people seeking asylum. The activities undertaken by RDOs likewise vary and range from undertaking systemic advocacy to building schools, providing material aid and access to emergency relief funds, or offering migration support. However, the fact that groups of former refugees in Australia from very different backgrounds commonly engage in collective acts of helping shows us that there is something structuring in the experience of third-country resettlement; this experience creates a situation whereby groups of people are propelled to come together in somewhat predictable ways.

The predictability of refugee diaspora mobilization can be better understood if we appreciate *why* those involved in RDOs feel compelled to act in this way. After all, the individuals most actively involved in RDOs are volunteers and largely draw on their personal networks and resources to help, suggesting significant animating forces. To this, I have suggested that there are recurring figures of suffering evoked by refugee diaspora humanitarians to create momentum and effect. These figures are a collective (*a people*) who suffer and with whom diaspora humanitarians include themselves in this circle of suffering; people alone or struggling to fulfill their expected caring roles; and forgotten refugees living in the margins of the world, unheard and unhelped. These narratives help us understand how those involved in RDOs draw on their own understandings and beliefs about who they are helping and the causes of their suffering.

Why individuals feel compelled to act in response to this perceived suffering—to answer that phone that keeps on ringing, even when they are exhausted—reveals complex undercurrents of moral, affective, and political forces. These are forces that are as diverse as the individual and collective histories of the people involved. Yet, like humanitarian narratives, there are also common threads. For those most invested in RDOs, their perspective and positionality as people with a history of helping and being helped—as diasporas, as survivors, as resettled refugees—sheds light on the forces that animate refugee diaspora humanitarianism. Among these are questions of morality. Diaspora humanitarians spoke about helping as fulfilling their obligations to their community, as being an act of faith, as being an echo of the values passed on from mothers and fathers who stood up to injustices, and, perhaps more complicated, as a moral duty to repay the gift of resettlement and to give back for having themselves been helped. This act of repaying the gift is imbued with feelings of guilt that one has been given the "gift" of living in a country like Australia and is somehow indebted to the people still struggling in the difficult spaces they once inhabited. In this, guilt and empathy are closely linked affective forces. Refugee diaspora humanitarians spoke about the guilt they felt for those they left behind and whose suffering they could empathize with because they had been there themselves. Individuals drew on their own experiences to feel the pain of others, and at times, empathy and trauma seemed entwined in acts of helping. Yet dark affective forces are not the only emotions animating diaspora humanitarians. Many of those I spoke to described the satisfaction that came from helping and the pleasurable sociability of working together for the good of others. As with other forms of humanitarianism, there are also negotiations of power in the mobilization of RDOs. Some clearly saw their involvement in RDOs as a way of bringing about transformational change in their homelands or paving the way for their people to return, albeit with considerable variation in how organizations or individuals rejected or aligned themselves to more formal political processes. On a personal level, those who are known as helpers gained experience, networks, and status from their involvement in RDOs; it became, for some, part of their identity. Together, these animating forces paint a picture of distinct moralities and motivations that reinforce the idea that acts of helping strangers in need (humanitarianism) are situated in particular histories, understandings, and interrelationships between those who help and those in need.

Through an exploration of *how* RDOs work (chaps. 4 and 5), the distinctiveness of refugee diaspora humanitarianism as transnational practice becomes clearer still. While there is certainly no model or typology to describe these actors, there does seem to be gravitational pull toward certain modalities. For example, in terms of governance structures, the RDOs in this study were all small, volunteer-run organizations mostly involving people who self-identify in a diasporic way. Their voluntary nature is seen by those involved as both a strength (a demonstration of their convictions and evidence of their accountability) and a significant challenge, particularly for the capacity of these organizations to effect change and their longer-term sustainability. While many of these RDOs seem to mirror—at least on paper—the bureaucratized, democratic governance structures of incorporated associations or nongovernmental organizations, in practice they operate with a high degree of informality. This does not mean that there are no rules, norms, or responsibilities governing RDOs, but rather that they are more often guided by understandings within trust-based social networks than by formal governance structures. Indeed, one of the more striking features of RDO governance is the hypervigilance to accountability practiced by many organizations to both donors *and* recipients, which is enabled by RDOs' embeddedness in transnational social networks that include both helpers and helped.

The RDOs in this research undeniably represent small economies. The financial resources RDOs mobilize largely come from their own social networks—from within diaspora communities in Australia—and seem infinitesimal when compared to the wider humanitarian system with organizational budgets in the millions or billions. RDOs make do by drawing on other (nonmonetary) resources, particularly the skills, knowledge, networks, and labor of volunteers, most of which is unaccounted for in organizational budgets. The resourcefulness and limited resources that shape refugee diaspora humanitarianism make RDOs extremely effective at turning small amounts of money into something tangible for the people they are helping, albeit at a very localized level. Indeed, the idea of *smallness* was a recurring theme in this research, with RDOs understanding the limits of what they could do in the context of enormous needs while also speaking of the value and significance of doing small things to improve the lives of those they reached out to or who reached out to them.

The distinctive transnational modalities of RDOs were described in this book using four crosscutting themes: mobility, (in)visibility, knowledge, and networks. In terms of *mobility*, refugee diaspora humanitarians move, connect, and organize across dispersed space. People involved in RDOs regularly travel to organize, both within Australia and overseas. For those who travel to refugee situations to help, their reasons for traveling are not solely humanitarian. Most travel also to visit, care for, create, or reunite with family and friends, suggesting that refugee diaspora humanitarianism and the ways in which transnational families connect exist side by side. Physical mobility enables diaspora humanitarianism in several ways: it provides opportunities for those in the wider diaspora to better understand the current situation for those they are trying to help, it facilitates needs identification and project planning, it allows RDO members to oversee or participate in the implementation of projects, it strengthens networks with people in the areas they are working, and it enables monitoring and accountability. The virtual mobilities of RDOs are also striking. Information and communication technologies have provided accessible means by which RDOs can organize across geographically dispersed locations and mobilize and sustain support by creating affective connections between people living worlds apart.

A second modalities theme explored in chapter 5 was that of *(in)visibility*—how those involved in RDOs are seen or not seen in different contexts and how this is used to their advantage. Here, I argue that refugee diaspora humanitarians use their visibility (Otherness) in safe humanitarian spaces such as Australia, Geneva, and New York to make claims about resources and protection needs and that being visible as a refugee or a representative of a people has purpose and effect. Conversely, these same people use their ability to blend in—their *in*visibility—in liminal humanitarian spaces (refugee and conflict situations). Refugee diaspora humanitarians spoke of how being (not) seen as "ordinary" allowed them to do things—to access places and people that more visible humanitarian actors would find difficult to reach. The flip side to this, however, is that blending in also renders RDOs invisible or inconsequential within broader humanitarian response systems.

RDOs are distinct in many ways because of the capacity of those involved to understand, make decisions, and act by drawing on different forms of knowledge. What refugee diaspora humanitarians know is often highly context-specific—being able to read nuances by virtue of someone's past experiences and connections to a people or place, for example. This knowledge distinguishes refugee diaspora humanitarians from institutional actors who more often understand a local situation, needs, and solutions by drawing on generalized knowledge synthesized from much longer and diverse organizational histories—knowledge evident and reinforced through industry frameworks, policies, and trainings—or experiential knowledge gained from working in different humanitarian contexts. While there are significant gaps (what RDOs *do not* know) relating to the technical knowledge needed to effectively implement projects, access to humanitarian coordination mechanisms, and the potential (two-way) disconnect between diaspora and local actors' understandings of a situation, refugee diaspora humanitarianism also challenges some of the distinctions made and values placed on *expert* versus *local* knowledge, in some cases bridging the two. Indeed, refugee diaspora humanitarianism seems to foreground different forms of knowledge—that which is embodied, affective, and involves a closer proximity between helper and helped—that could complement the rationalized technical knowledge that is so valued in the upper echelons of the international humanitarian system and experienced as so alienating by the objects of humanitarian intervention.

Finally, the fourth crosscutting theme regarding RDO transnational modalities concerned *networks*. In conceptualizing RDO networks, I suggest that these organizations and the individuals involved are part of rhizomatic networks or "networks in motion" (Deleuze and Guttari 1987); this allows us to see how the event of resettlement does not necessarily remove a person from a social network, but shifts their positionality, capacities, and relationships within a transnational social field. Social networks are fundamental to how RDOs get things done. RDO networks in Australia, their networks with people living in displacement contexts, and their networks with people in the wider diaspora all significantly shape and enable refugee diaspora humanitarianism. The effectiveness of an RDO is in many ways dependent on the relative strength and levels of trust within its social networks.

Refugee diaspora humanitarianism requires a confluence of factors. It requires people who have lived as refugees to be able to permanently settle in a country like Australia, where they have new possibilities to associate and to act. It requires former refugees to self-identify and come together as a diaspora to help those who they identify with as their people. It also requires an enabling context that allows people to collectively organize and act. As such, the motivations, modalities, and implications of refugee diaspora humanitarianism must be understood on their own terms if we are to realize the possibilities of a stronger refugee protection system, a more diverse and effective humanitarian response system, and a world in which (transnational) communities are seen as vital actors in finding solutions to forced displacement.

FORCED DISPLACEMENT AND RESPONSES FROM BELOW

The world of diaspora humanitarianism has only recently emerged in scholarly and policy discussions (see DEMAC 2016b; Horst et al. 2015; IOM 2015), and a focus on *refugee* diasporas has been less visible in discussions thus far. This research was designed to intentionally focus on refugee diasporas as people who are not only motivated by their identification with a people (diasporas) but who also have lived experience of forced displacement and being the objects of humanitarian assistance. The positionality and perspective of refugee diasporas make them, I believe, distinct humanitarian actors. In arguing this, I have shown that—despite the obvious heterogeneity of refugee populations—there is something structuring in the experience of becoming a resettled refugee.

Third-country resettlement creates a situation whereby a small number of individuals from a much larger population are granted the legal right to move from a situation of precarity (i.e., in need of international protection) to a safer, wealthier place of privilege. This act itself—resettlement—brings with it a multitude of challenges, obligations, and opportunities. For people who resettle, there are the challenges of remaking a life again in yet another place, of negotiating the obligations and guilt of being a former refugee in a country like Australia (of having received "the gift" of resettlement), and of finding ways to meaningfully relate to the people one has (physically) left behind along the way. But the resettlement context also provides opportunities to act in new ways—to mobilize as a diaspora, to travel, and to access resources, ideas, and networks that were previously unavailable. Indeed, the evidence suggested by this research is that, while not inevitable, the formation of RDOs to undertake helping work with displaced people in other parts of the world is a common experience.

Refugee diaspora humanitarianism is, in many ways, an organic movement *from below*. As discussed in chapter 4, while most RDOs are registered as incorporated associations, they operate loosely and with a high degree of informality. Moreover, these organizations come and go as interest within diaspora communities and the needs of their people waxes and wanes. Refugee diaspora humanitarianism is, in many ways, a counterpoint to institutional and large-scale responses to forced displacement. In reflecting on the broader significance of this, it is worth noting Robin Cohen and Nicholas Van Hear's article, "Visions of Refugia: Territorial and Transnational Solutions to Mass Displacement" (2017). Here, the authors describe as I have the failure of nation-states and the international governance architecture (the refugee regime and humanitarian system) to effectively protect the millions of people around the world who are forcibly displaced. In putting forward possible solutions to this "problem of mass displacement," Cohen and Van Hear offer the utopic idea of "Refugia," a "transnational or cross-national entity, a set of connections (*mise en relation*) between different sites developed through initiatives mainly taken by refugees and displaced people themselves" (2017, 497). They write:

> We suggest that Refugia already exists in a fragmentary and highly imperfect form. In countries that have long hosted large numbers of refugees and will likely do so for the foreseeable future—Turkey, Jordan, Lebanon, Iran, Pakistan, Kenya, Ethiopia and Uganda among others—refugees have established tenuous communities in the face of challenging conditions and poor prospects. These populations have links with more fortunate kin and friends in global cities further afield—not just in the neighbourhoods of New York, London, Paris, Berlin and Sydney, but in Istanbul, Cairo, Mumbai, Rio and many others in the emerging world, where people of diverse ethnicities and backgrounds are thrown together. Taken together, people in these dispersed locations constitute transnational communities through their diasporic connections. The transformational step towards a transnational polity would be to move beyond ethnic identification to a global affinity of the displaced. (Cohen and Van Hear 2017, 498)

What Cohen and Van Hear envision is displaced populations coming together and creating opportunities for people to move, negotiate, and access resources through being identified and identifiable as "Refugians." Refugians would live within territories (nation-sates) as they already do but would be connected to each other through an "archipelago of the displaced"—a key idea being that Refugia is "self-organized and self-managed, requiring not political or cultural conformity but simply subscribing to principles and deeds of solidarity and mutual aid" (Cohen and Van Hear 2017, 502). The most compelling part of this vision of Refugia is the prospect of people who are displaced being able to organize "in the interstices of the nation state system and the international governmental architecture" (Cohen and Van Hear 2017, 502)—of not being forced to live in the margins or dependent on the capacities and whims of states and a flawed humanitarian governance system, but instead having greater agency and power through being recognized and legitimized as a collective.

There were many ideas in this article that I could relate to in terms of how the RDOs in this study organized and connected transnationally. For example, there were echoes of Refugia in the ways diaspora humanitarians evoked forgotten refugees as figures of suffering. Many conversations I had seemed to suggest that the suffering of displacement was one that could be recognized and shared regardless of other forms of self-identification (e.g., ethnic, religious, national). Recall, for example, how John spoke of the effects of being labeled "a refugee" and being told "you cannot do, you cannot do" in chapter 3. This affinity of the displaced could also be seen during my fieldwork in Geneva, where I observed a small group of refugee diaspora advocates, many of whom were cognizant that they did not (or could not) represent a community but seemed to speak with confidence about theirs or others' experiences of displacement and humanitarian governance from the perspective of *being a refugee*. The same goes for my fieldwork in Indonesia, where the founder of a refugee-led organization said to a member of a newly forming refugee association, "No one else is going to help you. You are on your own"; the two then proceeded to enthusiastically discuss creative solutions to the problems that they shared. The obvious differences between these individuals—one a university-educated woman from Ethiopia, the other a young Hazara man who had grown up as a refugee in Pakistan with limited access to formal education—were less apparent in this context, as they shared the common goal and experience of surviving as refugees in Indonesia.

Yet the idea of Refugia as a fully realized transnational entity seems wildly utopic (or even dystopic) in the context of the rise of nationalism in many parts of the world and the persistent hegemony of the international system of sovereign states. While Cohen and Van Hear are cognizant of this (they describe their vision as a "pragmatic utopia"), they also point out that Refugia already exists in embryonic form: "Camps and communities near and in countries riven by conflicts, neighbourhoods in global cities, transnational political practices, money transfers, emergent communities and activities in disparate locations en route: all are fragments that, taken separately, do not seem to promise much. However, in the aggregate they could add up to Refugia, imperfectly prefigured" (2017, 501).

The appeal of Refugia, then, is that it is already happening. It does not require grand design, at least in its imperfect form. Taken as a movement involving fragmentary pieces rather than an orchestrated structure, Refugia is not likely to be mired with the political shortsightedness and gross discrepancies in power and wealth evident among those negotiating the future of the international refugee regime and humanitarian responses to people considered "out of place" (Malkki 1992). The idea of solutions coming from below—of people finding creative ways to connect with and support one another—seems to offer more possibility for those currently, or likely to be, displaced. The implication of Refugia echoes that of my own study. Both suggest that there is some hope to be found in enabling manifestations of self-governance, solidarity, and mutual aid.

While undertaking this research, I have also seen that there is an appetite to further support the growth of transnational networks of refugee-led organizations into some sort of polity—that maybe Cohen and Van Hear's vision of Refugia is not so far off. It is embryonic, but it is possible to see how the themes of self-governance—of community-based protection—will create more leaders within refugee communities. In fact, the coming together of leaders from disparate backgrounds and regions as refugees *is* already happening. In June 2018, the Global Summit of Refugees was held in Geneva, bringing together refugee-led networks and advocates from across the world for the first time to discuss how refugee voices can be heard more centrally in global dialogue on forced displacement.[1] This summit sparked the formation of the Global Refugee-led Network in 2019, a network that is demanding refugees be given a space at the table.[2] In 2021, an even more promising step is the US$10 million philanthropic funding of the Resourcing Refugee Leadership initiative, a "coalition effort focused on resourcing and positioning refugee-led organizations to influence refugee response"; the initiative itself is refugee-led.[3] The people I have written about in this book are among the groups that have been at the center of this movement toward refugee self-representation and self-determination. They are agitating. They are organizing. And about this there is much more to be learned and said.

TAPESTRIES OF CARE

As to the broader significance of this research, I want to suggest that the mobilization of RDOs to help familiar strangers must be understood in terms of everyday humanitarianism and that more attention should be paid to collective acts of caring in their many and varied forms. The need for finely grained studies of everyday humanitarians and their ethics, effects, and practices has never been greater at a time when the humanitarian landscape is changing and (potentially) diversifying, and the suffering caused by conflict and displacement shows no sign of abating. Yet there are few studies outside of those on the formal and institutionalized humanitarian system that explore situated acts of people helping strangers in need (Borstein's *Disquieting Gifts: Humanitarianism in New Delhi* [2012] being a notable exception). In fact, discussions about everyday humanitarianism and what this means are only just starting to emerge and thus far paint a gloomy picture. For example, according to a description of the Everyday Humanitarianism: Ethics, Affects and Practices conference held at the London School of Economics and Political Sciences in 2016, "In this 'post-humanitarian' age, solidarity is driven by converging logics of consumption and utilitarianism where doing good for others is about mundane micro-practices that aim at personal gratification, such as the click of the mouse or an e-signature. At the same time, moral universals and political questions of justice and equality may fade into the background or become treated as irrelevant" (Celebnorthsouth 2016).

The conference program reveals that interest in everyday acts of helping has been largely focused on undifferentiated Western publics—on individuals acting in tandem with dominant humanitarian actors to "do good," largely mediated through online technologies, celebrity, and the mass media that enables a "humanitarian marketplace" (Richey and Chouliaraki 2017). While these trends are notable and not to be refuted, the depth of this research reinforces the idea that "the everyday" looks very different for different individuals and groups, even within populations in the Global North. The people who were involved in RDOs in this study, for example, were exposed to similar media discourses, technologies, and possibilities to help as other Australians, yet they chose to act by painstakingly forming their own organizations. More so, these acts required significant animating forces as well as personal and collective investments of time and resources.

And so, when Lisa Ann Richey and Lilie Chouliaraki ask, "Do we live in an age of 'post-humanitarianism' where doing good for others is intrinsically linked with feelings of gratification for the self?" (2017, 314), I want to say *no*. How people try to do good for others is based on their capacity and positionality in relation to those who suffer and is complicated by moralities and motivations that are as diverse as each person's individual and collective history. For people who have once been the object of humanitarian assistance—former refugees now resettled in Australia—their histories, positionality, capacity, and motivations to help will differ from those of an Anglo-Australian, middle-class young person who has traveled overseas as a "voluntourist" (Douglas and Greenhill 2017) and who relates to others' suffering through mediated messages (Angelina Jolie holding a refugee baby in a camp) and the call to donate to UNHCR or to tweet #WithRefugees. How both relate to the suffering of strangers and choose to act are equally important, and both are more complicated than acts linked primarily to self-gratification.

What this study of refugee diaspora humanitarianism sheds light on is the everyday *situated* ethics and collective practices of care of a particular group of people: refugees resettled in Australia. And while this research did not start out as an exploration of the ethics of their care, through the process it became important to understand *why* these individuals and groups chose to act in this way. Through my research, I came to see these acts beyond their policy and structural significance and to grasp what they tell us about how people perceive another's suffering, their relationship to this suffering, and how this compels us to act in certain ways. Refugee diaspora humanitarianism is about how groups of people come together to try to do good that goes beyond—or perhaps sits between—acts of caring for kith and kin and acts of caring for an abstract and distant other (i.e., humanitarianism based on liberal altruism). These acts help us to understand suffering beyond the "suffering subject" (Robbins 2013) but as a collective experience—the suffering of *a people*.

In understanding refugee diaspora humanitarians as perceiving and responding to the suffering of a people, we can see how their actions are framed in ways that focus on remaking or strengthening social fabrics of care and in which the helpers include themselves within this social fabric. Their actions move beyond addressing the bare life (*zōe*) of the suffering subject and toward the *bios*—the story of the political and social being who suffers (Agamben 2005). In many ways, refugee diaspora humanitarianism challenges the idea that Didier Fassin suggests when he writes about the duality and hierarchy that lies in the figures of "aid workers" and "victims," "between the *zoē* of 'local populations' who can only passively await both bombs and humanitarian workers, fearing the former and mistrusting the latter, and the *bios* of those 'citizens of the world,' the aid workers who come, with courage and devotion, to render them assistance" (2010b, 231). In fact, refugee diaspora humanitarians muddy these distinctions. As a person who identifies with a collective people who suffer, the diaspora humanitarian is both victim and helper.

I want to further suggest that caring about the social group and not just bodies to be saved is fundamentally important. This is what Van Hear and Cohen suggest when they purport that collective transfers by diaspora groups to conflict-affected populations are different in nature to private remittances to households or extended family members. Despite being smaller in scale, collective transfers have significance beyond their immediate economic and material effects, helping to "recreate or repair the social fabric shredded by years of conflict, not least by helping to re-establish social linkages ruptured during war, and re-building trust and confidence" (Van Hear and Cohen 2017, 173). Refugee diaspora humanitarianism as everyday humanitarianism is about rebuilding social networks of trust. In this way, the number of lives saved by RDOs may not be the most important question when considering their implications and effect. Perhaps better questions are: How many people were connected to one another through the actions of RDOs? How was the suffering of a people healed or transformed by individuals coming together and acting in this way?

This study did not set out to compare or contrast refugee diaspora humanitarianism with other (dominant) forms of humanitarianism but to try to understand these practices on their own terms. At the same time, it is inevitable that this form of caring for strangers will be held up against other humanitarian practices. Indeed, by labelling the actions of RDOs *humanitarian*, I invite this comparison. I do this because I believe much can be learned through mutual exchange between diverse actors about practices of caring. As Joel Robbins suggests, an "anthropology of the good can . . . [help] us do justice to the different ways people live for the good, and finding ways to let their efforts inform our own" (2013, 459). For dominant humanitarian organizations interested in learning about how alleviating suffering can also involve empowering and being accountable to affected populations, refugee diaspora humanitarians have much to offer. Likewise, much could be learned by RDOs from institutional actors about governance, needs identification, coordination, and implementation.

In the end, there is no either-or of humanitarianism. There is no right way to help. Refugee diaspora humanitarianism does not hold any definitive answers or alternatives for how to improve the lives of those who have been forced from their homes. The fact that this diversity of care practices exists in and of itself is what is important and what could and should be nurtured. What refugee diaspora humanitarianism suggests is that the social fabric of care is—and should be—a rich tapestry; as humans, we can only hope to draw from networks of support in a variety of forms when we need it, and we can also act in a variety of ways as helpers. Erica Bornstein reminds us that giving challenges people "to think relationally about their place in the world" and that, "in this age of abundance and scarcity, models of renunciation and giving away are powerful reminders of the relations that make us members of groups" (2012, 174). The different actors who help in times of need include those who work for large humanitarian organizations whose *raison d'être* is to save lives, but it also includes neighbors, community leaders, faith networks, civil society movements, "nongovernmental individuals" (Hilhorst and Jansen 2010), and RDOs. These are everyday humanitarians whose actions and reasons for acting vary greatly. For all of these actors, the ethics, practices, and effects of their helping should not be "untouchable" to researchers (Fassin 2010d) but discerned for what they do and what it means for those involved. For me, this diversity implies the possibility of a richer tapestry of care.

At the very start of this book, I included a quote from Bornstein that spoke of the subtle shades of humanitarian efforts of people who are less visible and who provide care "inaudibly, without recognition and without status" (2012, 11). It is my hope that this book has cast light on one such group of humanitarians whose caring has largely gone unrecognized. For a country like Australia, which is rightly proud of offering a permanent home to over 800,000 refugees since Federation, continuing to frame refugees as the recipients of this country's benevolence or, worse, as people who signify potential threat or ongoing neediness misses the considerable and breathtaking ways in which many former refugees go about doing good in the world. Refugee diaspora humanitarianism may not be the panacea to the suffering of forced displacement or the precarious situations in which a large proportion of the world's displaced live, but these distinct actors and their actions suggest other possibilities and ways of caring involving solidarity, listening, and reknitting social fabrics. They are "social gestures to strangers and to distant kin" (Bornstein 2012, 174). And, for those who suffer through forced displacement—whose lives have been made worse by conflict and violence, domination and invisibility—it matters that groups of familiar strangers continue to connect and to care.

EPILOGUE

THIS BOOK BEGAN WITH A story about the Cisarua Refugee Learning Centre (CRLC) in Indonesia and the important role played by three people—Muzafar Ali, Tahira Razai, and Khadim Dai—in forming this school and in nurturing the transnational networks of care and support that have grown around this school and community. I made the point that resettled refugees are significant but often invisible actors in the provision of protection and support to those who fall within (or out of) the international refugee regime. I want to end this monologue by returning to CRLC and how this refugee-led initiative has fared in the context of the Covid-19 pandemic, which has had a significant impact on the possibilities for this school, community, and network of supporters.

The onset of the Covid-19 pandemic at the start of 2020 has changed the world in many ways, and its implications have been felt by the refugee community in Cisarua no less than anywhere else. While the social distancing and restrictions on mobility brought about by the pandemic may have required a less dramatic transition for a group whose mobility was already highly curtailed and who had, by necessity, established effective ways of connecting online, Covid-19 has created an even bigger disruption to the meager resettlement pathways available to refugees stuck in Indonesia. Global resettlement places in 2020 were at an all-time low, with only a trickle of resettlement taking place from Indonesia. In addition, challenges have presented themselves in terms of how CRLC's network of individual supporters in countries like Australia—many of whom are struggling with upheaval and the onset of great uncertainty and restrictions in their own worlds—will remain invested in this community going forward. At the time of writing, fundraising efforts had slowed down markedly, with many of the opportunities reduced for would-be donors to meet face-to-face and connect with each other and this community.

At the same time, Muzafar, Tahira, and Khadim remain invested and connected with the refugee community in Cisarua, and the ripples of this connection are still being felt. As this book tried to show, it is much harder for refugee diaspora humanitarians to disengage from helping people who they relate to as friends, former neighbors, or even as strangers whose lives they are achingly familiar with. As Muzafar offered when I recently asked him about his involvement with CRLC during the Covid-19 pandemic: "Covid has been an opportunity for me to play a more active role with the CRLC team and the community. The notion of closeness and distance has been squashed by self-isolation of individuals. It is easy for the community to contact me because this has become the norm. I have never felt this strongly connected with my community since I came to Australia."

Indeed, Muzafar reports that his involvement with the CRLC has significantly increased during the pandemic, as he worked with the center to develop a Covid-19 strategy, assigning teachers and members of the management team to establish regular contact with parents to check in about the challenges they were facing, stay updated about their physical and mental health, and make sure information about Covid-19 was being received from reliable sources and measures were in place to keep families safe. Muzafar also worked with the CRLC team to organize regular meetings with other refugee-led learning centers in Cisarua to share information. Additionally, he worked on modifying the CRLC budget to respond to the demands of shifting to online classes (e.g., by allocating extra funds to cover teachers' internet and communication costs). Echoing the findings of this book about the nonquantifiable nature of refugee diaspora humanitarianism and the importance of bearing witness, Muzafar reported that his increased involvement with CRLC was "mostly talking and listening with managers and the rest of the team."

Tahira has also remained connected to the CRLC management team and board of directors from her home in Toronto, providing and mobilizing support for teachers to transition to online modes of delivery and to sustain the community through this new crisis. Since arriving in Canada in 2017, Tahira helped form a "group of five" to sponsor one of CRLC's other former managers, Khalil Payeez, as part of Canada's private sponsorship program, facilitating resettlement pathways within this social network. Khalil arrived in Toronto at the very start of the pandemic, in early 2020. And so the network deepens and transforms, as Khalil becomes another (potential) bridge builder between a small group of refugees struggling to survive in Indonesia, refugee diaspora communities scattered across the world, and the wider social networks and resources that they mobilize along the way. When I contacted Khalil about mentioning him in this book, he informed me that he has started the process of sponsoring a family and two individuals that he knew from his time in Cisarua for resettlement.

Khadim also continues to expand his networks in Los Angeles, finding new ways to tell his own and others' stories of displacement through photography and film in the hope of shedding light on the experiences of and injustices faced by refugees.[1] In 2019, Khadim's efforts to secure scholarships for ten young refugees living in Cisarua to study in New Mexico were thwarted when the students' visas were denied.[2] In 2019 and 2020, Khadim supported three students from Afghanistan to attain scholarships to study in the United States. As he wrote: "My dream is to bring some young talent to the US and help them finish their studies and be a voice for refugees. I believe this investment will grow and help refugees in the long run."

As for me, I was invited to serve on the board of Cisarua Learning Inc. in 2019. I had already been readily drawn into the CRLC family of supporters in 2015, when I first connected with Muzafar Ali as I was on my way to Indonesia with members of an Oromo refugee diaspora organization (RDO); this was two weeks after he arrived in Australia. I also continue to serve on the board of another RDO—Eritrean Australian Humanitarian Aid (EAHA) Inc.—filling in paperwork and ensuring reporting requirements are met so that my esteemed Eritrean Australian friends can continue to do what they do best: care and connect. In late 2020, EAHA provided emergency financial support to keep a well-established community-run school in Khartoum afloat during a time when refugees in Sudan are ever-more precariously placed. In other words, EAHA picked up a starfish stranded on the beach and threw it back in.

February 2021

APPENDIX

Names that appear in book and affiliated organizations or communities

Name	Full name	Organization	Diaspora community	Country of birth/origin
Abdul	Pseudonym		Eritrean	Eritrea
Adem	Pseudonym		Oromo	Australia
Alaa	Pseudonym		Palestinian	Syria
Aliya	Pseudonym		Oromo	Australia
Anna	Anna Hutchens	Refugee Action Program, Brotherhood of St Laurence	N/A	N/A
Anwar	Anwar Alishek	Eritrean Australian Humanitarian Aid	Eritrean	Eritrea
Berhan	Berhan Jaber	Various	Eritrean	Eritrea
Carmen	Pseudonym		Assyrian	Iraq
Elizabeth	Pseudonym		South Sudanese	Kenya
Germa	Pseudonym		Oromo	Sudan
Hadi	Pseudonym		Iraqi	Iraq
Hamid	Pseudonym		Rohingya	Myanmar
Hassan	Pseudonym		Oromo	Ethiopia

(*Continued*)

Name	Full name	Organization	Diaspora community	Country of birth/origin
James	Pseudonym		Karen	Myanmar
John	Pseudonym		Zo	Myanmar
Jordan	Pseudonym		Karen	Myanmar
Joseph	Pseudonym		Eastern Orthodox	Lebanon
Ladan	Pseudonym		Ogaden	Somalia
Leyla	Pseudonym		Assyrian	Iraq
Mae Sie	Mae Sie Win	Karenni Federation of Australia	Karenni	Myanmar
Marama	Marama Kufi	Oromia Support Group Australia/ Oromo Relief Association Australia	Oromo	Ethiopia
Melika	Melika Sheikh-Eldin	AMES Australia	Eritrean	Eritrea
Mohammed	Pseudonym		Eritrean	Eritrea
Muzafar	Muzafar Ali	Cisarua Refugee Learning Centre	Hazara	Afghanistan
Naj	Pseudonym		Hazara	Afghanistan
Raj	Pseudonym		Lhotshampa	Bhutan
Rosanna	Pseudonym		Bahai'i	Iran
Sabira	Pseudonym		Hazara	Pakistan
Sarah	Pseudonym		Mandaean	Iraq
Youssef	Pseudonym		Oromo	Ethiopia

NOTES

Introduction

1. The term *familiar strangers* has been used by a range of scholars writing about diverse subject matters—notably by sociologist Stanley Milgram in the 1970s to describe interactions between strangers in urban environments (Milgram, "The Familiar Stranger: An Aspect of Urban Anonymity"), but more recently in historical studies of the Georgian diaspora in the Soviet empire (Scott, *Familiar Strangers: The Georgian Diaspora and the Evolution of Soviet Empire*), Chinese-speaking Muslims (Lipman, *Familiar Strangers: A History of Muslims in Northwest China*), and social networks online (Perez et al., "Familiar Strangers Detection in Online Social Networks"), as well as in particular contexts (Zhou et al., "'Familiar Strangers' in the Big Data Era: An Exploratory Study of Beijing Metro Encounters"). I do not draw intentionally on this scholarship in my use of the term *familiar strangers*. Although there are common threads across this literature of bringing together the idea of a person who is both known (familiar) and unknown (strange), I do not seek to create or argue for an overarching or meta concept in the use of the term. Rather, bringing these words together in this book is a shorthand to evoke the positionality of RDOs and their helping work. They are humanitarians because they are reaching out to help someone—a stranger—in need. But the stranger they seek to help is somehow familiar or known to them because of a perceived or shared affinity to a collective identity.

2. I use this imperfect term (*Global North*) to denote countries that, by and large, are structurally advantaged by global capitalism. I am aware that using such a shorthand term contributes to a tendency to deemphasize diversity within the Global North/South, such that there are those who are advantaged by global capitalism in countries that are considered the Global South, just as there are people disadvantaged by global capitalism in countries in the Global North.

3. This included 5.7 million returnees, the majority of whom returned to South Sudan, Burundi, Syria, or Côte d'Ivoire, where there remain considerable challenges, conflict, and insecurity; 57,500 refugees were resettled to a third country, and 56,700 attained "local integration" through naturalization or regularization of status in a country of asylum. UNHCR, *Global Trends: Forced Displacement in 2021.*

4. This term is usually attributed to Renato Rosaldo, who made this comment at the Anthropology and the Field conference on April 18, 1994: "The context was a comparison of ethnography by post-exotic anthropologists and cultural studies scholars, a discussion for what, in the absence of extended co-residence, guarantees interactive 'depth.'" Clifford, "Spatial Practices: Fieldwork, Travel, and the Disciplining of Anthropology," 219. See also Geertz, "Deep Hanging Out."

1. Humanitarianism and the International Refugee Regime

1. For an interesting discussion of the problematics of what is meant when *humanity* is evoked to justify different forms of humanitarian action, see De Lauri, "The Taliban and the Humanitarian Soldier"; Asad, "Reflections on Violence, Law, and Humanitarianism."

2. There have also been counter-critiques by scholars who suggest that the "objects" of humanitarianism are not passive bodies ("bare life") and that the "political" is always present in humanitarian contexts, as evidenced by practices such as squatting in refugee camps and the ways in which refugees turn "exceptional" spaces into "homes." See Agier, *On the Margins of the World*; Brun and Fábos, "Making Homes in Limbo?"; Rygiel "Bordering Solidarities: Migrant Activism" and "Bordering Solidarities: Forging Transgressive Citizenships"; Sanyal, "Squatting in Camps."

3. There have also been critiques of where the temporal boundaries of humanitarian interventions should lie, with Barnett arguing that as humanitarian actors have broadened their scope to addressing root causes of suffering, their interventions have extended well after the advent of an emergency and into multisectoral responses, as well as into efforts to prevent emergencies. See Barnett, *Empire of Humanity*. The boundaries between humanitarian intervention and development have become increasingly blurred. See also Frerks, "Refugees between Relief and Development"; Hilhorst and van Leeuwen, "Rethinking the Relation between Relief and Development."

4. http://www.unocha.org/about-us/who-we-are; See Agier, "Humanity as an Identity and Its Political Effects," 34, for a useful discussion on the apparatus of humanitarian government.

5. See https://www.unocha.org/our-work/coordination/humanitarian-coordination-leadership.

6. In his chapter titled "Heart of Humaneness: The Moral Economy of Humanitarian Intervention," Fassin describes the historical and cultural legacy of humanitarianism as rooted in European—and even more so, French—philosophical

traditions (271–274). In his conclusion, he makes this Western focus apparent, arguing: "We need to recognize that humanitarian workers are generally motivated by a sense of responsibility toward the world, its violence, and its injustice. But this sense of responsibility is all the more reason to hold them to account for what they say and what they do, *before the societies whose values they proclaim* and, even more, *before those to whom they offer assistance*" (286, italics added).

7. When writing of fields, I refer here to Bourdieu's analytic concept of field as "a space within which an effect of field is exercised, so that what happens to any object that traverses this space cannot be explained solely by the intrinsic properties of the object in question. The limits of the field are situated at the point where the effects of the field cease." Bourdieu and Wacquant, *An Invitation to Reflexive Sociology*, 100.

8. UNHCR is also increasingly working with stateless persons, many of whom are also refugees.

9. *Prima facie* refugee status determination (PFRSD) means being recognized as a refugee without going through an individual RSD process. PFRSD usually happens in situations of mass displacement as an expedient way of granting refugee legal status to people who are fleeing a situation where it is clear that international protection is required. Albert, *Prima facie Determination of Refugee Status*.

10. Statistics from 2019 are used here to illustrate the attainment of solutions before the Covid-19 pandemic, which further reduced options such as third country resettlement. In 2019, 107,800 refugees were resettled in third countries; in 2020, this was reduced to 34,400 places. In 2021 resettlement increased to 57,500 places globally, still well below pre-pandemic levels.

11. This statistic is somewhat misleading, as two of these durable solutions are only available to refugees. That is, of the 79.5 million persons of concern to UNHCR, the majority (45.7 million people) were internally displaced and are not eligible for resettlement and not counted in integration numbers because they are already within their home country. However, I have included this percentage of the total displaced population to illustrate the lack of solutions articulated by the international refugee regime overall.

12. Much as these fall short of meeting actual basic needs. See JSS, *The Living Conditions of People Seeking Asylum in Australia*.

13. This argument could be extended to other realms beyond helping. If a refugee reaches a high level in sport or business, this becomes newsworthy. For example, we could point here to the considerable international attention paid to the Refugee Team at the 2016 and 2021 Olympic Games.

14. http://www.huffingtonpost.com.au/entry/syrian-refugee-bride-zipper_n_12217154.

15. http://www.aljazeera.com/news/2016/03/refugees-volunteer-firefighters-australia-160327060730544.html.

16. http://www.buzzfeed.com/rossalynwarren/meet-the-syrian-refugee-who-is-leading-the-help-for-flood-vi?utm_term=.gmMbW5l33#.tgzoerORR.

17. http://lancasteronline.com/news/local/refugee-who-came-to-lancaster-county-helps-louisiana-flood-victims/article_eb43ee40-6e14-11e6-b271-3b65990f0c11.html.

18. http://www.abc.net.au/news/2016-06-20/former-african-refugee-now-helping-north-queensland-seniors/7525840.

19. When writing about labelling, I reference Wood, who writes that labelling is a generic process in human society that also has "a relationship expressing power at various levels of interpersonal and institutional interaction." See Wood, *Labelling in Development Policy: Essays in Honour of Bernard Schaffer*, 2.

20. Agier (2011) is particularly vehement in his critique of humanitarian government as the cause of refugee suffering. He writes: "The unwanted return of refugees to their 'homes' (an added displacement) or the human or economic problems which push the closure of a camp that is ten or fifteen years old, are lived as an act of aggression, a form of violence which is added onto the violence already experienced by the beneficiaries of humanitarianism." Agier, *Managing the Undesirables: Refugee Camps and Humanitarian Government*, 33–34.

21. It is important to note here that people may occupy more than one of these spaces at a time. For example, IDPs may also be living in camps or people seeking asylum may also be in urban settings. In these cases, both sets of implications for humanitarian interventions may apply.

22. The same can be said for refugees in many other long-established camps in different parts of the world. In recent years, there have been repeated moves to close the world's largest refugee camp, Dadaab in Kenya, and "encourage" (force) Somalis to return to their country of origin by removing humanitarian assistance.

23. The African Union Convention for the Protection and Assistance of Internally Displaced Persons in Africa (Kampala Convention), which came into force in 2012, is significant in this regard.

24. The International Organization for Migration (IOM), UNHCR, Jesuit Refugee Services (JRS), and Church World Service (CWS) are all humanitarian INGOs working with refugees and asylum seekers in Indonesia.

2. The Ecology of Refugee Diaspora Humanitarianism

1. To explain by way of example, consider the Syrian diaspora in Australia. While many Syrian Australians mobilized to help in response to the unfolding crisis in their country of origin, none were directly involved in this study. This is because it was only after the Syrian conflict began in 2011 that Syrian nationals became persons of concern to the international refugee regime. The Syrian diaspora in Australia is made up of two groups: those who arrived pre-2011 (almost exclusively as skilled migrants, students and through family reunion programs) and those who have arrived post-2011 (who include people who have personally experienced the violent conflict in their homeland and were forcibly displaced). At the time that I was identifying RDOs to include in this study, no Syrian diaspora organizations involving

former refugees were identified because Syrians were only just starting to be granted refugee and humanitarian visas, and few had actually arrived. Since I completed my fieldwork, several Syrian RDOs have emerged, and their activities are focused on places where Syrian refugees are living in extremely difficult circumstances (e.g., Lebanon, Jordan, and Turkey).

2. It is worth noting here that, particularly in anthropological studies of diaspora communities, there can be a tendency to reify ethnicity to explain beliefs and practices. Without denying the significance of factors including ethnicity, culture, gender, class, and so on, I focus in this research on the commonalities of experience that refugee displacement and resettlement bring and of the possibilities they create, which go beyond questions of ethnicity and culture.

3. Apart from the 2.8 percent of the Australian population who identify as Indigenous, all other Australians are migrants or the descendants of migrants. Even the largest self-identified ethnic group—Anglo Australians—can be considered an ethnic minority (36.1 percent in 2016). In the question about ancestry in the 2016 population census, only 33.5 percent of respondents self-identified as Australian. The census indicated that one-third of the population was born outside of Australia (33.3%) and nearly half the population (49% of stated responses) had one or both parents born overseas. See Australian Bureau of Statistics, "2016 Census QuickStats."

4. Others have written extensively and excellently on this topic. See Danforth, *The Macedonian Conflict: Ethnic Nationalism in a Transnational World*; and Ndhlovu, *Becoming an African Diaspora in Australia: Language, Culture, Identity.*

5. Interview with K02, Sydney, March 27, 2015.

6. Recruitment information used the phrase *organizations and groups* in anticipation that some collective action would be undertaken by more informal groups that did not identify as an organization or were wary of calling themselves an organization if they were not legally incorporated in Australia. This proved to be the case.

7. For example, in looking at the top countries of origin for refugee and humanitarian entrants over the past twenty years (table 2.1), communities from the former Yugoslavia were excluded from targeted recruitment. This was because it was unlikely that there would be current involvement in humanitarian action by former Yugoslav refugees due to the evolution and (largely) the resolution of the refugee situation in this region.

8. RDOs predominantly targeted their *advocacy* at the Australian government, UNHCR, the UN Human Rights Council, and international NGOs and focused their advocacy on raising the profile or attention given to their target population to enhance protection. *Migration support* included filling in visa application forms and sponsoring individuals or groups of people for resettlement in Australia. Decisions about who and how to support their migration were made on a collective, rather than a family or individual, basis. For example, many RDOs worked with existing community structures or community-based organizations overseas to identify cases in priority need of resettlement.

9. It is hard to find accurate estimates of the number of people living in Australia who identify as Oromo, particularly as statistics tend to gather "country of origin" information, which would include Oromo within the "Ethiopia-born" category (there would also be people who identify as Oromo who were born in countries of asylum, including Sudan, Kenya, and Uganda). The 2016 census recorded 11,791 Ethiopia-born persons in Australia, with 18,065 persons indicating that their mother and 17,885 that their father was Ethiopia-born. One interviewee estimated the size of the Oromo community in Australia (including second generation) as "no less than 12,000" (Interview with RDO 9, Melbourne, April 3, 2015).

10. AOCAV's vision as stated on its website is for "an inclusive and vibrant community committed to facilitating development and growth, whilst maintaining the rich cultural heritage of the Oromo people.n Accessed March 6, 2022, https://www.aocav.com/aboutus.html.

11. At the time of writing in 2019, UNHCR was advising refugees in Indonesia that resettlement places were so limited that it may take a decade if at all.

12. I participated in this visit.

13. In 2016, UNHCR's budget for Sudan was US$167 million, and its expenditure (i.e., amount of funding actually received) was US$80 million, meaning less than half of the estimated budget was met.

14. Since the military reseized control of the Myanmar government in a coup in February 2021, the prospect of return for many refugees in Thailand has again been put on hold.

15. Sadly, those who did manage to cross into Syria and ended up in the Yarmouk refugee camp near Damascus subsequently got caught up in the Syrian conflict that then ignited in 2011 and were forced to flee yet again.

16. The states that did provide resettlement to this group included Belgium, Chile, Finland, Italy, Norway, Sweden, Switzerland, and the United Kingdom (not Australia).

17. Each application for a Global Special Humanitarian Program visa involves a thirty-six-page legal document (application form 842), and all documents in languages other than English must be fully translated.

18. See https://www.youtube.com/watch?v=1JcuNoalTIo.

19. Chaldeans and Assyrians are often spoken about together, as Christian minorities from the historical region of Mesopotamia. The term *Assyrian* is frequently used to describe the broader ethnic group and Chaldeans as Catholic Assyrians.

20. According to Sargon Donabed (2015), Assyria—the homeland of the Assyrian people—is located within the borders of northern Iraq, southeastern Turkey, northwestern Iran, and northeastern Syria. Donabed, *Reforging a Forgotten History: Iraq and the Assyrians in the Twentieth Century.*

21. See https://www.assyrianaidsociety.org.

22. Internal Displacement Monitoring Centre, 2015, "Iraq IDPs Caught between a Rock and a Hard Place as Displacement Crisis Deepens," accessed October 16, 2017,

https://www.internal-displacement.org/publications/iraq-idps-caught-between-a-rock-and-a-hard-place-as-displacement-crisis-deepens.

23. Figure taken from financial reports, January 2014 to February 2016, available at http://assyrianaidsociety.org.

3. Forces That Compel

1. Bornstein and Redfield illustrate the historical roots of the dominant humanitarian actors by showing how some of the largest INGOs (in terms of budget expenditure) were all established in Western Europe or North America between 1863 and 1987. The majority were established in the postwar period between 1942 and 1987 in Britain, the United States, France, and Switzerland. Bornstein and Redfield, *Forces of Compassion: Humanitarianism between Ethics and Politics.*

2. See Forsythe, "Contemporary Humanitarianism: The Global and the Local," for an excellent analysis of the interests of powerful states within the UN humanitarian system. See Gökalp, "The UAE's Humanitarian Diplomacy: Claiming State Sovereignty, Regional Leverage and International Recognition," on how UAE, as a major donor to the humanitarian system, leverages its geopolitical and economic interests through its humanitarian diplomacy.

3. Interview with CBO 16, Sydney, May 7, 2015.

4. Interview with CBO 27, Melbourne, November 17, 2015.

5. Interview with CBO 15, Sydney, May 7, 2015.

6. Ladan (interview with CBO 3, Melbourne, March 7, 2015), Jordan (interview with CBO 10, Melbourne, April 12, 2015), Carmen (interview with CBO 14, Sydney, May 6, 2015).

7. Interview with CBO 17, Melbourne, May 21, 2015.

8. Interview with CBO 15, Sydney, May 7, 2015.

9. Interview with CBO 1, Melbourne, February 23, 2015.

10. Interview with CBO 25, Melbourne, November 17, 2015.

11. Interview with CBO 24, Melbourne, November 17, 2015.

12. Interview with CBO 11, Melbourne, April 14, 2015.

13. Interview with CBO 13, Melbourne, April 30, 2015.

14. Interview with CBO 2, Melbourne, March 2, 2015.

15. Interview with CBO 5, Melbourne, March 22, 2015.

16. Interview with CBO 15, Sydney, May 7, 2015.

17. Interview with CBO 11, Melbourne, April 14, 2015.

18. Interview with CBO 14, Sydney, May 6, 2015.

19. Interview with CBO 27, Melbourne, November 17, 2015.

20. Interview with CBO 6, Melbourne, March 23, 2015.

21. Interview with CBO 21, Albury, August 5, 2015.

22. Interview with CBO 17, Melbourne, May 21, 2015.

23. Interview with CBO 3, Melbourne, March 7, 2015.

24. Interview with CBO 10, Melbourne, April 12, 2015.
25. Interview with CBO 25, Melbourne, November 17, 2015.
26. Interview with CBO 2, Melbourne, March 2, 2015.
27. Interview with CBO 4, Melbourne, March 18, 2015.
28. Interview with CBO 3, Melbourne, March 7, 2015.
29. Interview with CBO 14, Sydney, May 6, 2015.
30. Interview with CBO 25, Melbourne, November 17, 2015.
31. Interview with CBO 24, Melbourne, November 17, 2015.
32. Interview with CBO 17, Melbourne, May 21, 2015.
33. Interview with CBO 9, Melbourne, April 3, 2015.
34. Interview with CBO 18, Sydney, May 26, 2015.
35. Zia Sahill, video posted on Facebook on December 20, 2015, https://www.facebook.com/zsahill/videos/10205193366889220/.
36. Interview with CBO 13, Melbourne, April 30, 2015.
37. Interview with CBO 14, Sydney, May 6, 2015.
38. Interview with CBO 19, Sydney, May 26, 2015.
39. Interview with CBO 1, Melbourne, February 23, 2015.
40. Interview with CBO 15, Sydney, May 7, 2015.
41. Interview with CBO 12, Melbourne, April 17, 2015.
42. Interview with CBO 7, Sydney, March 26, 2015.
43. Interview with CBO 23, Melbourne, October 21, 2015.
44. Interview with CBO 21, Albury, August 5, 2015.
45. Interview with CBO 20, Melbourne, August 1, 2015.
46. Interview with CBO 20, Melbourne, August 1, 2015.
47. Interview with CBO 2, Melbourne, March 2, 2015.
48. Interview with CBO 27, Melbourne, November 17, 2015.
49. Interview with CBO 25, Melbourne, November 17, 2015.
50. Interview with CBO 14, Sydney, May 6, 2015.
51. Interview with CBO 20, Melbourne, August 1, 2015.
52. Interview with CBO 19, Sydney, May 26, 2015.
53. Interview with CBO 1, Melbourne, February 23, 2015.
54. Interview with CBO 6, Melbourne, March 23, 2015.
55. Interview with CBO 4, Melbourne, March 18, 2015.
56. Interview with CBO 2, Melbourne, March 2, 2015.
57. Interview with CBO 23, Melbourne, October 21, 2015.
58. Interview with CBO 11, Melbourne, April 14, 2015.
59. Interview with CBO 14, Sydney, May 6, 2015.
60. Interview with CBO 25, Melbourne, November 17, 2015.
61. Interview with CBO 16, Sydney, May 7, 2015.
62. This process of diasporization has been explored by others in greater detail. See Danforth, *The Macedonian Conflict: Ethnic Nationalism in a Transnational World*;

Jakubowicz, "Living as a Diaspora: The Politics of Exclusion in Relation to Refugees and Disabled People"; and Ndhlovu, Becoming an African Diaspora in Australia: Language, Culture, Identity.

63. Interview with CBO 8, Sydney, March 27, 2015.
64. Interview with CBO 19, Sydney, May 26, 2015.
65. Interview with CBO 16, Sydney, May 7, 2015.
66. Interview with CBO 11, Melbourne, April 14, 2015.
67. Interview with CBO 5, Melbourne, March 22, 2015.
68. Interview with CBO 11, Melbourne, April 14, 2015.
69. Interview with CBO 29, Adelaide, November 28, 2015.
70. Interview with CBO 23, Melbourne, October 21, 2015.
71. Interview with CBO 21, Albury, August 5, 2015.
72. Interview with CBO 23, Melbourne, October 21, 2015.
73. Interview with CBO 4, Melbourne, March 18, 2015.

4. Modalities

1. https://akademossociety.org/.
2. See, for example, Consumer Affairs Victoria, n.d., "Becoming an Incorporated Association," accessed October 12, 2017, https://www.consumer.vic.gov.au/clubs-and-not-for-profits/incorporated-associations/become-an-incorporated-association.
3. Incorporated associations like RDOs are mostly registered at a state or territory government level, such as with Consumer Affairs Victoria or the New South Wales Office of Fair Trading. It is possible to also register a not-for-profit association with the Australian Securities and Investment Commission, which operates nationally. Associations registered with state authorities can operate in other states and territories of Australia but must report annually to the authority in the state or territory where their association was first registered.
4. This correlates with Van Hear and Cohen's findings that religious institutions play an important mediating role in diasporas' transnational engagements "by channelling financial contributions from the diaspora through temples, churches and mosques. Many of these forms of engagement, which might appear to be organized through formal institutions, are actually reliant on informal networks which are created and sustained mostly (but not only) through these institutions." Van Hear and Cohen, "Diasporas and Conflict: Distance, Contiguity and Spheres of Engagement," 176.
5. See also the case study of Dr. S in Bornstein, *Disquieting Gifts: Humanitarianism in New Delhi*, 74–78.
6. Interview with RDO 17, Melbourne, May 21, 2015.
7. Interview with RDO 6, Melbourne, March 23, 2015.
8. Interview with RDO 9, Melbourne, April 3, 2015.

9. This support was given by organizations such as Diaspora Action Australia and the Ecumenical Migration Centre at the Brotherhood of St. Laurence in Melbourne and STARTTS in Sydney.

10. Interview with KI 2, Sydney, March 27, 2015.

11. Interview with RDO 18, Sydney, May 26, 2015.

12. Interview with KI 4, Sydney, May 7, 2015.

13. Interview with RDO 6, Melbourne, March 23, 2015.

14. Interview with RDO 11, Melbourne, April 14, 2015.

15. Interview with RDO 20, Melbourne, August 1, 2015.

16. Interview with RDO 7, Sydney, March 26, 2015.

17. Interview with RDO 14, Sydney, May 6, 2015.

18. http://www.sphereproject.org/.

19. Interview with KI 6, Melbourne, May 6, 2015.

20. Interview with RDO 14, Sydney, May 6, 2015.

21. Interview with KI 6, Melbourne, May 6, 2015.

22. See Ghorashi and Boersma, "The 'Iranian Diaspora' and the New Media: From Political Action to Humanitarian Help," for a description of performative giving among the Iranian diaspora in America.

23. In the years since completing fieldwork, I have followed many online crowdfunding campaigns initiated by diaspora members in Australia that have raised substantial amounts of money to respond to crises affecting their communities overseas. In 2022, the Ukrainian diaspora's incredibly fast mobilization of resources in response to the Russian invasion of Ukraine using cryptocurrency online communities has taken this online fundraising to the next level. Purtill, "Crypto and blockchain are being used in unprecedented ways in the Russia-Ukraine war."

24. *Hawâla* is an informal value transfer system based not on the movement of cash or on telegraph or computer network wire transfers between banks, but on the performance and honor of a huge network of money brokers. *Hawâla* is used widely in Muslim communities, although not exclusively. "Hawala," Wikipedia, https://en.wikipedia.org/wiki/Hawala, accessed March 10, 2022.

25. Interview with RDO 15, Sydney, May 7, 2015.

26. Interview with RDO 11, Melbourne, April 14, 2015.

27. Interview with KI 1, Melbourne, March 11, 2015.

28. Interview with RDO 11, Melbourne, April 14, 2015.

29. Interview with RDO 21, Albury, August 5, 2015.

30. Interview with RDO 7, Sydney, March 26, 2015.

31. Interview with RDO 3, Melbourne, March 7, 2015.

32. Interview with RDO 10, Melbourne, April 12, 2015.

33. Interview with RDO 9, Melbourne, April 3, 2015.

34. Interview with RDO 13, Melbourne, April 30, 2015.

35. Interview with RDO 25, Melbourne, November 17, 2015.

36. Interview with RDO 4, Melbourne, March 18, 2015.
37. Interview with RDO 17, Melbourne, May 21, 2015.

5. Modalities

1. When people are resettled as refugees in Australia, they are granted a permanent residency visa on arrival. After four years, permanent residents can apply for citizenship, which entitles them to an Australian passport. An Australian passport enables visa-free travel or visa on arrival to 169 countries around the world, with Australia ranked eighth in terms of travel freedom, according to the Visa Restrictions Index. For those who are permanent residents but not citizens (people who have lived in Australia for less than four years or have not applied for citizenship), most can travel outside Australia on a Convention Travel Document (CTD); however, the number of states that recognize CTDs is limited. Countries that have not signed the Refugee Convention may not allow individuals to enter their territory on CTDs.
2. Interview with RDO 2, Melbourne, March 2, 2015.
3. Interview with RDO 23, Melbourne, October 23, 2015.
4. Interview with RDO 11, Melbourne, April 14, 2015.
5. In 2013, this felt like a notable event and modality, even though the Covid-19 pandemic and the resulting transformation of work practices have meant this kind of virtual connectivity is now commonplace.
6. Interview with RDO 29, Adelaide, November 28, 2015.
7. Interview with RDO 3, Melbourne, March 7, 2015.
8. Interview with RDO 18, Sydney, May 26, 2015.
9. See van de Port, "'It Takes a Serb to Know a Serb': Uncovering the Roots of Obstinate Otherness in Serbia," for a similar argument—that you cannot "know a Serb" unless you are one—about the assertion of Serb identity.
10. While the risks for these individuals may have been different because of their ability to blend in (through appearance, language, understanding of context), it should not be assumed that there were no risks. See DEMAC, *Diaspora Humanitarianism: Transnational Ways of Working*; and Foulkes, "Emergency Aid: Obstacles to Going Local."
11. Interview with RDO 10, Melbourne, April 12, 2015.
12. Restrictions on access were introduced because of serious security threats, namely, refugees being kidnapped, tortured, and extorted by smugglers and traffickers. Humphris, *Refugees and the Rashaida: Human Smuggling and Trafficking from Eritrea to Sudan and Egypt.*
13. Two connected RDOs were involved in funding the construction of the six classrooms.
14. This forum was cohosted by Diaspora Action Australia and the Melbourne Refugee Studies Program and was held on November 27, 2015, at the University of Melbourne, Australia.

15. Interview with RDO 18, Sydney, May 26, 2015.
16. Interview with RDO 13, Melbourne, April 30, 2015.
17. Interview with RDO 2, Melbourne, March 2, 2015.
18. Interview with RDO 10, Melbourne, April 12, 2015.
19. Interview with RDO 11, Melbourne, April 14, 2015.
20. Interview with KI 1, Melbourne, March 11, 2015.
21. For example, many INGOs reference The Sphere Project's *Humanitarian Charter and Minimum Standards in Humanitarian Response*. See http://www.sphereproject.org/.
22. Interview with RDO 23, Melbourne, October 21, 2015.
23. Interview with RDO 3, Melbourne, March 7, 2015.
24. Interview with RDO 7, Sydney, March 26, 2015.
25. Interview with RDO 19, Sydney, May 26, 2015.
26. Interview with RDO 15, Sydney, May 7, 2015.
27. Interview with KI 2, Sydney, March 27, 2015.
28. Interview with RDO 7, Sydney, March 26, 2015.
29. Interview with RDO 17, Melbourne, May 21, 2015.
30. Interview with RDO 2, Melbourne, March 2, 2015.
31. Interview with RDO 10, Melbourne, April 12, 2015.
32. Interview with RDO 11, Melbourne, April 14, 2015.
33. Interview with RDO 3, Melbourne, March 7, 2015.

6. Implications and Imaginings

1. Note, for example, the World Humanitarian Summit in 2016 convened by then UN Secretary General Ban Ki-moon to "generate commitments to reduce suffering and deliver better for people caught in humanitarian crises." See https://agendaforhumanity.org/summit.html. For an example of humanitarian innovation, see https://www.unhcr.org/innovation/

2. In discussing CBP, I do not offer an in-depth analysis of its implementation. Rather, I take policy discussions as part of the ongoing process of envisioning and shaping humanitarian responses in situations of forced displacement—that is, policies inform practices and vice versa, but the link between the two is not always as expected. The impact of these policies on refugees is a question that warrants separate investigation, but understanding its direction helps us understand future possibilities that hopefully draw on lessons from the past.

3. A UNHCR definition of protection is being "protected from persistent internal or external violence or threats of violence, and their effects, and from coercion and systematic deprivation of basic rights." See UNHCR, *Understanding Community-Based Protection*, 4.

4. For example, Sandvik, "The Physicality of Legal Consciousness," describes how refugees in Uganda learn about, understand, and perform particular narratives

of suffering that they believe will facilitate their chances of being accepted by a third country for resettlement, and how UNHCR's legal protection officers seek to distinguish "true authenticity" in narrative performances.

5. A widely recognized interagency model of humanitarian protection is the "egg model," which emerged as the agreed protection framework from ICRC-led workshops. This model has three key elements: (1) division of all agency actions around concerning violations and protection into three main spheres or levels of programming: responsive, remedial, and environment-building; (2) description of all forms of protective action into five main modes of action: denunciation, persuasion, mobilization, substitution, and support to services; (3) endorsement of the principle of interagency complementarity as central to all protection programming. See Slim and Eguren, *Humanitarian Protection*, 25.

6. As an aside, one could question several other assumptions in this case study, including whether the "expected ways" in which people help each other were, in fact, "dismantled" or "destroyed" by the exceptional circumstances brought about the tsunami or simply adapted to the change in possibilities and, presumably, adapted again once the INGOs left.

7. UNHCR Exchange hosts a webpage where information about "what has worked in the field" in terms of CBP is shared, with many examples of how communities are conceptualized in relatively bounded and geographically localized terms (for example, see UNHCR Sudan 2014 for report from community asset mapping in Khartoum)

8. A keynote speaker at the *Diasporas in Action* conference at Melbourne University in 2016, Chukwu-Emeka Chikezie, insightfully commented that diasporas are unacknowledged leaders in humanitarian practice; sending cash transfers (i.e., remittances) to people caught up in humanitarian crises well before the popularity of "cash-based transfers" was heralded by dominant actors as a more efficient, effective, and empowering means of providing humanitarian assistance.

9. Interview with HO 3, Skype (Copenhagen, Denmark), August 3, 2105.

10. Ibid.

11. Since this research was undertaken, a number of important initiatives have been developed to engage diaspora as actors in humanitarian response systems. This includes the European-based Diaspora Emergency Action and Coordination (DEMAC) initiative and the International Organization for Migration's global iDiaspora platform and various pilot programs.

12. Interview with HO 4, phone (Armidale, Australia), August 12, 2015.

13. Ibid.

14. Interview with RDO 1, Melbourne, February 23, 2015.

15. Interview with RDO 21, Albury, August 5, 2015.

16. This may be similar to other countries in the Global North. One interviewee who lived in Denmark, noted: "We have hardly any approaches towards migration for development and diaspora engagement in development. . . . (We) have no targeted

diaspora approach and neither does anybody else, according to our knowledge." Interview with HO 3, Skype (Copenhagen, Denmark), August 3, 2105.

17. To wit, of the thirty-three people who were charged with terrorist-related offenses in Australia, mostly relating to volunteering as foreign fighters, twenty-two were from second- and third-generation Lebanese-Muslim background.

18. Other examples include former immigration minister Kevin Andrews' 2007 statement in relation to cutting the refugee intake from Africa that "some groups don't seem to be settling and adjusting into the Australian way of life." See Farouque et al., "Minister Cuts African Refugee Intake."; the infamous Children Overboard affair in 2001 where ministers in the Howard Administration publicly lied about asylum seekers throwing their children into the sea in a presumed ploy to secure rescue and passage to Australia; and, more recently, the introduction of the term "*Illegal* Maritime Arrival" for any person seeking asylum in Australia by boat, despite the fact that international law clearly establishes the legality of people's right to seek asylum regardless of their mode of arrival.

19. The founding members of the DLN are Diaspora Action Australia, Research for Development Impact Network, Australian Council for International Development, Oxfam Australia, Refugee Council of Australia, Australian Red Cross, and the University of Melbourne Refugee Studies Program. In 2021, an Australian Research Council Linkage Project Grant was awarded through the work of the DLN to explore how Australia-based migrants respond in times of crisis overseas.

20. Australia started moving down the ranks of resettlement states from 2017. In 2021, Australia was ranked 14 in terms of resettlement numbers. See Garnier, "The Ongoing Impacts of the COVID-19 Pandemic on Refugee Resettlement."

7. Helping Familiar Strangers

1. https://www.networkforrefugeevoices.org/global-summit-of-refugees.html.
2. https://globalrefugeenetwork.org/index.php/en/.
3. https://www.resourcingrlos.org/.

Epilogue

1. See Dai, K. 2020. "Refugee Life: A Pictorial History by Khadim Dai." *CEC Journal: Issue 7: Hurt and Repair.* Bartos Institute for Constructive Engagement of Conflict. Accessed October 12, 2021, https://scalar.usc.edu/works/cec-journal-issue-7/refugee-life.

2. Harlow, O. 2018. "Film Aims to Help Bring Afghan Refugees to Study in N.M." *Santa Fe New Mexican,* July 31, 2018.

BIBLIOGRAPHY

Agamben, G. 2005. *State of Exception*. Chicago: University of Chicago Press.

Agenda for Humanity. 2016. *The Grand Bargain—A Shared Commitment to Better Serve People in Need*. Istanbul, Turkey.

Agier, M. 2008. *On the Margins of the World: The Refugee Experience Today*. Cambridge, UK: Polity.

Agier, M. 2010. "Humanity as an Identity and Its Political Effects (A Note on Camps and Humanitarian Government)." *Humanity: An International Journal of Human Rights, Humanitarianism and Development* 1, no. 1 (Fall): 29–45.

Agier, M. 2011. *Managing the Undesirables: Refugee Camps and Humanitarian Government*. Cambridge, UK: Polity.

Albert, M. 2010. *Prima Facie Determination of Refugee Status: An Overview of Its Legal Foundation* (Working Paper Series No. 55). Oxford: Refugee Studies Centre.

Al-Sharmani, M. 2010. "Transnational Family Networks in the Somali Diaspora in Egypt: Women's Roles and Differentiated Experiences." *Gender, Place and Culture: A Journal of Feminist Geography* 17, no. 4: 499–518.

Altman, T. 2015. "Righteous Citizens: The New Voluntarism and the Neoliberal Welfare Landscape." In *Association of Social Anthropologists of the Commonwealth Conference*. Exeter, UK.

Amnesty International. 2014. *"Because I Am Oromo": Sweeping Repression in the Oromia Region of Ethiopia*. London: Amnesty.

Appadurai, A. 1996. *Modernity at Large: Cultural Dimensions of Globalization*. Minneapolis: University of Minnesota Press.

Appadurai, A. 2013. *The Future as Cultural Fact: Essays on the Global Condition*. London: Verso.

Asad, T. 2015. Reflections on Violence, Law, and Humanitarianism. *Critical Inquiry* 41: 390–427.

Australian Bureau of Statistics. 2017. "2016 Census QuickStats." Accessed September 29, 2017, http://www.censusdata.abs.gov.au/census_services/getproduct/census/2016/quickstat/036.

Bakewell, O. 2008. "Research Beyond the Categories: The Importance of Policy Irrelevant Research into Forced Migration." *Journal of Refugee Studies* 21, no. 4: 432–453.

Barnett, M. 2005. "Humanitarianism Transformed." *Perspectives on Politics* 3, no. 4: 723–740.

Barnett, M. 2011. *Empire of Humanity: A History of Humanitarianism*. Ithaca, NY: Cornell University Press.

Barnett, M., and T. G. Weiss. 2011. *Humanitarianism Contested: Where Angels Fear to Tread*. Oxon, UK: Routledge.

Barth, F. 1969. "Introduction." In *Ethnic Groups and Boundaries: The Social Organization of Cultural Difference*, edited by F. Barth, 9–38. Boston: Little, Brown.

Basch, L. G., N. G. Schiller, and C. Szanton Blanc. 1994. *Nations Unbound: Transnational Projects, Postcolonial Predicaments, and Deterritorialized Nation-States*. Switzerland: Gordon and Breach.

Bauman, Z. 2000. *Liquid Modernity*. Cambridge, UK: Polity.

Belot, H. 2016. "Peter Dutton Defends 'Honest' Comments on Lebanese-Muslim Refugees." *ABC News Online*, November 25, 2016.

Benner, M. T., A. Muangsookjarouen, E. Sondorp, and J. Townsend. 2008. "Neglect of Refugee Participation." *Forced Migration Review* 30: 25.

Bennett, C., and M. Foley. 2016. *Time to Let Go: Remaking Humanitarian Action for the Modern Era*. London: Humanitarian Policy Group, Overseas Development Institute.

Benthall, J., and R. Lacey, eds. 2014. *Gulf Charities and Islamic Philanthropy in the 'Age of Terror' and Beyond*. Berlin: Gerlach.

Bernal, V. 2006. "Diaspora, Cyberspace and Political Imagination: The Eritrean Diaspora Online." *Global Networks* 6, no. 2: 161–179.

Berry, K., and S. Reddy. 2010. *Safety with Dignity: Integrating Community-Based Protection into Humanitarian Programming*. London: Humanitarian Practice Network, Overseas Development Institute.

Bessa, T. 2009. "From Political Instrument to Protection Tool? Resettlement of Refugees and North-South Relations." *Refuge* 26, no. 1: 91–100.

Betts, A. 2010. "Survival Migration: A New Protection Framework." *Global Governance* 16, no. 3: 361–382.

Betts, A., and W. Jones. 2016. *Mobilizing the Diaspora: How Refugees Challenge Authoritarianism*. Cambridge, UK: Cambridge University Press.

Bevir, M. 2013. *Governance: A Short Introduction*. Oxford: Oxford University Press.

Bornstein, E. 2012. *Disquieting Gifts: Humanitarianism in New Delhi*. Standford, CA: Stanford University Press.

Bornstein, E., and P. Redfield, eds. 2010. *Forces of Compassion: Humanitarianism Between Ethics and Politics.* Santa Fe, NM: School for Advanced Research Press.

Bourdieu, P. 1988. *Homo Academicus/Pierre Bourdieu.* Translated by Peter Collier. Stanford, CA: Stanford University Press.

Bourdieu, P. 2010. "Sociologists of Belief and Beliefs of Sociologists." *Nordic Journal of Religion and Society* 23, no. 1: 1–7.

Bourdieu, P., and L. J. D. Wacquant. 1992. *An Invitation to Reflexive Sociology.* Chicago: University of Chicago Press.

Brees, I. 2010. "Refugees and Transnationalism on the Thai–Burmese Border." *Global Networks* 10, no. 2: 282–299.

Brinkerhoff, J. M. 2008. "Diaspora Philanthropy in an At-Risk Society: The Case of Coptic Orphans in Egypt." *Nonprofit and Voluntary Sector Quarterly* 37, no. 3: 411–433.

Brinkerhoff, J. M. 2011. "David and Goliath: Diaspora Organizations as Partners in the Development Industry." *Public Administration and Development* 31, no. 1: 37–49.

Brinkerhoff, J. M. 2012. "Creating an Enabling Environment for Diasporas' Participation in Homeland Development." *International Migration* 50, no. 1: 75–95.

Brun, C., and A. Fábos. 2015. "Making Homes in Limbo? A Conceptual Framework." *Refuge* 31, no. 1: 5–18.

Butler, K. D. 2001. "Defining Diaspora, Refining a Discourse." *Diaspora: A Journal of Transnational Studies* 10, no. 2: 189.

Celebnorthsouth. 2016. Everyday Humanitarianism: Ethics, Affects and Practices. Accessed August 29, 2017, https://celebnorthsouth.wordpress.com/activities/upcoming-conference-everyday-humanitarianism-ethics-affects-and-practices/.

Charter4Change. 2016. *Charter for Change: Localization of Humanitarian Aid.* Accessed November 28, 2016, https://charter4change.files.wordpress.com/2016/02/charter-for-change-july-20152.pdf.

Chouliaraki, L. 2013. *The Ironic Spectator: Solidarity in the Age of Post-Humanitarianism.* Cambridge, UK: Polity.

Cisarua Learning. n.d. *About Cisarua Learning.* Accessed November 29, 2019, https://cisarualearning.com/new-page-3.

Clifford, J. 1994. Diasporas. *Cultural Anthropology,* no. 3: 302.

Clifford, J. 1997. "Spatial Practices: Fieldwork, Travel, and the Disciplining of Anthropology." In *Anthropological Locations: Boundaries and Grounds of a Field Science,* edited by A. Gupta and J. Ferguson, 185–222. Berkeley: University of California Press.

Cohen, R., and N. Van Hear. 2017. "Visions of Refugia: Territorial and Transnational Solutions to Mass Displacement." *Planning Theory and Practice* 18, no. 3: 494–504.

Collier, P. 2000. *Economic Causes of Civil Conflict and Their Implications for Policy.* Washington, DC: World Bank.

Collyer, M. 2006. "'Citizens without Borders'?: Discussions of Transnationalism and Forced Migrants at the Ninth Conference of the International Association for the Study of Forced Migration, São Paulo, Brazil, January 2005." *Refuge* 23, no. 1: 94–100.

Commonwealth of Australia. 2011. *The People of Australia: Australia's Multicultural Policy*. Canberra: Department of Immigration and Border Protection.

Conradson, D., and D. McKay. 2007. "Translocal Subjectivities: Mobility, Connection, Emotion." *Mobilities* 2, no. 2: 167–174.

Crisp, J. 2018. "As the World Abandons Refugees, UNHCR's Constraints Are Exposed." *Refugees Deeply*, September 2018. Accessed March 1, 2020, https://www.newsdeeply.com/refugees/community/2018/09/13/as-the-world-abandons-refugees-unhcrs-constraints-are-exposed.

CRLC. 2019. "LIVE from the CRLC." Accessed November 26, 2019, https://youtu.be/oYUvEBvWVYw.

Danforth, L. 1995. *The Macedonian Conflict: Ethnic Nationalism in a Transnational World*. Princeton, NJ: Princeton University Press.

de Koker, L. 2014. "Lack of Real Action on Remittances Increases Terrorist Financing Risk." *The Conversation*. Accessed November 14, 2017, https://theconversation.com/lack-of-real-action-on-remittances-increases-terrorist-financing-risk-34706.

De Lauri, A. 2019. "The Taliban and the Humanitarian Soldier: Configurations of Freedom and Humanity in Afghanistan." *ANUAC* 8, no. 1: 31–57.

Deleuze, G., and F. Guttari. 1987. *A Thousand Plateaus: Capitalism and Schizophrenia*. Minneapolis: University of Minnesota Press.

DEMAC. 2016a. *Diaspora at the World Humanitarian Summit*. Accessed November 13, 2017, http://www.demac.org/sharing-knowledge/diaspora-whs.

DEMAC. 2016b. *Diaspora Humanitarianism: Transnational Ways of Working*. Accessed March 19, 2022, https://reliefweb.int/report/world/diaspora-humanitarianism-transnational-ways-working.

De Montclos, M.-A. P. 2008. "Humanitarian Aid, War, Exodus, and Reconstruction of Identities: A Case Study of Somali 'Minority Refugees' in Kenya." *Nationalism and Ethnic Politics* 14, no. 2: 289–321.

De Montclos, M.-A. P., and P. M. Kagwanja. 2000. "Refugee Camps or Cities? The Socio-economic Dynamics of the Dadaab and Kakuma Camps in Northern Kenya." *Journal of Refugee Studies* 13, no. 2: 205–222.

DePoe, J. M. n.d. "Knowledge by Acquaintance and Knowledge by Description." Accessed August 1, 2016, http://www.iep.utm.edu/knowacq/.

Development Initiatives. 2019. *Global Humanitarian Assistance Report 2019*. Accessed March 19, 2022, https://devinit.org/resources/global-humanitarian-assistance-report-2019/.

Diaspora Action Australia. n.d. *The Diaspora Learning Network*. Accessed August 28, 2017, http://diasporaaction.org.au/diaspora-learning-network/.

Diaspora Learning Network. 2016. Diasporas in Action: Working Together for Peace, Development and Humanitarian Response. Conference Outcomes, University of Melbourne, Australia, September 26–27, 2016.

Donabed, S. G. 2015. *Reforging a Forgotten History: Iraq and the Assyrians in the Twentieth Century*. Edinburgh: Edinburgh University Press.

Douglas, T., and A. Greenhill. 2017. "What Is Voluntourism?" *Interaction* 45, no. 1: 33–35.

Dudley, S. 2006. "Re-shaping Karenni-ness in Exile: Education, Nationalism and Being in the Wider World." In *Exploring Ethnic Diversity in Burma*, edited by M. Gravers, 77–106. Copenhagen: NIAS.

Dunn, E. C. 2014. "Humanitarian Reason: A Moral History of the Present." *The Political and Legal Anthropology Review* 37, no. 1: 191–193.

EAHA. n.d. "Eritrean Australian Humanitarian Aid: About Us." Accessed October 19, 2015, https://eahaid.wordpress.com/about/.

Ealom, J. 2021. "When Big Philanthropy Takes a Backseat." *Medium*. Accessed March 17, 2021, https://medium.com/needslist/a-new-approach-to-a-decades-old-problem-2f7a715db38f.

Eiseley, L. C. 1978. *The Star Thrower*. New York: Times Books.

Essed, P., and R. Wesenbeek. 2004. "Contested Refugee Status: Human Rights, Ethics and Social Responsibilities." In *Refugees and the Transformation of Societies: Agency, Policies, Ethics, and Politics*, edited by P. Essed, G. Frerks, and J. Schrijvers, 53–65. New York: Berghahn Books.

Farouque, F., A. Petrie, and D. Miletic. 2007. "Minister Cuts African Refugee Intake." *The Age*, October 2, 2007. Accessed November 3, 2016, http://www.theage.com.au/articles/2007/10/01/1191091031242.html.

Fassin, D. 2010a. "Heart of Humaneness: The Moral Economy of Humanitarian Intervention." In *Contemporary States of Emergency : The Politics of Military and Humanitarian Interventions*, edited by D. Fassin and M. Pandolfi, 269–294. New York: Zone Books.

Fassin, D. 2010b. *Humanitarian Reason: A Moral History of the Present*. Los Angeles: University of California Press.

Fassin, D. 2010c. "Inequality of Lives, Hierarchies of Humanity: Moral Commitments and Ethical Dilemmas of Humanitarianism." In *In the Name of Humanity: The Government of Threat and Care*, edited by I. Feldman and M. Ticktin, 238–255. Durham, NC: Duke University Press.

Fassin, D. 2010d. "Noli Me Tangere: The Moral Untouchability of Humanitarianism." In *Forces of Compassion: Humanitarianism Between Ethics and Politics*, edited by P. Redfield and E. Bornstein, 35–52. Santa Fe, NM: School for Advanced Research Press.

Fassin, D., and M. Pandolfi. 2010. *Contemporary States of Emergency: The Politics of Military and Humanitarian Interventions*. New York: Zone Books.

Feldman, I. 2012. *Palestinian Refugee Experience in a Changing Humanitarian Order.* Rochester, NY: Social Science Research Network.

Feldman, I., and M. Ticktin. 2010. "Introduction: Government and Humanity." In *In the Name of Humanity: The Government of Threat and Care,* edited by I. Feldman and M. Ticktin, 1–26. Durham, NC: Duke University Press.

Feller, E. 2006. "Asylum, Migration and Refugee Protection: Realities, Myths and the Promise of Things to Come." *International Journal of Refugee Law* 18, no. 3–4: 509–536.

Ferguson, J. 2009. "The Uses of Neoliberalism." *Antipode* 41, no. S1: 166–184.

Ferguson, J., and A. Gupta. 2002. "Spatializing States: Toward an Ethnography of Neoliberal Governmentality." *American Ethnologist* 29, no. 4: 981–1002.

Fine, G. A. 1993. "Ten Lies of Ethnography: Moral Dilemmas of Field Research." *Journal of Contemporary Ethnography* 22, no. 3: 267–294.

Forsythe, D. P. 2009. "Contemporary Humanitarianism: The Global and the Local." In *Humanitarianism and Suffering: The Mobilization of Empathy,* edited by R. A. Wilson and R. D. Brown, 58–87. Cambridge, UK: Cambridge University Press.

Foucault, M. 1977. *Discipline and Punish: The Birth of the Prison.* New York: Vintage Books.

Foucault, M. 2010. *The Government of Self and Others.* Edited by A. I. Davidson. Basingstoke, UK: Palgrave Macmillan.

Foulkes, I. 2015. "Emergency Aid: Obstacles to Going Local." *IRIN News,* September 24, 2015. Accessed May 16, 2016, http://www.irinnews.org/analysis/2015/09/24.

Frerks, G. 2004. "Refugees between Relief and Development." In *Refugees and the Transformation of Societies: Agency, Policies, Ethics, and Politics,* edited by P. Essed, G. Frerks, and J. Schrijvers, 167–178. New York: Berghahn Books.

Fullilove, M. 2008. *World Wide Webs: Diasporas and The International System.* Sydney: Lowy Institute for International Policy.

Gamlen, A. 2019. *Human Geopolitics: States, Emigrants, and the Rise of Diaspora Institutions.* Oxford: Oxford University Press.

Garnier, A. 2022. "The Ongoing Impacts of the COVID-19 Pandemic on Refugee Resettlement." In *Asylum Insight.* Accessed March 16, 2022, https://www.asyluminsight.com/garnier.

Geertz, C. 1998. "Deep Hanging Out." *New York Review of Books* 45, no. 16: 69–72.

Gert, B. 2016. "The Definition of Morality." Accessed November 8, 2016, https://plato.stanford.edu/entries/morality-definition/.

GHA. 2014. *Global Humanitarian Assistance: Defining Humanitarian Assistance.* Accessed March 19, 2022, https://web.archive.org/web/20171102215158/http://www.globalhumanitarianassistance.org/data-guides/defining-humanitarian-aid.

Ghorashi, H., and K. Boersma. 2009. "The 'Iranian Diaspora' and the New Media: From Political Action to Humanitarian Help." *Development and Change* 40, no. 4: 667–691.

Giddens, A. 1984. *The Constitution of Society*. Berkeley: University of California Press.
Gleeson, M. 2016. *Offshore: Behind the Wire on Manus and Nauru*. Sydney: UNSW Press.
Glick Schiller, N. 2004. "Transnationality." In *A Companion to the Anthropology of Politics*, edited by J. Vincent and D. Nugent, 448–467. Malden, MA: Blackwell.
Glick Schiller, N. 2012. "Transnationality, Migrants and Cities." In *Beyond Methodological Nationalism: Research Methodologies for Cross-Border Studies*, edited by A. Amelina, D. Nergiz, T. Faist, and N. Glick Schiller, 23–40. New York: Routledge.
Glick Schiller, N., and N. B. Salazar. 2013. "Regimes of Mobility Across the Globe." *Journal of Ethnic and Migration Studies* 39, no. 2: 183–200.
Goetz, A. M., and R. Jenkins. 2005. *Reinventing Accountability: Making Democracy Work for Human Development*. New York: Palgrave Macmillan.
Goffman, E. 1959. *The Presentation of Self in Everyday Life*. New York: Anchor Books.
Gökalp, D. 2020. "The UAE's Humanitarian Diplomacy: Claiming State Sovereignty, Regional Leverage and International Recognition." *CMI Working Paper* 1: 1–11.
Gropas, R. 2013. *The Migration-Development Nexus: Time for a Paradigm Shift* (Policy Paper). Jacques Delors Institute, Notre Europe.
Guilhot, N. 2012. "The Anthropologist as Witness: Humanitarianism between Ethnography and Critique." *Humanity: An International Journal of Human Rights, Humanitarianism, and Development* 3, no. 1: 81–101.
Hage, G. 2005. "A Not So Multi-sited Ethnography of a Not So Imagined Community." *Anthropological Theory* 5, no. 4: 463–475.
Hage, G. 2012. *White Nation: Fantasies of White Supremacy in a Multicultural Society*. Hoboken, NJ: Taylor and Francis.
Hall, S. 1997. *Representation: Cultural Representations and Signifying Practices*. London: SAGE.
Hannam, K., M. Sheller, and J. Urry. 2006. "Editorial: Mobilities, Immobilities and Moorings." *Mobilities* 1, no. 1: 1–22.
Hansen, P. 2004. *Migrant Remittances as a Development Tool: The Case of Somaliland*. Migration Policy Research (vol. 3). Geneva: IOM.
Harley, T., and H. Hobbs. 2020. "The Meaningful Participation of Refugees in Decision-Making Processes: Questions of Law and Policy." *International Journal of Refugee Law* 32, no. 2: 200–226.
Harrell-Bond, B. 2002. "Can Humanitarian Work with Refugees be Humane?" *Human Rights Quarterly* 24, no. 1: 51–85.
Harrell-Bond, B., and E. Voutira. 2007. "In Search of 'Invisible' Actors: Barriers to Access in Refugee Research." *Journal of Refugee Studies* 20, no. 2: 281–298.
Harvey, D. 2005. *A Brief History of Neoliberalism*. Oxford: Oxford University Press.
Hathaway, J. C. 2005. *The Rights of Refugees under International Law*. Cambridge, UK: Cambridge University Press.
Higgins, C. 2017. *Asylum by Boat: Origins of Australia's Refugee Policy*. Sydney: NewSouth.

Hilhorst, D., and B. J. Jansen. 2010. "Humanitarian Space as Arena: A Perspective on the Everyday Politics of Aid." *Development and Change* 41, no. 6: 1117–1139.

Hilhorst, D., and M. van Leeuwen. 2004. "Rethinking the Relation between Relief and Development: 'Villagization' in Rwanda." In *Refugees and the Transformation of Societies: Agency, Policies, Ethics, and Politics*, edited by P. Essed, G. Frerks, and J. Schrijvers, 179–189. New York: Berghahn Books.

Hirt, N. 2015. "One Eritrean Generation, Two Worlds: The Established Diaspora, the New Exiles and Their Relations to the Homeland." *Horn of Africa Bulletin* 27, no. 5: 23–28.

Horst, C. 2006a. "Buufis amongst Somalis in Dadaab: The Transnational and Historical Logics behind Resettlement Dreams." *Journal of Refugee Studies* 19, no. 2: 143–157.

Horst, C. 2006b. "Introduction: Refugee Livelihoods: Continuity and Transformations." *Refugee Survey Quarterly* 25, no. 2: 6–22.

Horst, C. 2008a. "A Monopoly on Assistance: International Aid to Refugee Camps and the Neglected Role of the Somali Diaspora." *Africa Spectrum* 43, no. 1: 121–131.

Horst, C. 2008b. "The Transnational Political Engagements of Refugees: Remittance Sending Practices amongst Somalis in Norway." *Conflict, Security and Development* 8, no. 3: 317–339.

Horst, C. 2013. "The Depoliticization of Diasporas from the Horn of Africa: From Refugees to Transnational Aid Workers." *African Studies* 72, no. 2: 228–245.

Horst, C., S. Lubkemann, and R. N. Pailey. 2015. "The Invisibility of a Third Humanitarian Domain." In *The New Humanitarians in International Practice*, edited by D. Dijkzeul and Z. Sezgin, 213–255. London: Routledge.

Hugo, G., S. Vas Dev, J. Wall, M. Young, V. Sharma, and K. Parker. 2011. *Economic, Social and Civic Contributions of First and Second Generation Humanitarian Entrants*. Canberra: Report to Department of Immigration and Citizenship.

Humphris, R. 2013. "Refugees and the Rashaida: Human Smuggling and Trafficking from Eritrea to Sudan and Egypt." *New Issues in Refugee Issues*, Research Paper No. 254. Geneva: UNHCR.

IASC. 1994. *Definition of Complex Emergencies*. Accessed August 31, 2016, https://interagencystandingcommittee.org/system/files/legacy_files/WG16_4.pdf.

IOM. 2015. *Diaspora Engagement in Humanitarian Response*. Briefing Paper, May 2015. Washington, DC: IOM.

Isotalo, R. 2009. "Politicizing the Transnational: On Implications for Migrants, Refugees, and Scholarship." *Social Analysis* 53, no. 3: 60–84.

Jakubowicz, A. 2002. "Living as a Diaspora: The Politics of Exclusion in Relation to Refugees and Disabled People." *ISAA Review* 2, no. 3: 6–12.

Jansen, S., and S. Lofving, eds. 2009. *Struggles for Home: Violence, Hope and the Movement of People*. New York: Berghahn Books.

Johnson, P. J., and K. Stoll. 2008. "Remittance Patterns of Southern Sudanese Refugee Men: Enacting the Global Breadwinner Role." *Family Relations* 57, no. 4: 431–443.

JSS. 2015. *The Living Conditions of People Seeking Asylum in Australia*. Sydney: Jesuit Social Services.

Kira, I. A., and P. Tummala-Narra. 2015. "Psychotherapy with Refugees: Emerging Paradigm." *Journal of Loss and Trauma* 20, no. 5: 449–467.

Kloos, S. 2012. "Humanitarian Reason: A Moral History of the Present, by Fassin, Didier" *Social Anthropology/Anthropologie Sociale* 20, no. 3: 331–361.

Koinova, M. 2011. "Diasporas and Secessionist Conflicts: The Mobilization of the Armenian, Albanian and Chechen Diasporas." *Ethnic and Racial Studies* 34, no. 2: 333–356.

Krause, M. 2014. *The Good Project: Humanitarian Relief NGOs and the Fragmentation of Reason*. Chicago: University of Chicago Press.

Laqueur, T. W. 2009. "Mourning, Pity, and the Work of Narrative in the Making of 'Humanity.'" In *Humanitarianism and Suffering: The Mobilization of Empathy*, edited by R. A. Wilson and R. D. Brown, 31–57. Cambridge, MA: Cambridge University Press.

Lipman, J. N. 1997. *Familiar Strangers: A History of Muslims in Northwest China*. Seattle: University of Washington Press.

Lischer, S. K. 2005. *Dangerous Sanctuaries: Refugee Camps, Civil War, and the Dilemmas of Humanitarian Aid*. Ithaca, NY: Cornell University Press.

Little, A., and N. Vaughan-Williams. 2017. "Stopping Boats, Saving Lives, Securing Subjects: Humanitarian Borders in Europe and Australia." *European Journal of International Relations* 23, no. 3: 533–556.

Loescher, G., A. Betts, and J. Milner. 2008. *The United Nations High Commissioner for Refugees (UNHCR): The Politics and Practice of Refugee Protection Into the Twenty-first Century*. London: Routledge.

Lum, B., M. Nikolko, Y. Samy, and D. Carment. 2013. "Diasporas, Remittances and State Fragility: Assessing the Linkages." *Ethnopolitics* 12, no. 2: 201–219.

Maley, W. 2016. *What Is a Refugee?* Melbourne: Scribe.

Malkki, L. H. 1992. "National Geographic: The Rooting of Peoples and the Territorialization of National Identity among Scholars and Refugees." *Cultural Anthropology* 7, no. 1: 24–44.

Malkki, L. H. 1995. *Purity and Exile: Violence, Memory, and National Cosmology among Hutu Refugees in Tanzania*. Chicago: University of Chicago Press.

Malkki, L. H. 1996. "Speechless Emissaries: Refugees, Humanitarianism, and Dehistoricization." *Cultural Anthropology* 11, no. 3: 377–404.

Malkki, L. H. 2015. *The Need to Help: The Domestic Arts of International Humanitarianism*. Durham, NC: Duke University Press.

Marcus, G. E. 1995. "Ethnography in/of the World System: The Emergence of Multi-Sited Ethnography." *Annual Review of Anthropology* 24: 95–117.

Massey, D. 1993. "Power-Geometry and a Progressive Sense of Place." In *Mapping the Futures: Local Cultures, Global Change*, edited by H. Bird, B. Curtis, T. Putnam, G. Robertson, and L. Tickner, 59–69. London: Routledge.

McAdam, J., and F. Chong. 2014. *Refugees: Why Seeking Asylum is Legal and Australia's Policies Are Not*. Sydney: UNSW Press.

Milgram, S. 1972. "The Familiar Stranger: An Aspect of Urban Anonymity." *The Division 8 Newsletter*, Division of Personality and Social Psychology. Washington.

Missbach, A. 2013. "The Waxing and Waning of the Acehnese Diaspora's Long-Distance Politics." *Modern Asian Studies* 47, no. 3: 1055–1082.

Missbach, A. 2015. *Troubled Transit: Asylum Seekers Stuck in Indonesia*. Singapore: Institute of Southeast Asian Studies.

Mojab, S., and R. Gorman. 2007. "Dispersed Nationalism: War, Diaspora and Kurdish Women's Organizing." *Journal of Middle East Women's Studies* 3, no. 1: 58–85.

Monsutti, A. 2004. "Cooperation, Remittances, and Kinship among the Hazaras." *Iranian Studies* 37, no. 2: 219–240.

Monsutti, A. 2008. "Afghan Migratory Strategies and the Three Solutions to the Refugee Problem." *Refugee Survey Quarterly* 27, no. 1: 58–73.

Ndhlovu, F. 2014. *Becoming an African Diaspora in Australia: Language, Culture, Identity*. Hampshire, UK: Palgrave Macmillan.

Neumann, K., S. M.Gifford, A. Lems, and S. Scherr. 2014. "Refugee Settlement in Australia: Policy, Scholarship and the Production of Knowledge, 1952–2013." *Journal of Intercultural Studies* 35, no. 1: 1–17.

Nyberg-Sørensen, N. 2007. *Living Across Worlds: Diaspora, Development and Transnational Engagement*. Washington, DC: International Organization for Migration.

Nyberg-Sørensen, N., N. Van Hear, and P. Engberg-Pedersen. 2002. "The Migration-Development Nexus: Evidence and Policy Options." *International Migration* 40, no. 5: 49.

O'Hagan, J., and M. Hirono. 2014. "Fragmentation of the International Humanitarian Order? Understanding 'Cultures of Humanitarianism' in East Asia." *Ethics and International Affairs* 28, no. 4: 409–424.

OHCHR. 2015. *Report of the Detailed Findings of the Commission of Inquiry on Human Rights in Eritrea*. Geneva: Office of the High Commissioner for Human Rights.

Okolie, A. 2003. "Identity: Now You Don't See It; Now You Do." *Identity: An International Journal of Theory and Research* 3, no. 1: 1–7.

Olliff, L. 2010. *What Works: Employment Strategies for Refugee and Humanitarian Entrants*. Sydney: Refugee Council of Australia.

Ortner, S. 1984. "Theory in Anthropology since the Sixties." *Comparative Studies in Society and History* 26: 126–166.

Ortner, S. 2016. "Dark Anthropology and Its Others: Theory since the Eighties." *HAU: Journal of Ethnographic Theory* 6, no. 1: 47–73.

Otten, C. 2014. "Last Remaining Christians Flee Iraq's Mosul." *Al Jazeera*, July 22, 2014. http://www.aljazeera.com/news/middleeast/2014/07/last-remaining-christians-flee-iraq-mosul-201472118235739663.html.

Pacitto, J., and E. Fiddian-Qasmiyeh. 2013. "Writing the 'Other' into Humanitarian Discourse: Framing Theory and Practice in South-South Humanitarian Responses to Forced Displacement." *New Issues in Refugee Research* 93, no. 257: 1–37.

Parker, B. 2016. "MSF Pulls Out of World Humanitarian Summit." *IRIN News,* May 5, 2016. Accessed December 9, 2016, http://www.irinnews.org/news/2016/05/05/msf-pulls-out-world-humanitarian-summit.

Perez, C., B. Birregah, and M. Lemercier. 2013. "Familiar Strangers Detection in Online Social Networks." 2013 IEEE/ACM International Conference on Advances in Social Networks Analysis and Mining, Advances in *Social Networks Analysis and Mining.* ACM and IEEE.

Phillips, J., and J. Simon-Davies. 2014. *Migration to Australia: A Quick Guide to the Statistics.* Canberra: Parlimentary Library of Australia.

Piper, M., P. Power, and G. Thom. 2013. *Refugee Resettlement: 2012 and Beyond.* Geneva: UNHCR Policy Development and Evaluation Service.

Poole, A. 2013. "Ransoms, Remittances, and Refugees: The Gatekeeper State in Eritrea." *Africa Today* 60, no. 2: 67–82.

Price, C. A. 1990. *Australia and Refugees 1921–1976.* Canberra ACT: National Population Council.

Purtill, J. 2022. "Crypto and Blockchain Are Being Used in Unprecedented Ways in the Russia-Ukraine War." *ABC News Science,* March 2, 2022. https://www.abc.net.au/news/science/2022-03-02/russia-ukraine-war-testing-ground-cryptocurrencies-blockchain/100869596.

Putnam, R. D. 2000. *Bowling Alone: The Collapse and Revival of American Community.* New York: Simon and Schuster.

Radio Free Asia. 2015. "Karenni Refugee Camp Fire Destroys Hundreds of Homes in Eastern Myanmar." *Radio Free Asia,* April 7, 2015. http://www.rfa.org/english/news/myanmar/karenni-refugee-camp-fire-destroys-homes-04072015150842.html.

Redfield, P. 2012. "The Unbearable Lightness of Ex-Pats: Double Binds of Humanitarian Mobility." *Cultural Anthropology* 27, no. 2: 358–382.

Redfield, P., and E. Bornstein, eds. 2010. "An Introduction to the Anthropology of Humanitarianism." In *Forces of Compassion: Humanitarianism Between Ethics and Politics,* 3–30. Santa Fe, NM: School for Advanced Research Press.

Refugee Council of Australia. n.d. *How Many Refugees Have Come to Australia?.* Accessed March 19, 2022, https://www.refugeecouncil.org.au/how-many-refugees-have-come/

Reid-Henry, S. 2013. "On the Politics of Our Humanitarian Present." *Environment and Planning D: Society and Space* 31: 753–760.

Reid-Henry, S. 2014. "Humanitarianism as Liberal Diagnostic: Humanitarian Reason and the Political Rationalities of the Liberal Will-to-Care." *Transactions of the Institute of British Geographers* 39: 418–431.

Richey, L. A., and L. Chouliaraki. 2017. "Everyday Humanitarianism: Ethics, Affects and Practices." *New Political Science* 39, no. 2: 314–316.
Richey, L. A., and S. Ponte. 2011. *Brand Aid: Shopping Well to Save the World*. Minneapolis: University of Minnesota Press.
Robbins, J. 2013. "Beyond the Suffering Subject: Toward an Anthropology of the Good." *Journal of the Royal Anthropological Institute* 19: 447–462.
Robins, S. 2009. "Humanitarian Aid Beyond 'Bare Survival': Social Movement Responses to Xenophobic Violence in South Africa." *American Ethnologist* 36, no. 4: 637–650.
Russell, B. 1997. *The Problems of Philsophy*. New York: Oxford University Press.
Rygiel, K. 2011. "Bordering Solidarities: Migrant Activism and the Politics of Movement and Camps at Calais." *Citizenship Studies* 15: 1–19.
Rygiel, K. 2012. "Bordering Solidarities: Forging Transgressive Citizenships In and Through Transit." *Citizenship Studies* 16, no. 5/6: 807–825.
Said, E. 1978. *Orientalism*. Harmondsworth, UK: Penguin.
Salamon, L. M. 1987. "Of Market Failure, Voluntary Failure, and Third-Party Government: Toward a Theory of Government-Nonprofit Relations in the Modern Welfare State." *Journal of Voluntary Action Research* 16, no. 1–2: 29–49.
Salehyan, I. 2005. "Dangerous Sanctuaries: Refugee Camps, Civil War, and the Dilemmas of Humanitarian Aid." *Journal of Peace Research* 42, no. 5: 644–645.
Sandvik, K. B. 2009. "The Physicality of Legal Consciousness: Suffering and the Production of Credibility in Refugee Resettlement." In *Humanitarianism and Suffering: The Mobilization of Empathy*, edited by R. A. Wilson and R. D. Brown, 223–244. Cambridge, UK: Cambridge University Press.
Sanyal, R. 2011. "Squatting in Camps: Building and Insurgency in Spaces of Refuge." *Urban Studies* 48, no. 5: 877–890.
Schapendonk, J. 2012. "Mobilities and Sediments: Spatial Dynamics in the Context of Contemporary Sub-Saharan African Migration to Europe." *African Diaspora: Transnational Journal of Culture, Economy and Society* 5, no. 2: 117–142.
Schwartzman, H. B. 1992. *Ethnography in Organizations*. Evanston, IL: Northwestern University.
Scott, E. 2016. *Familiar Strangers: The Georgian Diaspora and the Evolution of Soviet Empire*. Oxford: Oxford University Press.
Sezgin, Z. 2015. Diaspora Action in Syria and Neighbouring Countries. In *The New Humanitarians in International Practice*, edited by D. Dijkzeul and Z. Sezgin, 232–255. London: Routledge.
Shandy, D. J. 2006. "Global Transactions: Sudanese Refugees Sending Money Home." *Refuge* 23, no. 2: 28–35.
Sharma, K., A. Kashyap, and P. R. Ladd, eds. 2011. *Realizing the Development Potential of Diasporas*. New York: United Nations University Press.
Sheller, M., and J. Urry. 2006. "The New Mobilities Paradigm." *Environment and Planning A: Economy and Space* 38, no. 2: 207–226.
Sinatti, G., and C. Horst. 2014. "Migrants as Agents of Development: Diaspora Engagement Discourse and Practice in Europe." *Ethnicities* 15, no. 1: 1–19.

Slim, H. 2003. "Humanitarianism with Borders? NGOs, Belligerent Military Forces and Humanitarian Action." ICVA Conference on "NGOs in a Changing World: Dilemmas and Challenges." Geneva: International Council of Voluntary Agencies.

Slim, H. 2022. "Solidarity, Not Neutrality, Will Characterize Western Aid to Ukraine." Ethics & International Affairs. Accessed June, 19, 2022, https://www.ethicsandinternationalaffairs.org/2022/solidarity-not-neutrality-will-characterize-western-aid-to-ukraine/

Slim, H., and L. E. Eguren. 2004. *Humanitarian Protection: An ALNAP Guidance Booklet*. London: ALNAP.

Smillie, I., and L. Minear. 2004. *The Charity of Nations: Humanitarian Action in a Calculating World*. Bloomfield, CT: Kumarian.

Soh-Leong, L. 2009. "'Loss of Connections Is Death': Transnational Family Ties Among Sudanese Refugee Families Resettling in the United States." *Journal of Cross-Cultural Psychology* 40, no. 6: 1028–1040.

Stevens, D. 2013. "What Do We Mean by Protection?" *International Journal on Minority and Group Rights* 20, no. 2: 233–262.

Suski, L. 2009. "Children, Suffering, and the Humanitarian Appeal." In *Humanitarianism and Suffering: The Mobilization of Empathy*, edited by R. A. Wilson and R. D. Brown, 202–222. Cambridge, UK: Cambridge University Press.

Sweis, R. K. 2019. "Doctors with Borders: Hierarchies of Humanitarians and the Syrian Civil War." *International Journal of Middle East Studies* 51, no. 4: 587–601.

Tesfahuney, M. 1998. "Mobility, Racism and Geopolitics." *Political Geography* 17, no. 5: 499–515.

The Nation. 2017. "UN Pushes Self-Reliance as Donor Funding for Kenya Dwindles." *The Nation*, November 25, 2017. https://nation.africa/kenya/news/UN-refugee-donor-funding-Kenya-dwindles/1056-4202704-n3a88oz/index.html.

The Sphere Project. 2018. *Humanitarian Charter and Minimum Standards in Humanitarian Response*. Geneva: The Sphere Project.

Ticktin, M. 2011. *Casualties of Care: Immigration and the Politics of Humanitarianism in France*. San Diego: University of California Press.

Ticktin, M. 2014. "Transnational Humanitarianism." *Annual Review of Anthropology* 43: 273–289.

Tofighian, O. 2020. "Introducing Manus Prison Theory: Knowing Border Violence." *Globalizations* 17, no. 7: 1138–1156.

Tölölyan, K. 2007. "The Contemporary Discourse of Diaspora Studies." *Comparative Studies of South Asia, Africa, and the Middle East* 27: 647–655.

Tsing, A. L. 2005. *Friction: An Ethnography of Global Connection*. Princeton, NJ: Princeton University Press.

Tsourapas, G. 2019. "The Syrian Refugee Crisis and Foreign Policy Decision-Making in Jordan, Lebanon, and Turkey." *Journal of Global Security Studies* 4, no. 4: 464–481.

Türk, V. 2011. "Restructuring Refuge and Settlement: Responding to the Global Dynamics of Displacement." *Refuge* 28, no. 2: 117–126.

Türk, V. 2019. "Preventing Displacement, Addressing Root Causes and the Promise of the Global Compact on Refugees." *Forced Migration Review* 62: 64–67.

Türk, V., and M. Garlick. 2016. "From Burdens and Responsibilities to Opportunities: The Comprehensive Refugee Response Framework and a Global Compact on Refugees." *International Journal of Refugee Law* 28, no. 4: 656–678.

Turner, S. 2016. "What Is a Refugee Camp: Explorations of the Limits and Effects of the Camp." *Journal of Refugee Studies* 29, no. 2: 139–148.

Uehling, G. 1998. "Is there 'Refuge' in the Refugee Category?" In *Power, Ethics, and Human Rights: Anthropological Studies of Refugee Research and Action*, edited by R. M. Krulfeld and J. L. MacDonald, 123–144. Landham, MD: Rowman and Littlefield.

UNHCR. 2004. "Framework for Durable Solutions for Refugees and Persons of Concern." *Refugee Survey Quarterly* 23, no. 1: 179–200.

UNHCR. 2013. *Understanding Community-Based Protection* (Protection Policy Paper). United Nations High Commissioner for Refugees (UNHCR).

UNHCR. 2014a. "Sharp Increase in Number of Eritrean Refugees and Asylum-Seekers in Europe, Ethiopia and Sudan," November 14, 2014. Accessed October 19, 2015, http://www.unhcr.org/5465fea1381.html.

UNHCR. 2014b. The 1951 Refugee Convention. http://www.unhcr.org/pages/49da0e466.html.

UNHCR. 2017. *Global Trends: Forced Displacement in 2016*. Geneva: UNHCR.

UNHCR. 2019. *Global Trends: Forced Displacement in 2018*. Geneva: UNHCR.

UNHCR. 2020a. *Global Trends: Forced Displacement in 2019*. Geneva: UNHCR.

UNHCR. 2020b. "Sudan: Population Dashboard. Refugees and Asylum-Seekers." September 30, 2020. Accessed March 6, 2022, https://reporting.unhcr.org/document/539.

UNHCR. 2021. *Global Trends: Forced Displacement in 2020*. Geneva: UNHCR.

UNHCR. 2022. *Global Trends: Forced Displacement in 2021*. Geneva: UNHCR.

UNHCR Sudan. 2014. Community Asset Mapping Resource: Khartoum, Sudan. Khartoum: UNHCR.

Urry, J. 2007. *Mobilities*. Cambridge, UK: Polity.

US Committee for Refugees and Immigrants. 2004. *World Refugee Survey 2004*. Washington, DC: US Committee for Refugees and Immigrants.

van de Port, M. 1999. "'It Takes a Serb to Know a Serb': Uncovering the Roots of Obstinate Otherness in Serbia." *Critique of Anthropology* 19, no. 1: 7–30.

Van Hear, N. 1998. *New Diasporas: The Mass Exodus, Dispersal and Regrouping of Migrant Communities*. London: UCL Press.

Van Hear, N. 2006. "Refugees in Diaspora: From Durable Solutions to Transnational Relations." *Refuge* 23, no. 1: 9–15.

Van Hear, N. 2009. "The Rise of Refugee Diasporas." *Current History* 108, no. 717: 180–185.

Van Hear, N., and R. Cohen. 2017. "Diasporas and Conflict: Distance, Contiguity and Spheres of Engagement." *Oxford Development Studies* 45, no. 2: 171–184.

VICE News. 2016. "Blackout: Leaks from Eritrea, Africa's North Korea." Accessed March 19, 2022, https://www.youtube.com/watch?v=XBacsi5eXoA.

Wahlbeck, Ö. 2002. "The Concept of Diaspora as an Analytical Tool in the Study of Refugee Communities." *Journal of Ethnic and Migration Studies* 28, no. 2: 221–238.

Walters, W. 2010. "Foucault and Frontiers: Notes on the Birth of the Humanitarian Border." In *Governmentality: Current Issues and Future Challenges,* edited by U. Brocklin, B. Krasmann, and T. Lemke. New York: Routledge.

Wheeler, N. J. 2000. "Saving Strangers: Humanitarian Intervention in International Society." Oxford: Oxford University Press.

Wigley, B. 2006. *The State of UNHCR's Organization Culture: What Now?* Geneva: United Nations High Commissioner for Refugees.

Wikipedia. n.d. "Humanitarianism." Accessed September 15, 2017, https://en.wikipedia.org/wiki/Humanitarianism.

Williams, D. C. 2012. "Changing Burma from Without: Political Activism among the Burmese Diaspora." *Indiana Journal of Global Legal Studies* 19, no. 1: 121–142.

Williams, J. M. 2015. "From Humanitarian Exceptionalism to Contingent Care: Care and Enforcement at the Humanitarian Border." *Political Geography* 47: 11–20.

Wilson, R. A., and R. D. Brown, ds. 2009. *Humanitarianism and Suffering: The Mobilization of Empathy.* Cambridge, UK: Cambridge University Press.

Wise, A. 2004. "Nation, Transnation, Diaspora: Locating East Timorese Long-Distance Nationalism." *SOJOURN: Journal of Social Issues in Southeast Asia* 19, no. 2: 151–180.

Wood, G. 1985. "Labels: A Shadow Across Reality: An Introductory Note." In *Labelling in Development Policy: Essays in Honour of Bernard Schaffer,* edited by G. Wood, 1–5. London: SAGE.

Young, A. 2016. *The Challenges of Unsolicited Bilateral Donations in Pacific Humanitarian Responses.* Melbourne: Australian Red Cross.

Zetter, R., and K. Long. 2012. "Unlocking Protracted Displacement." *Forced Migration Review* 40: 34–37.

Zhou, J., Y. Yang, H. Ma, and Y. Li. 2020. "'Familiar Strangers' in the Big Data Era: An Exploratory Study of Beijing Metro Encounters." *Cities* 97.

Zinterer, T. 2005. "Diaspora Networks as High Risk or High Potential: The Transnational Turn in National Policy Discourses on Migrants." *Conference Papers—International Studies Association,* 1–19.

INDEX

Note: All figures, tables and maps are signified by italics

LOUISE OLLIFF is Postdoctoral Fellow in the School of Regulation and Global Governance (RegNet) at Australian National University (ANU), Senior Policy Advisor for the Refugee Council of Australia, and Adjunct Fellow at the Humanitarian and Development Research Initiative (HADRI) at Western Sydney University.

www.ingramcontent.com/pod-product-compliance
Lightning Source LLC
Chambersburg PA
CBHW030401270326
41926CB00009B/1214

* 9 7 8 0 2 5 3 0 6 3 5 6 4 *